LETTRE
A M. DACIER.

DE L'IMPRIMERIE DE FIRMIN DIDOT,
IMPRIMEUR DU ROI ET DE L'INSTITUT.

LETTRE

A M. DACIER,

SECRÉTAIRE PERPÉTUEL DE L'ACADÉMIE ROYALE
DES INSCRIPTIONS ET BELLES-LETTRES,

RELATIVE A L'ALPHABET

DES HIÉROGLYPHES PHONÉTIQUES

EMPLOYÉS PAR LES ÉGYPTIENS POUR INSCRIRE SUR LEURS MONUMENTS LES TITRES, LES NOMS ET LES SURNOMS DES SOUVERAINS GRECS ET ROMAINS;

Par M. CHAMPOLLION le jeune.

A PARIS,

CHEZ FIRMIN DIDOT PÈRE ET FILS,

LIBRAIRES, RUE JACOB, N° 24.

M. DCCC. XXII.

LETTRE A M. DACIER

RELATIVE A L'ALPHABET

DES HIÉROGLYPHES PHONÉTIQUES.

Monsieur,

Je dois aux bontés dont vous m'honorez l'indulgent intérêt que l'Académie royale des Inscriptions et Belles-Lettres a bien voulu accorder à mes travaux sur les écritures égyptiennes, en me permettant de lui soumettre mes deux mémoires sur l'écriture *hiératique* ou sacerdotale, et sur l'écriture *démotique* ou populaire; j'oserai enfin, après cette épreuve si flatteuse pour moi, espérer d'avoir réussi à démontrer que ces deux espèces d'écriture sont, l'une et l'autre, non pas alphabétiques, ainsi qu'on l'avait pensé si généralement, mais *idéographiques*, comme les hiéroglyphes mêmes, c'est-à-dire peignant les *idées* et non les *sons* d'une langue; et croire être parvenu, après dix années de recherches assidues, à réunir des données presque complètes sur la théorie générale de ces deux espèces d'écriture, sur l'origine, la nature, la forme et le nombre de leurs signes, les règles de leurs combinaisons au moyen de ceux de ces signes qui remplissent des fonctions purement logiques ou grammaticales, et avoir ainsi jeté les premiers fondements de ce qu'on pourrait appeler la *grammaire* et le *dictionnaire* de ces deux écritures employées dans le grand nombre de monuments dont l'interprétation répandra tant de lumière sur l'histoire générale de l'Egypte. A l'égard de l'écriture *démotique* en particulier, il a suffi de la précieuse inscription de Rosette pour en reconnaître l'ensemble; la critique est redevable d'abord aux lumières de votre illustre confrère M. Silvestre de Sacy, et successivement à celles de feu Akerblad et de M. le docteur Young, des premières notions exactes qu'on a tirées de ce monument, et c'est de cette même inscription que j'ai déduit la série des signes démotiques qui, prenant une valeur syllabico-alphabétique, exprimaient dans les textes *idéographiques* les noms propres des personnages étrangers à l'Égypte. C'est ainsi encore que le nom des Ptolémées a été retrouvé et sur cette même inscription et sur un manuscrit en papyrus récemment apporté d'Égypte.

Il ne me reste donc plus, pour compléter mon travail sur les trois espèces d'écritures égyptiennes, qu'à produire mon mémoire sur les *hiéroglyphes* purs. J'ose espérer que mes nouveaux efforts obtiendront aussi un accueil favorable de votre célèbre compagnie, dont la bienveillance a été pour moi un si précieux encouragement.

Mais dans l'état actuel des études égyptiennes, lorsque de toutes parts les monuments affluent et sont recueillis par les souverains comme par les amateurs, lorsqu'aussi, et à leur sujet, les savants de tous les pays s'empressent de se livrer à de laborieuses recherches, et s'efforcent de pénétrer intimement dans la connaissance de ces monuments écrits qui doivent servir à expliquer tous les autres, je ne crois pas devoir remettre à un autre temps d'offrir à ces savants et sous vos honorables auspices, une courte mais importante série de faits nouveaux, qui appartient naturellement à mon Mémoire sur l'écriture *hiéroglyphique*, et qui leur épargnera sans doute la peine que j'ai prise pour l'établir, peut-être aussi de graves erreurs sur les époques diverses de l'histoire des arts et de l'administration générale de l'Égypte : car il s'agit de la série des *hiéroglyphes* qui, faisant exception à la nature générale des signes de cette écriture, étaient doués de la faculté d'*exprimer les sons* des mots, et ont servi à inscrire sur les monuments publics de l'Égypte, les *titres*, les *noms* et les *surnoms des souverains grecs ou romains* qui la gouvernèrent successivement. Bien des certitudes pour l'histoire de cette contrée célèbre doivent naître de ce nouveau résultat de mes recherches, auquel j'ai été conduit très-naturellement.

L'interprétation du texte *démotique* de l'Inscription de Rosette par le moyen du texte grec qui l'accompagne, m'avait fait reconnaître que les Égyptiens se servaient d'un certain nombre de caractères *démotiques* auxquels ils avaient attribué la faculté d'exprimer des sons, pour introduire dans leurs textes idéographiques les *noms propres* et les *mots étrangers à la langue égyptienne*. On sent facilement l'indispensable nécessité d'une telle institution dans un système d'écriture idéographique. Les Chinois, qui se servent également d'une écriture idéographique, emploient aussi un procédé tout-à-fait semblable et créé pour le même motif.

Le monument de Rosette nous présente l'application de ce système auxiliaire d'écriture que nous avons appelé *phonétique*, c'est-à-dire exprimant les sons, dans les noms propres des rois *Alexandre*, *Ptolémée*, des reines *Arsinoé*, *Bérénice*, dans les noms propres de six autres personnages, *Aétès*, *Pyrrha*, *Philinus*, *Aréia*, *Diogène*, *Irène*, dans le mot grec ΣΥΝΤΑΞΙΣ et dans ΟΥΗΝΝ (1).

Un manuscrit sur papyrus, en écriture démotique, récemment acquis pour le cabinet du roi, nous a donné aussi les noms *Alexandre*, *Ptolémée*, *Bérénice* et *Arsinoé*, semblables à ceux du monument de Rosette, de plus les noms phonétiques du roi *Eupator* et de la reine *Cléopâtre*, et ceux de trois personnages grecs, *Apollonius*, *Antiochus* et *Antigone* (2).

---

(1) Voyez ma Planche I, n° 1 à 12, et l'explication des planches.

(2) V. ma pl. I, n° 13 à 21. Ce manuscrit *démotique* est du nombre des papyrus en diverses langues que la bibliothèque du Roi vient d'acheter de M. Cazati, et sur lesquels M. St-Martin a donné, dans le *Journal des Savants* du mois de septembre, une intéressante notice. D'après ma traduction du protocole de ce contrat démotique, c'est un acte public du règne d'Évergète II, et dans lequel sont nommées trois Cléopâtres, *Cléopâtre sa sœur et sa femme*, *Cléopâtre*

Vous avez sans doute remarqué, Monsieur, dans mon Mémoire sur l'écriture démotique égyptienne, que ces noms étrangers étaient exprimés phonétiquement au moyen de signes plutôt *syllabiques* qu'*alphabétiques*. La valeur de chaque caractère est reconnue et invariablement fixée par la comparaison de ces divers noms; et de tous ces rapprochements est résulté l'alphabet ou plutôt le syllabaire *démotique* figuré sur ma planche I, colonne deuxième.

L'emploi de ces caractères phonétiques une fois constaté dans l'écriture *démotique*, je devais naturellement en conclure que puisque les signes de cette écriture populaire étaient, ainsi que je l'ai exposé, empruntés de l'écriture *hiératique* ou sacerdotale, et puisque encore les signes de cette écriture *hiératique* ne sont, comme on l'a reconnu par mes divers mémoires, qu'une représentation abrégée, une véritable *tachygraphie* des *hiéroglyphes*, cette troisième espèce d'écriture, l'*hiéroglyphique* pure, devait avoir aussi un certain nombre de ses signes doués de la faculté d'exprimer les sons; en un mot, qu'il existait également une série d'*hiéroglyphes phonétiques*. Pour s'assurer de la vérité de cet aperçu, pour reconnaître l'existence et discerner même la valeur de quelques-uns des signes de cette

---

fille du roi (Philométor) et *Cléopâtre sa mère*. M. Raoul-Rochette se propose de publier ce manuscrit égyptien avec quelques autres papyrus du cabinet du Roi. Ce savant fera un véritable présent à l'archéologie égyptienne.

espèce, il aurait suffi d'avoir sous les yeux, écrits en *hiéroglyphes* purs, deux noms propres de rois grecs préalablement connus, et contenant plusieurs lettres employées à la fois dans l'un et dans l'autre, tels que *Ptolémée* et *Cléopâtre*, *Alexandre* et *Bérénice*, etc.

Le texte hiéroglyphique de l'inscription de Rosette, qui se serait prêté si heureusement à cette recherche, ne présentait, à cause de ses fractures, que le seul nom de *Ptolémée*.

L'obélisque trouvé dans l'île de Philæ, et récemment transporté à Londres, contient aussi le nom hiéroglyphique d'un Ptolémée (voy. ma planche I, n° 23), conçu dans les mêmes signes que dans l'Inscription de Rosette, également renfermé dans un cartouche (1), et il est suivi d'un second cartouche qui doit contenir nécessairement le nom propre d'une femme, d'une reine Lagide, puisque ce cartouche est terminé par les signes hiéroglyphiques du genre féminin, signes qui terminent aussi les noms propres hiéroglyphiques de toutes les déesses égyptiennes sans exception (2). L'obélisque était *lié*, dit-on, à un socle portant une inscription grecque qui est une supplique des prêtres d'Isis à Philæ, adressée au roi Ptolémée, à Cléopâtre sa sœur, et à Cléopâtre sa femme (3). Si cet obélisque et l'inscription hié-

---

(1) Voy. mes *Observations sur l'obélisque égyptien de l'île de Philæ*, dans la Revue encyclopédique, cahier de mars 1822; et le cartouche de l'inscription de Rosette, à la suite de ce mémoire pl. I, n° 22.

(2) Voyez ma planche I, n° 21.

(3) On doit à M. Letronne une savante explication de cette inscrip-

roglyphique qu'il porte étaient une conséquence de la supplique des prêtres qui, en effet, y parlent de la consécration d'un monument analogue, le cartouche du nom féminin ne pouvait être nécessairement que celui d'une Cléopâtre. Ce nom et celui de Ptolémée qui, dans le grec, ont quelques lettres semblables, devaient servir à un rapprochement comparatif des signes hiéroglyphiques composant l'un et l'autre; et si les signes semblables dans ces deux noms exprimaient dans l'un et l'autre cartouche *les mêmes sons*, ils devaient constater leur nature *entièrement phonétique*.

Une comparaison préliminaire nous avait aussi fait reconnaître que, dans l'écriture démotique, ces deux mêmes noms écrits phonétiquement employaient plusieurs caractères tout-à-fait semblables (1). L'analogie des trois écritures égyptiennes dans leur marche générale, devait nous faire espérer la même rencontre et les mêmes rapports dans ces mêmes noms écrits *hiéroglyphiquement* : c'est ce qu'a aussitôt confirmé la simple comparaison du cartouche hiéroglyphique renfermant

---

tion grecque, et publiée sous ce titre: *Éclaircissements sur une inscription grecque, contenant une pétition des prêtres d'Isis, dans l'île de Philæ, à Ptolémée Évergète second, copiée à Philæ, par M. Cailliaud, en octobre* 1816; lus à l'Académie royale des Inscriptions et Belles-Lettres. Paris, imprimerie royale, 1822, in-8°. A l'égard des deux reines *Cléopâtre* nommées à la fois dans l'Inscription, voyez, d'après la citation de M. Letronne, les *Annales des Lagides*, par M. Champollion-Figeac, tome II, page 168.

(1) Voyez planche I, n° 2 ou 14 et 17.

(8)

le nom de Ptolémée (1) avec celui de l'obélisque de Philæ, que nous considérions, d'après l'inscription grecque, comme contenant le nom de Cléopâtre (2).

Le premier signe du nom de *Cléopâtre* qui figure une espèce de *quart de cercle*, et qui représenterait le K, ne devait point se trouver dans le nom de Ptolémée : il n'y est point en effet.

Le second, un *lion en repos* qui doit représenter le Λ est tout-à-fait semblable au quatrième signe du nom de Ptolémée, qui est est aussi un Λ (Πτολ).

Le troisième signe du nom de Cléopâtre est une *plume* ou *feuille* qui représenterait la voyelle brève E; l'on voit aussi à la fin du nom de Ptolémée deux *feuilles* semblables qui ne peuvent y avoir, vu leur position, que la valeur de la diphtongue AI, de ΑΙΟΣ.

Le quatrième caractère du cartouche hiéroglyphique de Cléopâtre, représentant une espèce de *fleur avec sa tige recourbée*, répondrait à l'O du nom grec de cette reine. Il est en effet le troisième caractère du nom de Ptolémée (Πτό).

Le cinquième signe du nom de Cléopâtre, qui a la forme d'un parallélogramme et qui doit représenter le Π, est de même le premier signe du nom hiéroglyphique de Ptolémée.

Le sixième signe répondant à la voyelle A de ΚΛΕΟΠΑΤΡΑ est un *épervier*, et ne se voit pas dans le nom de Ptolémée, ce qui doit être en effet.

---

(1) Voyez ma planche I, n° 22.
(2) Voyez ma planche I, n° 24.

Le septième caractère est une *main ouverte*, représentant le T; mais cette main ne se retrouve pas dans le mot Ptolémée, où la seconde lettre, le T, est exprimée par un *segment de sphère*, qui néanmoins est aussi un T; car on verra plus bas pourquoi ces deux signes hiéroglyphiques sont homophones.

Le huitième signe de ΚΛΕΟΠΑΤΡΑ, qui est une *bouche* vue de face, et qui serait le P, ne se trouve pas dans le cartouche de Ptolémée, et ne doit point y être non plus.

Enfin, le neuvième et dernier signe du nom de la reine, qui doit être la voyelle A, est en effet *l'épervier* que nous avons déjà vu représenter cette voyelle dans la troisième syllabe du même nom. Ce nom propre est terminé par les deux signes hiéroglyphiques du genre féminin; celui de Ptolémée l'est par un autre signe qui consiste en un trait recourbé, et qui équivaut au Σ grec, comme nous le verrons bientôt.

Les signes réunis de ces deux cartouches analysés phonétiquement, nous donnaient donc déjà douze signes répondant à onze consonnes et voyelles ou diphtongues de l'alphabet grec : A, AI, E, K, Λ, M, O, Π, P, Σ, T.

La valeur phonétique déjà très-probable de ces douze signes deviendra incontestable, si, en appliquant ces valeurs à d'autres cartouches ou petits tableaux circonscrits, contenant des noms propres et tirés des monuments égyptiens hiéroglyphiques, on en fait sans effort une lecture régulière, produisant des noms propres de souverains, étrangers à la langue égyptienne.

Parmi les cartouches recueillis sur les divers édifices de Karnac à Thèbes, et publiés dans la *Description de l'Égypte* (A., t. III, pl. 38), j'ai remarqué un de ces cartouches numéroté 13 (1), composé de signes déjà connus pour la plupart d'après l'analyse précédente, et qui se trouvent dans l'ordre suivant : l'*épervier*, A ; le *lion en repos*, Λ ; un *grand vase à anneau*, encore inconnu ; le *trait recourbé*, Σ ; la *plume seule*, E ou toute autre voyelle brève ; le signe vulgairement nommé *signe de l'eau*, inconnu ; la *main ouverte*, T ; la *bouche de face*, P ; deux *sceptres horizontaux affrontés*, encore inconnu. Ces lettres réunies donnent AΛ.ΣE.TP. ; et en assignant *au vase à anneau* la valeur du K, à l'hiéroglyphe de l'eau la valeur du N, et au signe final la valeur du Σ, on a le mot AΛKΣENTPΣ, qui est écrit ainsi, lettre pour lettre, en écriture démotique, dans l'inscription de Rosette et dans le papyrus du cabinet du roi, à la place du nom grec AΛEΞANΔPOΣ (2).

Ce nouveau nom nous donne ainsi trois caractères phonétiques de plus, répondant aux lettres grecques K, N et Σ.

Il est facile de justifier la valeur que nous leur assignons.

Le vase à anneau est une nouvelle forme du K, déjà désigné dans le nom KΛEOΠATPA, par un quart de cercle. On a déjà vu aussi que la lettre T était également représentée par deux signes différents ; mais l'on

---

(1) V. ma Planche I, n° 25.   (2) Idem, n° 1 et n° 13.

ne devra pas s'étonner de cette synonymie et de cette multiplicité de signes pour exprimer le même son, chez un peuple dont l'écriture est essentiellemeut idéographique.

On ne peut point, en effet, considérer l'écriture *phonétique* des Égyptiens, soit *hiéroglyphique*, soit *démotique*, comme un système aussi fixe et aussi invariable que nos alphabets. Les Égyptiens étaient habitués à représenter directement leurs idées; l'expression des sons n'était, dans leur écriture idéographique, qu'un moyen auxiliaire; et lorsque l'occasion de s'en servir se présenta plus fréquemment, ils songèrent bien à étendre leurs moyens d'exprimer les sons, mais ne renoncèrent point pour cela à leurs écritures idéographiques, consacrées par la religion et par leur usage continu pendant un grand nombre de siècles. Ils procédèrent alors, comme l'ont fait dans des conjonctures absolument pareilles les Chinois, qui, pour écrire un mot étranger à leur langue, ont tout simplement adopté les signes idéographiques dont la prononciation leur paraît offrir le plus d'analogie avec chaque syllabe ou élément du mot étranger qu'il s'agit de transcrire. On conçoit donc que les Égyptiens voulant exprimer soit une voyelle, soit une consonne, soit une syllabe d'un mot étranger, se soient servis d'un signe hiéroglyphique *exprimant* ou *représentant* un objet quelconque dont le nom, en langue parlée, contenait ou dans son entier, ou dans sa première partie, le son de la voyelle, de la consonne ou de la syllabe qu'il s'agissait d'écrire.

C'est ainsi que parmi les hiéroglyphes phonétiques dont le son est déjà reconnu, l'*épervier*, qui exprimait la *vie*, *l'ame*, ⲃⲁⲉ, ⲃⲁⲓ, *ahé*, *ahi*, ou tout autre *oiseau* en général, en égyptien ⲃⲁⲗⲏⲧ *halét*, est probablement devenu le signe du son A ; que l'hiéroglyphe dit *signe de l'eau*, qui, dans les textes idéographiques, représente certainement la préposition égyptienne ⲛ *de*, est devenu le signe de l'articulation N ; que la *bouche*, en égyptien ⲣⲟ *ro*, a été choisie pour représenter la consonne grecque P, etc. Nous concevrons de même comment le son T a été exprimé indifféremment, soit par le *segment de sphère*, puisque ce caractère, dans l'écriture idéographique, est le signe de l'article féminin ϯ *ti* ou ⲧⲉ *té*, soit par une *main ouverte*, qui se disait ⲧⲟⲧ *tot* (*vola, manus*) en langue égyptienne. Il en est de même de tous les autres sons rendus par des caractères différents, comme nous l'établirons bientôt par des exemples plus nombreux. Cette multiplicité de signes n'a donc d'autre origine que les procédés propres à la méthode que nous venons d'exposer.

Bien plus, les caractères démotiques employés pour exprimer phonétiquement les noms propres, caractères que nous connaissions déjà par l'inscription de Rosette, se trouvent n'être autre chose que les caractères *hiératiques qui répondent exactement aux caractères hiéroglyphiques* dont nous venons de reconnaître aussi l'emploi phonétique.

Nous avons vu que le son K était rendu, dans les noms Κλεοπατρα et Αλεξανδρος, par deux signes qui diffèrent de forme (le *quart de cercle* et le *vase à anneau*); mais l'homophonie de ces deux caractères ne saurait être douteuse, puisque le signe initial du nom démotique de Cléopâtre (1) n'est autre que l'équivalent hiératique de l'hiéroglyphe représentant le *vase à anneau* que nous avons justement supposé être le signe du son K, dans le cartouche hiéroglyphique ΑΛΚΣΑΝΤΡΣ. Ces deux caractères homophones doivent donc être admis. Nous trouverons ailleurs d'autres exemples d'homophonies pareilles, tous procédant de la même cause.

Quant au second des caractères hiéroglyphiques qui représentent le son Σ dans ΑΛΚΣΑΝΤΡΣ (les *deux sceptres horizontaux affrontés* (2)), lequel diffère essentiellement du *trait recourbé* qui, dans ΠΤΟΛΜΗΣ, représente aussi le son Σ, l'homophonie de ces deux signes est, nous osons le dire, incontestable; car ces deux signes hiéroglyphiques *sont rendus dans les textes hiératiques par un seul et même caractère*, comme vous pouvez le reconnaître, Monsieur, dans le Tableau général des signes hiératiques, que j'ai présenté l'année dernière à l'Académie (3), et comme il est facile de s'en assurer en comparant le manuscrit hiératique gravé dans la *Description de l'Égypte* (4), avec le grand manuscrit hiéroglyphique publié dans le même ouvrage (5). Cette

---

(1) Voyez ma planche I, n° 17.
(2) *Idem*, planche I, n° 25.
(3) Tableau général des signes hiératiques et hiéroglyphiques comparés, Ire classe, n° 14; VIe classe, n° 8 et n° 9.
(4) Antiquités, vol. II, pl. 62, pag. 1 et 2.
(5) *Idem*, planche 74, de la colonne 120 à la colonne 104.

collation de ces deux légendes démontrera l'emploi indifférent des deux signes l'un pour l'autre dans les textes idéographiques, et la collation de certains autres manuscrits, tels que la page 4 du même manuscrit de la bibliothèque royale, ou la page 8 du manuscrit de M. Fontana (1), comparées, la première avec les colonnes 87 à 83 pl. 74, et la seconde avec les colonnes 93 à 86 de la même planche 74 du grand manuscrit hiéroglyphique, donnera en outre pour équivalent *hiératique* du signe hiéroglyphique représentant deux sceptres affrontés, un caractère (2) qui est exactement le même que le signe démotique représentant aussi l'articulation Σ dans les mots ΑΛΚΣΑΝΤΡΣ (3) (Alexandre) et ΣΝΤΚΣΣ (4) (συνταξις) du texte populaire de l'inscription de Rosette. Enfin, comme dernière preuve de la valeur commune de ces deux signes, nous citerons un second cartouche hiéroglyphique phonétique, contenant le nom d'Alexandre, et sculpté à Karnac (*Description de l'Égypte, Antiquités*, vol. 3, pl. 38, n° 15) (5), dans lequel les deux Σ de ce nom sont rendus par le signe composé des *deux sceptres horizontaux*, répété deux fois.

On peut donc considérer comme bien déterminée la

---

(1) *Copie figurée d'un rouleau de papyrus trouvé en Égypte, publié par M. Fontana et expliqué par M. de Hammer*, Vienne, Strauss, 1822.

(2) Voyez ma planche I, n° 27.
(3) *Idem*, planche I, n° 1 et 13.
(4) *Idem*, planche I, n° 11.
(5) *Idem*, planche I, n° 26, à la suite de ce Mémoire.

valeur *phonétique* des quinze signes hiéroglyphiques tirés des trois cartouches qui viennent d'être analysés.

On trouve sculpté au plafond de la grande porte triomphale de Karnac à Thèbes (*Desc. de l'Égypte*, *Ant.* vol. 3, pl. 5o), le cartouche phonétique d'un PTOLÉMÉE, suivi des titres *toujours vivant*, *chéri de Phtha*, en caractères idéographiques. Il est accompagné d'un cartouche qui est nécessairement un nom de femme, puisqu'il est terminé par les signes idéographiques du genre féminin, comme le nom hiéroglyphique de la reine Cléopâtre déjà retrouvé. Dans ce nouveau nom de reine Lagide, nous reconnaissons facilement, au moyen des caractères hiéroglyphico-phonétiques déjà fixés, le nom de Bérénice orthographié BPNHKΣ presque comme dans le papyrus démotique du cabinet du roi; et ce nom propre (1) nous donne un nouveau signe phonétique, celui du B, représenté par une espèce de *patère* (2), et de plus de

---

(1) Voyez ma planche I, n° 32 et 33.

(2) C'est sans doute par la forme de ce même signe, qui a quelque analogie avec la représentation d'une *corbeille*, que M. le docteur Young a été conduit à reconnaître le nom de *Bérénice* dans le cartouche qui le contient en effet. Mais ce savant anglais pensa que les hiéroglyphes qui forment les noms propres, pouvaient exprimer des syllabes entières, qu'ils étaient ainsi une sorte de *rébus*, et que le signe initial du nom de Bérénice, par exemple, représentait la syllabe Bɪp qui veut dire *corbeille* en langue égyptienne. Ce point de départ faussa en très-grande partie l'analyse phonétique qu'il a tentée sur les noms de *Ptolémée* et de *Bérénice*, où il a cependant reconnu la valeur phonétique de quatre signes : ce sont le Π, une des formes du T, une des formes du M, et celle de l'I ; mais l'ensemble de son alphabet

nouvelles formes du K et du Σ qui reparaîtront dans plusieurs autres cartouches. Quant à ces variations en général, trouvez bon, Monsieur, que, pour ne pas donner à la lettre que vous me permettez de vous adresser, une trop grande étendue, je cesse de les faire remarquer à mesure que nous les rencontrerons, les ayant soigneusement réunies dans l'alphabet complet, formant la dernière des planches qui accompagnent ma lettre. Mais vous pouvez, Monsieur, vous assurer sans peine de l'homophonie de ces signes variés, puisque chacun d'eux se retrouvera dans plusieurs autres noms propres dont la lecture ne vous offrira pas d'ailleurs la moindre incertitude.

Réunissant donc l'ensemble des signes phonétiques qui viennent d'être isolément recueillis et qui composent l'alphabet général, je vais successivement mettre sous vos yeux et très-sommairement, d'après les planches de la Description de l'Égypte, les noms propres tracés en hiéroglyphes phonétiques sur ceux des monuments de cette contrée qui nous sont si bien connus par ce

---

syllabique établi sur ces deux noms seulement, fut tout-à-fait inapplicable aux nombreux noms propres phonétiques inscrits sur les monuments de l'Égypte. Toutefois M. le docteur Young a fait en Angleterre, sur les monuments écrits de l'ancienne Égypte, des travaux analogues à ceux qui m'ont occupé pendant tant d'années; et ses recherches sur le texte intermédiaire et le texte hiéroglyphique de l'inscription de Rosette, comme sur les manuscrits que j'ai fait reconnaître pour *hiératiques*, présentent une série de résultats très-importants. Voyez *Encyclopædia britannica, supplément*, vol. IV, par. I. Edimburgh, december 1819.

magnifique ouvrage, graces à la fidélité de nos voyageurs, et aux lumières qui ont dirigé son exécution (1).

Parmi ces noms, plusieurs appartiennent à la période grecque de l'histoire d'Égypte.

On lira donc avec nous :

1° Le nom d'*Alexandre*, sculpté deux fois sur les édifices de Karnac. Il eût été bien surprenant en effet de ne point retrouver le nom de ce conquérant, écrit sur les monuments de l'antique capitale de l'Égypte. Il y est orthographié ΑΛΚΣΑΝΤΡΣ (2) et ΑΛΚΣΝΤΡΕΣ (3) comme dans l'écriture démotique. Ce nom illustre remplit toute la capacité des cartouches. Il est à regretter qu'on n'ait point copié les légendes d'hiéroglyphes qui les précèdent ou qui les suivent : elles nous eussent donné les titres et les qualifications de ce nouveau souverain.

2° Le nom de *Ptolémée*, commun à tous les Lagides. Tantôt il occupe le cartouche entier, comme on le voit deux fois dans la sixième ligne du texte hiéroglyphique de la pierre de Rosette (4), à Dendera (5), sur le mo-

---

(1) On sait que M. Jomard est le commissaire du gouvernement chargé de diriger l'exécution de cet ouvrage.

(2) Description de l'Égypte, Antiquités, vol. III, planche 38, n° 13. Voyez à la fin de cette lettre planche I, n° 25.

(3) Description de l'Égypte, *idem*, planche 38, n° 15, et notre planche I, n° 26.

(4) Voyez notre planche I, n° 28.

(5) *Idem*, n° 29. Description de l'Égypte, vol. IV, pl. 28, n° 26.

nolithe de Qous (1), etc., etc. Tantôt, ce qui est plus ordinaire, il se montre accompagné des titres idéographiques *toujours vivant, chéri de Phtha* (2); *toujours vivant, chéri d'Isis* (3); *toujours vivant, chéri de Phtha et d'Isis.*

Le nom que portèrent tous les souverains de la dynastie macédonienne, et qui se lit ordinairement ΠΤΟΛΜΗΣ (4) et quelquefois ΠΤΛΟΜΗΣ (5), est presque toujours précédé d'un autre cartouche qui contient les surnoms particuliers du Ptolémée, tracés en hiéroglyphes idéographiques, tels que *Dieu sauveur, Dieu Évergète, Dieu Épiphane, Dieu Adelphe,* etc. Je me réserve de faire connaître la série entière de ces surnoms idéographiques dans un travail spécial. Il ne s'agit ici que des noms écrits phonétiquement. Toutefois lorsque ce même surnom n'est point, comme les précédents, une simple qualification, et lorsqu'il est réellement *un nom* emprunté à une *langue étrangère* aux Égyptiens, ce même surnom est alors écrit en hiéroglyphes phonétiques, et devient susceptible de lecture comme le nom même de *Ptolémée*. Vous trouverez bientôt, monsieur, deux exemples de cette particularité.

---

(1) *Idem*, n° 30. Description de l'Égypte, Antiq., vol. IV, pl. I, n° 3; et notre planche I, n° 30.

(2) Voyez notre planche I, n° 22 et 23, etc.

(3) *Idem*, n° 23 bis. Voyez aussi Description de l'Égypte, A. vol. I, planche 43, n° 3, etc.

(4) Voyez notre pl. I, n° 29 et 31.

(5) *Idem*, planche I, n° 30.

3° Le nom de *Bérénice* orthographié ΒΡΝΗΚΣ, se lit deux fois au plafond de la porte triomphale du sud à Karnac (1).

4° On remarque sur les bas-reliefs des temples de Philæ trois cartouches accolés (2); le premier contient, en écriture idéographique, *les dieux Évergètes chéris*, etc.; le second le nom de *Ptolémée* (ΠΤΟΛΜΗΣ) *toujours vivant, chéri d'Isis*, et le troisième le nom phonétique ΚΛΕΟΠΑΤΡΑ précédé du titre idéographique *sa sœur*: ces trois petits tableaux nous donnent la série suivante: *Les dieux Évergètes chéris du soleil,* etc., *Ptolémée toujours vivant chéri d'Isis, et sa sœur Cléopâtre*, qui ne peut se rapporter qu'à Ptolémée Évergète second, et à Cléopâtre sa sœur, et sa première femme, veuve de Philométor.

L'obélisque de Philæ qui se rapporte au même Évergète second, présente aussi le nom de *Cléopâtre* (3), mais il est précédé des deux désignations idéographiques *sa femme* et *sa sœur*. S'il faut entendre par là, comme nous le pensons, les deux Cléopâtres (Βασιλισση Κλεοπατρα τη Αδελφη και Βασιλισση Κλεοπατρα τη γυναικι) mentionnées dans l'inscription grecque du socle, le car-

---

(1) Planche I, n° 32 et 33. Voyez aussi Description de l'Égypte, Antiq. vol. III, pl. 50.

(2) Le dessin de ce bas-relief existe dans les riches portefeuilles d'un savant architecte, membre de l'Institut, qui doit bientôt faire jouir le public des importantes conquêtes qu'il a faites pour les arts dans ses voyages en Orient.

(3) Voyez ma planche I, n° 24.

touche hiéroglyphique ΚΛΕΟΠΑΤΡΑ se rapporte à la fois et à Cléopâtre fille d'Épiphane, veuve de Philométor, *sœur* et première femme d'Évergète second, et à Cléopâtre, fille de la précédente et de Philométor, et seconde *femme* de ce même Évergète. Au reste le nom de Cléopâtre, qui fut celui de plusieurs reines d'Égypte, se retrouve très-fréquemment sur les colonnes des portiques de Philæ, sur les corniches du grand temple d'Ombos, sur les monuments de Thèbes et de Dendera (1).

5° La frise intérieure de l'enceinte du grand temple d'Edfou nous offre un long cartouche renfermant la légende Ptolémée, *surnommé* Alexandre, *toujours vivant, chéri de Phtha* (2). Le nom est écrit ΠΤΟΛΜΗΣ et se trouve séparé du surnom ΑΡΚΣΝΤΡΣ, par un groupe idéographique (3) répondant au mot grec ἐπικαλουμενος qui, sur le contrat de Ptolémaïs, avertit aussi du *surnom* de *Ptolémée Alexandre*. Un cartouche (4) semblable dans lequel le nom et le surnom sont également écrits ΠΤΟΛΜΗΣ et ΑΡΚΣΝΤΡΣ accompagnés des titres idéographiques *toujours vivant, chéri de Phtha*, quoique avec des éléments différents, est sculpté sur le grand temple d'Ombos.

---

(1) *Idem* n° 34, 35 et 36. Voyez l'explication des planches.
(2) Même planche n° 40; et Description de l'Égypte, A, vol. I, pl. 60, n° 9.
(3) Même planche I, n° 38.
(4) Description de l'Égypte, A, vol. I, pl. 43, n° 8. Voyez notre planche I, n° 41.

Vous aurez sans doute remarqué, monsieur, le changement du Λ en P dans le surnom de Ptolémée *Alexandre*, tandis que le nom d'*Alexandre* le grand que nous avons lu sur les édifices de Karnac, porte deux fois le Λ conformément à l'orthographe grecque. Mais la confusion de ces deux lettres d'un même organe, l'emploi indifférent de ces deux liquides l'une pour l'autre, n'a rien qui doive étonner surtout dans l'Égypte ancienne où la confusion du Λ pour le P ou du P pour le Λ paraît avoir été telle, que l'emploi presque exclusif du Λ pour le P caractérisa fondamentalement le troisième dialecte de la langue égyptienne, le *Baschmourique*, que je persiste à considérer comme le langage vulgaire de l'Égypte moyenne. Nous trouverons d'ailleurs dans de nouveaux cartouches phonétiques, des exemples multipliés de l'usage indifférent de ces deux consonnes l'une pour l'autre.

6° Parmi les cartouches que les membres de la Commission d'Égypte ont dessinés sur les édifices de Dendéra, il en est un (1) qui vous intéressera, monsieur, sous plusieurs rapports. La légende suivante y est exprimée soit phonétiquement soit idéographiquement : ΠΤΟΛΜΗΣ (Ptolémée) *surnommé* ΝΗΟ ΚΗΣΡΣ (*jeune ou nouveau César*) *toujours vivant, chéri d'Isis*. Ce nom de *Ptolémée* et ce surnom de *jeune César* ou de *nouveau César* s'appliquent sans difficulté à un jeune prince dont

---

(1) Voyez ma planche I, n° 42; et Description de l'Égypte, Λ, vol. IV, planche 28, n° 15.

la mort fut aussi malheureuse que la naissance. On y reconnaît, en effet, ce fils dont la reine Cléopâtre se montra si orgueilleuse, parce que Jules-César en fut le père; cet enfant porta, selon Plutarque (1), le nom de *Cæsarion*, et Dion-Cassius (2) le désigne plus complètement sous ceux de *Ptolémée-Cæsarion;* c'est là certainement le Πτολεμαιος Νεο-Καισαρ du cartouche hiéroglyphique. Il est vrai que l'existence du nom de ce prince, gravé en caractères sacrés sur un des principaux temples de l'Égypte, fait supposer qu'il a dû être un de ses rois; l'histoire ne parle point de ses actions, mais elle a conservé le souvenir de son règne éphémère. Ptolémée-Cæsarion fut en effet reconnu et proclamé roi d'Égypte étant à peine âgé de sept ans. Il succédait à deux autres rois, ses oncles, victimes, bien jeunes aussi, des discordes publiques. Ce fut des Triumvirs vainqueurs à Philippes que Cæsarion reçut la couronne, parce que Cléopâtre sa mère les avait secondés. C'est encore Dion-Cassius qui le rapporte textuellement (3). Mais, liée au sort d'Antoine, Cléopâtre bientôt après eut Octave pour ennemi; et ce même enfant, Cæsarion, sembla quelque temps être le seul motif des guerres qui désolèrent alors la république romaine. Antoine, maître de l'Égypte et vainqueur de l'Orient, déclara le jeune Pto-

---

(1) In Cæsare, pag. 731.

(2) XLVII, pag. 345.

(3) Voyez les *Annales des Lagides*, par M. Champollion-Figeac, tome II, pages 343 à 381.

lémée le fils légitime de Jules-César, et lui décerna le titre de *roi des rois*, moins peut-être pour relever sa naissance et son rang, que pour abaisser Octave (1). Celui-ci, poursuivant à la fois Antoine son compétiteur et cet enfant roi qu'on disait fils, plus que lui, de Jules César, réussit enfin à leur arracher la vie; Cléopâtre se donna la mort, et l'antique monarchie égyptienne fut changée en une préfecture romaine.

Le passage de Dion Cassius nous donne approximativement l'époque où ce cartouche hiéroglyphique de Ptolémée Cæsarion a dû être inscrit sur le temple de Dendéra à côté de celui de *Cléopâtre* sa mère (2), car la couronne fut donnée à Cæsarion la onzième année de Cléopâtre, l'an 40 avant l'ère chrétienne. Le bas-relief du temple de Dendéra est le premier monument public connu qui rappelle le nom d'un jeune roi presque inaperçu dans l'histoire, et c'est sans aucun doute à ce même *Ptolémée-Cæsarion* que nous devons rapporter aussi les deux cartouches accolés, sculptés également à Dendéra (3), et qui, entièrement phonétiques, renferment les seuls mots ΠΤΟΛΜΗΣ ΚΗΣΛΣ (pour ΚΗΣΡΣ) *Ptolémée-Cæsar*.

Tels sont les principaux des noms de rois macédoniens

---

(1) *Idem, idem.*

(2) Planche I, n° 36. — Description de l'Égypte, A, vol. IV, pl. 28, n° 27.

(3) Planche I, n° 43.— Description de l'Égypte, A, vol. IV, pl. 28, n° 26 et 25.

d'Égypte, que j'ai retrouvés parmi les noms propres hiéroglyphiques gravés dans la *Description de l'Égypte*. Il est facile de sentir combien l'inspection des monuments mêmes pourrait en multiplier le nombre.

Vous partagerez sans doute aussi, monsieur, toute ma surprise, lorsque le même alphabet hiéroglyphique phonétique appliqué à une foule d'autres cartouches gravés dans le même ouvrage, vous donnera les titres, les noms et jusqu'aux surnoms des empereurs romains, énoncés en *langue grecque* et écrits avec ces mêmes hiéroglyphes phonétiques.

On y lit en effet :

1° Le titre impérial Αυτοκρατωρ, occupant à lui seul toute la capacité d'un cartouche (1), ou bien encore suivi des titres idéographiques *toujours vivant* (2), orthographié ΑΟΤΟΚΡΤΡ, ΑΟΤΚΡΤΟΡ, ΑΟΤΑΚΡΤΡ, et même ΑΟΤΟΚΛΤΛ (3), le Λ étant employé *baschmouriquement* (pardonnez-moi l'expression) pour le P.

Les cartouches renfermant ce titre sont presque toujours accolés ou mis en rapport avec un second cartouche contenant, comme nous le verrons bientôt, les *noms propres* des empereurs. Mais quelquefois aussi on trouve ce mot dans des cartouches absolument isolés. L'exemple le plus remarquable sans doute que je puisse

---

(1) Voyez ma planche II, n° 44, 45 et 46.

(2) Voyez ma planche II, n° 47.

(3) Description de l'Égypte, Ant., vol. IV, pl. 27, n° 13, etc.; et ma planche II, n° 48 et 49.

citer de cette particularité, est le bas-relief sculpté sur la seconde pierre du zodiaque circulaire de Dendéra, monument célèbre dont la munificence royale vient d'enrichir le Cabinet des Antiques. D'après la belle gravure publiée dans la Description de l'Égypte, on voit à droite une grande figure de femme sculptée de ronde bosse entre deux longues colonnes perpendiculaires d'hiéroglyphes. Au bas de la colonne de gauche est un cartouche (1) qui contient seulement le titre ΑΟΤΚΡΤΡ. Cette partie importante du monument n'est pas à Paris; la pierre a été sciée vers ce point même parce qu'on n'a eu pour objet que d'enlever le zodiaque circulaire seul, et on l'a ainsi isolé d'un bas-relief qui s'y rapportait selon toutes les probabilités. Quoi qu'il en soit, le cartouche dont je viens de donner la lecture, établit, d'une manière incontestable, que le bas-relief et le zodiaque circulaire ont été sculptés par des mains égyptiennes sous la domination des Romains. Notre alphabet acquiert par ce fait seul une haute importance, puisqu'il simplifie beaucoup une question si long-temps agitée, et sur laquelle la plupart de ceux qui l'ont examinée n'ont présenté que des opinions incertaines et souvent diamétralement opposées. Il eût été à désirer qu'un second cartouche accolé au premier nous donnât, comme sur beaucoup d'autres bas-reliefs égyptiens, le nom même de l'empereur. Mais si, en pareille matière, les conjectures étaient admissibles, plusieurs circonstances me porte-

---

(1) Voyez ma planche II, n° 50.

raient à croire que ce titre ainsi isolé pourrait appartenir ou à l'empereur Claude ou plutôt à l'empereur Néron, dont beaucoup de médailles frappées en Égypte ne portent en effet aussi pour toute légende que le titre seul ΑΥΤΟΚΡΑΤΩΡ (1).

2° Le titre de ΚΑΙΣΑΡ ou ΚΑΙΣΑΡΟΣ renfermé seul dans un cartouche ou suivi des épithètes idéographiques *toujours vivant, chéri d'Isis*, se montre isolé dans les édifices de Philæ et de Dendéra (2). Il est orthographié ΚΗΣΡΣ ou ΚΗΣΑΣ indifféremment.

3° D'autres cartouches portent les titres d'*empereur* et de *César* réunis sous les formes suivantes : ΑΟΤΟΚΡΤΡ ΚΗΣΡΣ, ΑΟΤΟΚΡΤΟΡ ΚΕΣΡΣ, ΑΟΤΚΡΤΡ ΚΗΣΡ, et même ΑΟΤΚΡΤΛ ΚΗΣΡΣ (3). Mais ces mêmes cartouches sont combinés avec d'autres renfermant le nom propre de l'empereur.

4° La corniche de la partie postérieure du temple de l'ouest à Philæ (4), est décorée de six bas-reliefs représentant tous un souverain la tête ornée de la coiffure royale appelée *Pschent* (coiffure dont l'inscription de Rosette nous a conservé le nom dans son texte grec et nous a retracé la forme dans son texte hiéroglyphique); ce personnage est assis sur un trône, et deux déesses debout lui présentent un emblème absolument

---

(1) Zoëga, *Numi Ægyptii imperatorii*, pages 14 et 22.
(2) Voyez l'explication des planches n° 51, 52, 53, 54, et 55, et pl. II.
(3) Planche II, n° 56, 57, 58, 59 et 60.
(4) Description de l'Égypte, Ant., tome I.

(27)

semblable à celui que portent dans leurs mains les chefs militaires, qui, sur un des bas-reliefs du palais de Médinet-Abou à Thèbes (1), précèdent et suivent un ancien conquérant égyptien dans une cérémonie triomphale. Cette composition m'a sur-le-champ rappelé l'article du décret porté par les prêtres réunis à Memphis et gravé sur la pierre de Rosette; article qui ordonne de représenter *dans les temples de l'Égypte l'image du roi Ptolémée Épiphane, à laquelle l'image du Dieu principal du temple présentera l'insigne de la Victoire* (2). Je m'attendais en quelque sorte à lire dans les *deux cartouches* (3) qui sont placés à droite et à gauche de ces bas-reliefs, le nom de *Ptolémée Épiphane*; mais on y trouve en réalité la légende ΑΟΤΚΡΤΡ ΚΗΣΡΣ (*l'empereur César*), *toujours vivant, chéri d'Isis*, qui ne peut se rapporter qu'à l'empereur Auguste, dont les médailles grecques frappées en Égypte n'offrent assez ordinairement que ces deux mêmes mots (4); et je fais remarquer ici cette similitude, dont vous verrez une multitude d'autres exemples, parce que l'autorité qui faisait inscrire les titres et les noms des empereurs sur les temples en écriture hiéroglyphique, était certainement la même qui réglait la légende de leurs médailles d'Égypte. Quant

---

(1) Description de l'Égypte, Ant., vol. II, planche 11.
(2) Inscription de Rosette, texte grec, ligne 39. Le texte démotique dit *l'image du Dieu*, ligne 23.
(3) Voyez ma planche II, n° 61.
(4) Zoëga, *Numi Ægyptii imperatorii*, pages 3, 8, etc.

au sujet des bas-reliefs de Philæ, puisqu'ils se rapportent à Auguste, ils pourraient rappeler sa victoire d'Actium qui, pour l'Égypte, devint l'origine d'une ère nouvelle et très connue.

5° Le nom de l'empereur *Tibère* se lit plusieurs fois sur les murs du temple de l'ouest à Philæ. Deux cartouches réunis y forment la légende suivante : ΑΟΤΚΡΤΡ-ΤΒΡΗΣ ΚΗΣΡΣ *toujours vivant* (1); et plusieurs autres encore groupés deux à deux, portent : ΑΟΤΚΡΤΡ ΤΒΛΗΣ ΚΗΣΡΣ *toujours vivant* (2). Cette même légende est aussi répétée neuf fois sur la frise de ce même temple (3), et n'est encore, presque lettre pour lettre, qu'une transcription de la légende des médailles grecques de Tibère frappées en Égypte (4).

6° Les monuments de Philæ offrent aussi deux autres cartouches accolés qui renferment les titres et le nom de *Domitien*, en ces termes : ΑΟΤΚΡΤΡ ΤΟΜΤΗΝΣ ΣΒΣΤΣ, *l'empereur Domitien Auguste* (5). Nous retrouvons des légendes de cet empereur beaucoup plus étendues sur les édifices de Dendéra; elles sont renfermées dans deux cartouches réunis, qui se lisent ou se traduisent sans difficulté ΑΟΤΚΡΤΡ-ΚΗΣΡΣ ΤΟΜΤΗΝΣ (*l'empereur César Domitien*), *surnommé* ΚΡΜΝΗΚΣ (*Germanicus*) (6). Ces

---

(1) Voyez ma planche II, n° 64.
(2) *Idem*, planche II, n° 63.
(3) *Idem*, planche II, n° 62.
(4) Voyez Zoëga, et Mionnet, Description etc., tome VI.
(5) Voyez ma planche III, n° 65.
(6) *Idem*, planche III, n° 66, 67, 68.

légendes sont en tout conformes à celles des médailles grecques de cet empereur, frappées en Égypte

7° Un monument d'un autre ordre, un obélisque, celui qu'on appelle à Rome l'*Obélisque Pamphile*, présente aussi le nom phonétique de *Domitien*, en l'honneur duquel il a été sans doute sculpté en Égypte, et érigé dans la capitale de l'empire. On remarque d'abord sur la face orientale de cet obélisque le titre idéographique *Roi*, suivi d'un cartouche renfermant le titre de ΚΗΣΡ (*César*), avec d'autres signes dont l'incertitude, dans la gravure de Kircher, ne me permet point de hasarder la lecture. Les cartouches de la face orientale et de la face méridionale renferment ces mots : ΚΗΣΡΣ ΤΜΗΤΙΗΝΣ (*César Domitien*) (1). Enfin les deux cartouches placés vers le bas de la face septentrionale du même obélisque, forment la légende : ΑΟΤΚΡΤΛΚΗΣΡΣ ΤΜΗΤΕΝΣ ΣΒΣΤΣ (2), l'empereur César Domitien Auguste.

8° Le nom de *Vespasien* son Père se lit dans un des cartouches supérieurs de la même face, compris dans la formule idéographique *qui a reçu la puissance venant de* ΟΥΣΠΣΗΝΣ *son père* (3); les quatre premiers signes de ce cartouche sont trop rapprochés sur la gravure de Kircher.

9° Il existe dans la partie orientale de l'île de Philæ,

---

(1) Voyez ma planche III, n° 69.
(2) *Idem*, planche III, n° 70, cartouches *a* et *b*.
(3) *Idem*, planche III, n° 70 bis.

un édifice fort élégant, mais dont la décoration hiéro-glyphique n'a jamais été terminée. Du nombre des parties complètes, sont deux entre-colonnements dont l'un a été dessiné, dans tous ses détails, par la Commission d'Égypte (1). Les cartouches dont il est chargé, se rapportent tous à l'empereur *Trajan.* L'image en pied de ce bon prince, faisant une offrande à Isis et à Arouéris, est accompagnée de deux cartouches contenant les mots ΑΟΤΚΡΤΡ ΚΗΣΡΣ ΝΡΟ· ΤΡΗΝΣ..... (*l'empereur César Nerva Trajan*) (2); et la légende ΤΡΗΝΣ ΚΗΣΡΣ (*Trajan César*) *toujours vivant* (3), renfermée dans un cartouche termine aussi la colonne perpendiculaire d'hiéroglyphes sculptée à la droite du bas-relief. La frise de ce même entre-colonnement est ornée de neuf petits cartouches. Celui du centre, un peu plus grand que les huit autres, soutenu par deux *Uréus* ou *aspics royaux*, renferme le nom de *Trajan*, ΤΡΗΝΣ, avec l'épithète idéographique *toujours vivant.* Combiné avec celui de droite et celui de gauche, il produit la légende suivante : *l'empereur toujours vivant; Trajan toujours vivant; César germe éternel d'Isis.* Les trois cartouches rangés à la droite de ces derniers, produisent les mots *Trajan toujours vivant, César, Germanicus, Dacicus, toujours vivant.* Enfin, les trois cartouches de la gauche donnent la légende : Nerva Trajan *toujours vivant,* Empereur César *tou-*

---

(1) Descript. de l'Égypte, Antiq., vol. II, pl. 27, n° 2.
(2) Voyez ma planche III, n° 71.
(3) *Idem*, planche III, n° 72.

jours vivant, Auguste (1) *toujours vivant chéri d'Isis*. Le nom de Trajan se lit encore sur le grand temple d'Ombos; deux cartouches dessinés dans les ruines de ce monument, forment en effet la série ΑΟΤΟΚΡΤΡ ΚΗΣΛ ΝΛΟΛ - ΤΡΗΝΣ (*l'empereur César-Nerva-Trajan*), surnommé ΚΡΜΝΗΚΣ, ΤΗΚΚΣ (*Germanicus, Dacicus*) (2); ce qui est encore, mot pour mot, la légende des médailles grecques de cet empereur frappées en Égypte.

10° C'est sur un des obélisques de Rome, celui qu'on appelle l'*Obélisque Barbérini*, que nous trouverons le nom du successeur de Trajan, Hadrien, qui aima tant l'Égypte et y laissa de si nombreux souvenirs. Ce monolithe portait, sur la première face, un grand cartouche aujourd'hui entièrement détruit, et qui, comme me l'indiquent les signes idéographiques dont il est précédé et ceux dont il est suivi, contenait le nom et les titres de l'empereur. Mais le nom d'Hadrien est heureusement conservé dans un cartouche placé devant la représentation en pied de ce prince, faisant une offrande au dieu *Phré* (le soleil), vers le haut de la quatrième face de l'obélisque. Ce cartouche, de très-petite proportion sur la gravure de Zoëga, m'a présenté toutefois, fort clairement, neuf hiéroglyphes phonétiques, dont la transcription en lettres grecques donne ἈΤΡΗΝΣ ΚΣΡ *Hadrien-César* (3).

---

(1) Voyez ma planche III, n° 75 *a*.
(2) *Idem*, planche III, n° 74.
(3) *Idem*, planche III, n° 76.

11º La lecture de ce nom ne peut vous offrir aucun doute en elle-même; elle deviendrait certaine, d'ailleurs, s'il pouvait en exister aucun, par le fait seul que le nom de l'impératrice *Sabine*, épouse d'Hadrien, se trouve aussi écrit en hiéroglyphes phonétiques sur le même obélisque. La première face de ce monolithe contient, en effet, une série de signes idéographiques, exprimant les idées : *pareillement son épouse, grandement chérie.* Cette série (1) est suivie de deux cartouches; le premier contient en toutes lettres, le nom de l'impératrice ΣΑΒΗΝΑ (2), suivi des signes idéographiques du genre féminin, comme le sont les noms des reines *Bérénice* et *Cléopâtre*, et du titre encore idéographique *déesse vivante, forte* ou *victorieuse*; le second cartouche qui suit immédiatement, renferme en écriture phonétique, le titre de Σεβαςη (*Auguste*), orthographié ΣΒΣΤΗ (3), et accompagné de la légende idéographique *déesse toujours vivante*. Vous remarquerez sans doute aussi, monsieur, que les deux cartouches relatifs à l'impératrice étant réunis, produisent la légende Σαϐινα ou Σαϐεινα σεϐαςη, qui est justement la seule que portent toutes les médailles grecques de la femme d'Hadrien, frappées en Égypte.

12º Je terminerai cette collection des noms hiéroglyphiques par celui du prince qui mérita si bien à-la-fois et des lettres et de l'humanité; je veux parler du pieux *Antonin*, dont le nom se lit à plusieurs reprises

---

(1) Voyez ma Planche III, nº 77.
(2) *Idem a.*
(3) Planche III, nº 77 *b.* et 79.

sur le *Typhonium* de Dendéra. Deux cartouches apposés produisent la légende suivante : ΑΟΤΟΚΡΤΟΡ ΚΣΡΣ ΑΝΤΟΝΗΝΣ (*l'empereur César-Antonin*), surnommé *toujours vivant* (1).

Mais il nous reste encore, monsieur, à jeter un coup-d'œil rapide sur la nature du système phonétique selon lequel ces noms sont écrits, à nous former une idée exacte de la nature des signes qu'il emploie, et à rechercher aussi les motifs qui purent faire choisir l'image de tel ou tel objet, pour représenter telle consonne ou voyelle plutôt que telle autre.

Quant à l'ensemble du système d'écriture phonétique égyptienne (et nous comprenons à-la-fois sous cette dénomination l'écriture phonétique populaire et l'écriture phonétique hiéroglyphique), il est incontestable que ce système n'est point une écriture purement *alphabétique*, si l'on doit entendre en effet par *alphabétique* une écriture représentant rigoureusement, et chacun dans leur ordre propre, tous le sons et toutes *les articulations* qui forment les mots d'une langue. Nous voyons, en effet, l'écriture phonétique égyptienne, pour représenter le mot *César*, d'après le génitif grec ΚΑΙΣΑΡΟΣ, se contenter souvent d'assembler les signes des consonnes Κ, Σ, Ρ, Σ, sans s'inquiéter de la diphtongue ni des deux voyelles que l'orthographe grecque exige impérieusement, et nous montrer, par exemple, les noms propres ΑΛΕΞΑΝΔΡΟΣ, ΒΕΡΕΝΙΚΗ ou plutôt ΒΕΡΕΝΙΚΗΣ,

---

(1) Voyez ma planche III, n° 78.

ΤΡΑΙΑΝΟΣ, etc., transcrits avec toutes leurs consonnes, il est vrai, mais perdant la plus grande partie de leurs voyelles : ΑΛΚΣΑΝΤΡΣ, ΒΡΝΗΚΣ, ΤΡΗΝΣ. On peut donc assimiler l'écriture phonétique égyptienne, à celle des anciens Phéniciens, aux écritures dites hébraïque, syriaque, samaritaine, à l'arabe cufique, et à l'arabe actuel; écritures que l'on pourrait nommer *semi-alphabétiques*, parce qu'elles n'offrent, en quelque sorte, à l'œil que le squelette seul des mots, les consonnes et les voyelles longues, laissant à la science du lecteur le soin de suppléer les voyelles brèves.

L'exposé des motifs qui déterminèrent les Égyptiens à prendre tel ou tel signe hiéroglyphique pour représenter tel ou tel son, exige un peu plus de développements : je suis forcé d'entrer dans des détails minutieux que je vous prie d'avance, monsieur, de me pardonner en faveur de l'importance de cette question en elle-même, et peut-être aussi des résultats singuliers auxquels son examen peut conduire.

J'ai déja fait pressentir que, pour rendre les *sons* et les *articulations*, et former ainsi une écriture phonétique, les Égyptiens prirent des hiéroglyphes figurant des objets physiques ou exprimant *des idées* dont le nom ou le mot correspondant en langue parlée commençait par la voyelle ou la consonne qu'il s'agissait de représenter. Le rapprochement que nous allons faire des signes hiéroglyphiques exprimant les consonnes avec les mots égyptiens exprimant les objets que ces mêmes hiéroglyphes représentent, lèvera toute incertitude sur la vérité du principe que nous venons d'énoncer, des analogies aussi multipliées ne pouvant être, en aucune manière, un pur effet du hasard. La consonne B est exprimée, 1°, par un hiéroglyphe figurant le petit vase contenant du feu, et qui, placé sur la main d'un bras d'homme, sculpté, soit en bois soit en métal, forme la patère dans laquelle les héros représentés sur les bas-reliefs égyptiens brûlent ordinairement l'encens devant les images des dieux : le mot Bⲣ̄ⲃⲉ *Berbe*, des livres coptes, convient très-bien à ce petit vase.

2° Le B est rendu sur l'obélisque Pamphile, par un quadrupède ; mais la gravure de Kircher est tellement négligée, que nous ne pouvons décider si cet animal est une vache Bⲁϩⲥⲓ (*Bahsi*), un chevreau Bⲁⲁⲙⲡⲉ (*Baampé*), un bouc Bⲁⲣⲏⲓⲧ (*Baréit*), un renard Bⲁϣⲱⲣ (*Baschôr*), le petit quadrupède nommé Bⲟⲓϣ (*Boischi*), ou enfin un schakal Bⲱⲛϣ (*Bônsch.*)

La consonne K est rendue : 1°, par *un vase à anneau*, espèce de *bassin*, et les dictionnaires égyptiens nous présentent les mots Ⲕⲉⲗⲱⲗ (*Kelôl*), Ⲕⲉⲗⲱⲗⲓ (*Kéloli*), Ⲕⲛⲓⲕⲓϫⲓ (*Knikidji*), et Ⲕⲁϫⲓ (*Kadji*), qui tous expriment des *vases*, des *bassins* pour puiser l'eau ;

2° Par une figure représentant soit un *angle* droit avec sa corde, soit une espèce de *triangle*, et le mot Ⲕⲟⲟϩ (*Kooh*), signifie un angle ;

3° Par une espèce de *hutte* ou sorte de *cabane*, en égyptien Ⲕⲁⲗⲓⲃⲓ (*Kalibi*), soit par une espèce d'*enceinte* entourée de murs, Ⲕⲧⲟ (*Kto*), et recouverte d'une *voûte* ou *plafond* Ⲕⲏⲡⲉ (*Képé*);

3.

4º Par une *coiffure* ou *capuchon*, ⲕⲗⲁϥⲧ (*Klaft*); c'est la coiffure ordinaire des personnages privés dans les bas-reliefs égyptiens.

Le Λ est rendu par un *lion* ou une *lionne* dans une attitude de repos parfait. Nous trouverons le motif du choix de cet animal pour représenter la consonne Λ, dans le mot égyptien ⲗⲁⲃⲟ (*Labo*) ou ⲗⲁⲃⲟⲓ (*Laboi*), employé dans les textes coptes, avec la signification de *Lionne* (1). Nous ferons observer que le mot exprimant l'idée de *Lionne*, en arabe لبوة *Lebouah*, et en hébreu לביה *Lébieh*, sont parfaitement semblables au mot égyptien ⲗⲁⲃⲟⲓ (*Laboi*); ajoutons même que ce mot, dont l'orthographe régulière paraît avoir été ⲗⲁϥⲟⲓ (*Lafoi*), n'est qu'un mot composé signifiant *très-velu*, *valdè hirsutus*, et que c'est dans ce sens qu'on aurait aussi quelquefois appliqué ce nom à l'ours dans la version égyptienne des livres saints (2).

Le trait brisé qu'on a cru représenter l'*eau* en écriture hiéroglyphique, y exprime, seulement, la préposition *de*, en égyptien ⲛ; c'est pour cela que ce signe idéographique est devenu celui du son N. Les petits vases qui représentent aussi la consonne N, ne sont autres que ces petits vases d'*albâtre* qu'on trouve si fréquemment en Égypte, et qui servaient à contenir des huiles parfumées ⲛⲉϩ (*Neh*); ces vases portent dans les écrivains grecs le nom d'Ἀλαϐαστρος ou d'Ἀλαϐαστρον.

---

(1) Kircher, *Scala magna*, pag. 164.
(2) Apocalypse, XIII, 2.

La consonne grecque P est exprimée hiéroglyphiquement 1° par l'image de la *bouche* ρο (*Ro*).

2° Par une fleur de *grenade* ρⲩⲁⲛ (*erman*) ou ροⲩⲁⲛ *roman*.

Enfin la consonne T est représentée 1° par l'image d'une *main* ⲧⲟⲧ; 2° par le caractère idéographique de l'article déterminatif du genre féminin ⲧ (*Ti*) ou ⲧⲉ (*Té*); 3° ou par le *niveau* des maçons, en langue égyptienne ⲧⲱⲡⲓ (*Tóri*) où ⲧⲱⲡⲉ (*Tóré*) suivant les dialectes.

Je ne doute point, monsieur, que si nous pouvions déterminer d'une manière certaine l'objet que figurent ou expriment tous les autres hiéroglyphes phonétiques compris dans notre alphabet, il ne me fût très-facile de montrer, dans les lexiques égyptiens-coptes, les noms de ces mêmes objets commençant par la consonne ou les voyelles que leur image représente dans le système hyéroglyphique phonétique.

Cette méthode, suivie pour la composition de l'alphabet phonétique égyptien, fait pressentir jusques à quel point on pouvait multiplier, si on l'eût voulu, le nombre des hiéroglyphes phonétiques, sans nuire pour cela à la clarté de leur expression. Mais tout semble prouver que notre alphabet les renferme en très-grande partie. Nous avons, en effet, le droit de tirer cette conséquence, puisque cet alphabet est le résultat d'une série de noms propres phonétiques, gravés sur les monuments de l'Égypte pendant un intervalle de près de *cinq siècles*, et sur divers points de cette contrée.

Quant aux signes des voyelles de l'alphabet hiéroglyphique, il est aisé de voir qu'ils s'emploient d'une manière assez confuse les uns pour les autres. On ne peut établir sur ce point que les règles générales suivantes :

1° L'épervier, l'ibis, et trois autres espèces d'oiseaux s'emploient constamment pour A ;

2° La feuille ou plume représente indifféremment les voyelles brèves Ă Ĕ, même parfois Ŏ.

3° Les deux feuilles ou plumes répondent indifféremment aux voyelles I, H, ou aux diphthongues IA, AI.

Tout ce que je viens d'exposer sur l'origine, la formation et les anomalies de l'alphabet *hiéroglyphique phonétique*, s'applique presque entièrement à l'alphabet *démotique-phonétique*, dont la seconde colonne de la planche IV contient toute la série des signes, tirés de l'inscription de Rosette et du papyrus nouvellement acquis pour le cabinet du roi.

Ces deux systèmes d'écritures phonétiques étaient aussi intimement liés entre eux que le système *idéographique sacerdotal* le fut avec le système *idéographique populaire* qui n'en était qu'une émanation, et avec le système *hiéroglyphique pur* dont il tirait son origine. Les lettres démotiques ne sont, en effet, pour la plupart, comme nous l'avons annoncé, que les signes *hiératiques* des hiéroglyphes phonétiques eux-mêmes. Il vous sera aisé, monsieur, de reconnaître toute la vérité de cette assertion, en prenant la peine de consulter le Tableau comparatif des signes hiératiques classés à côté du signe hiéroglyphique correspondant, Tableau que j'ai présenté à l'Académie des belles-lettres depuis plus d'une année. Il n'existe donc, au fond, entre les deux alphabets, l'*hiéroglyphique* et le *démotique*, d'autre différence que la forme seule des signes, la valeur et les motifs mêmes de cette valeur demeurant les mêmes. J'ajouterai, enfin, que ces signes phonétiques populaires n'étant autre chose que des caractères hiératiques sans altération, il ne put forcément exister en Égypte que *deux* systèmes d'écritures phonétiques seulement; 1° l'écriture *hiéroglyphique phonétique*, employée sur les grands monuments ; 2° l'écriture *hiératico-démotique*, celle des noms propres grecs du texte intermédiaire de Rosette et du papyrus démotique de la bibliothèque du Roi (*Supra*, p. 4.), et que nous trouverons peut-être un jour employée à transcrire le nom de quelque souverain grec ou romain dans des rouleaux de papyrus en écriture hiératique.

L'écriture phonétique fut donc en usage dans toutes les classes de la nation égyptienne, et elles l'employèrent long-temps comme un auxiliaire obligé des trois méthodes idéographiques. Lorsque, par l'effet de sa conversion au christianisme, le peuple égyptien reçut de ses apôtres l'écriture alphabétique grecque, obligé dès-lors d'écrire tous les mots de sa langue maternelle avec ce nouvel alphabet dont l'adoption l'isola pour toujours de la religion, de l'histoire et des institutions de ses ancêtres, tous les monuments étant, par ce fait, devenus muets pour ces néophites et pour leurs descendants, ces Égyptiens conservèrent toutefois quelque habitude de leur ancienne écriture phonétique ; et nous remarquons, en effet, que dans les plus anciens textes coptes, en dialecte thébain, la plupart des voyelles brèves sont totalement omises, et qu'ils ne présentent souvent, comme les noms hiéroglyphiques des empereurs romains, que des séries de consonnes interrompues de loin en loin par quelques voyelles presque toujours longues. Ce rapprochement nous a paru digne de remarque. Les auteurs grecs et latins ne nous ont transmis aucune notion formelle sur l'écriture phonétique égyptienne; il est fort difficile de déduire même l'existence de ce système, en pressant la lettre de certains passages où quelque chose de pareil semblerait être fort obscurément indiqué. Nous devons donc renoncer à connaître, par la tradition historique, l'époque où les écritures phonétiques furent introduites dans le système graphique des anciens Égyptiens.

Mais les faits parlent assez d'eux-mêmes pour nous autoriser à dire, avec quelque certitude, que l'usage d'une écriture auxiliaire destinée à représenter les sons et les articulations de certains mots, précéda, en Égypte, la domination des Grecs et des Romains, quoiqu'il semble très-naturel d'attribuer l'introduction de l'écriture semi-alphabétique égyptienne à l'influence de ces deux nations européennes, qui se servaient depuis long-temps d'un alphabet proprement dit.

Je fonde mon opinion, à cet égard, sur les deux considérations suivantes, qui vous paraîtront peut-être, monsieur, d'un assez grand poids, pour décider la question.

1° Si les Égyptiens eussent inventé leur écriture phonétique à l'imitation de l'alphabet des Grecs ou de l'alphabet des Romains, ils eussent naturellement établi un nombre de signes phonétiques égal aux éléments connus de l'alphabet grec ou de l'alphabet latin. Or, c'est ce qui n'est point; et la preuve incontestable que l'écriture phonétique égyptienne fut créée dans un tout autre but que celui d'exprimer les sons des noms propres des souverains grecs ou romains, se trouve dans la transcription égyptienne de ces noms eux-mêmes qui, pour la plupart, sont corrompus au point de devenir méconnaissables; d'abord par la suppression ou la confusion de la plus grande partie des voyelles, en second lieu par l'emploi constant des consonnes T pour Δ, K pour Γ, Π pour Φ; enfin par l'emploi accidentel du Λ pour le P, et du P pour le Λ.

2° J'ai la certitude que les mêmes signes *hiéroglyphiques-phonétiques* employés pour représenter les sons des noms propres grecs et romains, sont employés aussi dans des textes idéographiques gravés fort antérieurement à l'arrivée des Grecs en Égypte, et qu'ils ont déjà, dans certaines occasions, la même valeur représentative des sons ou des articulations, que dans les cartouches gravés sous les Grecs et sous les Romains. Le développement de ce fait précieux et décisif appartient à mon travail sur l'écriture hiéroglyphique pure. Je ne pourrais l'établir dans cette lettre sans me jeter dans des détails prodigieusement étendus.

Je pense donc, monsieur, que l'écriture *phonétique*

exista en Égypte à une époque fort reculée; qu'elle était d'abord une partie nécessaire de l'écriture idéographique; et qu'on l'employait aussi alors, comme on le fit après Cambyse, à transcrire (grossièrement il est vrai) dans les textes idéographiques, les noms propres des peuples, des pays, des villes, des souverains, et des individus étrangers dont il importait de rappeler le souvenir dans les textes historiques ou dans les inscriptions monumentales.

J'oserai dire plus : il serait possible de retrouver dans cette ancienne écriture phonétique égyptienne, quelque imparfaite qu'elle soit en elle-même, sinon l'origine, du moins le modèle sur lequel peuvent avoir été calqués les alphabets des peuples de l'Asie occidentale, et surtout ceux des nations voisines de l'Égypte. Si vous remarquez en effet, monsieur, 1° que chaque lettre des alphabets que nous appelons hébreu, chaldaïque et syriaque, porte un nom significatif, noms fort anciens puisqu'ils furent presque tous transmis par les Phéniciens aux Grecs lorsque ceux-ci en reçurent l'alphabet; 2° Que *la première consonne ou voyelle de ces noms* est aussi, dans ces alphabets, *la voyelle ou la consonne que la lecture représente*, vous reconnaîtrez avec moi, dans la création de ces alphabets, une analogie parfaite avec la création de l'alphabet phonétique égyptien : et si des alphabets de ce genre sont formés primitivement, comme tout le prouve, de signes représentant des idées ou objets, il est évident que nous devons reconnaître le peuple inventeur de cette méthode graphique, dans celui qui se servit spécialement d'une écriture idéographique ; c'est dire enfin, que l'Europe, qui reçut de la vieille Égypte les éléments des sciences et des arts, lui devrait encore l'inappréciable bienfait de l'écriture alphabétique.

Du reste je n'ai voulu qu'indiquer ici sommairement cet aperçu fécond en grandes conséquences, et il ressortait naturellement de mon sujet principal, l'*alphabet des hiéroglyphes phonétiques*, dont je me suis proposé d'exposer à la fois la théorie et quelques applications. Celles-ci offrent des résultats déja favorablement appréciés par l'illustre Académie dont les doctes travaux ont donné à l'Europe les premiers principes de la solide érudition, et ne cessent de lui en offrir les plus utiles exemples. Mes essais ajouteront peut-être quelque chose à la série des faits certains dont elle a enrichi l'histoire des vieux peuples ; celle des Égyptiens, qui remplissent encore le monde de leur juste renommée, y puisera quelques lumières nouvelles ; et c'est beaucoup sans doute, aujourd'hui, que de pouvoir faire, avec assurance, un premier pas dans l'étude de leurs monuments écrits, d'y recueillir quelques données précises sur leurs principales institutions auxquelles l'antiquité elle-même a fait une réputation de sagesse que rien du moins n'a encore démentie. Quant aux prodigieux monuments que l'Égypte érigea, nous pouvons enfin lire dans les cartouches qui les décorent, leur chronologie certaine depuis Cambyse, et les époques de leur fondation ou de leurs accroissements successifs sous les dynasties diverses qui la gouvernèrent, la plupart d'entre ces monuments portant à la fois des noms pharaoniques, des noms grecs et des noms romains, et les premiers, caractérisés par le petit nombre de leurs signes, résistant constamment à toute tentative pour y appliquer avec succès l'*alphabet* que je viens de faire connaître. Telle sera, je l'espère, l'utilité de ce travail que je suis très-flatté, monsieur, de produire sous vos honorables auspices; le public lettré ne lui refusera ni son estime, ni son suffrage, puisqu'il a pu obtenir ceux du vénérable Nestor de l'érudition et des lettres françaises, qui les honora et les enrichit par tant de travaux, et qui, d'une main à la fois protectrice et bienveillante, se complut toujours à soutenir et à diriger dans la difficile carrière qu'il a si glorieusement parcourue, tant de jeunes émules qui ont depuis complètement justifié un si vif intérêt. Heureux d'en jouir à mon tour, je n'oserai cependant répondre que de ma profonde gratitude, et du respectueux attachement dont je vous prie, monsieur, de me permettre de vous renouveler publiquement toutes les assurances.

Paris, le 22 septembre 1822 (1).

J. F. CHAMPOLLION le jeune.

---

(1) Un extrait de cette Lettre a été lu à l'Académie royale de Inscriptions et Belles-Lettres, le 27 septembre 1822.

EXPLICATION DES PLANCHES.

On réunit ici la lecture de tous les noms propres exprimés phonétiquement soit en écriture *démotique*, soit en écriture *hiéroglyphique*, et représentés sur nos trois premières planches.

Les noms *démotiques* doivent être lus de droite à gauche. Les signes qui composent les noms *hiéroglyphiques* renfermés dans des cartels ou cartouches, sont disposés de deux manières:

1° Ou ils sont rangés horizontalement; dans ce cas ils peuvent procéder soit de gauche à droite, soit de droite à gauche;

2° Où ils sont tracés en colonne perpendiculaire.

Dans l'un et l'autre cas les hiéroglyphes sont souvent placés deux à deux, trois à trois, etc., les uns au-dessus des autres.

La direction générale des signes hiéroglyphiques formant un nom propre ou une légende, est facile à connaître, et l'on doit en commencer la lecture par le côté de l'inscription vers lequel sont tournées les têtes des animaux qui se trouvent parmi ces signes. Cette règle ne souffre aucune exception.

Les noms et mots phonétiques sont transcrits ici en petites capitales grecques; et le sens des signes purement *hiéroglyphiques*, en lettres italiques.

Planche Ire.
Noms en écriture démotique.

INSCRIPTION DE ROSETTE.

1. ΑΛΚΣΑΝΤΡΣ (Alexandre).
2. ΠΤΛΟΜΗΣ (Ptolémée).
3. ΑΡΣΗΝΕ (Arsinoé).

4. ΒΡΝΙΙΚΕ (Bérénice).
5. ΑΗΕΤΟΣ (Aétès).
6. ΠΡΕ (Pyrrha).
7. ΠΗΛΗΝΣ (Philinus).
8. ΑΡΗΕ (Aréia).
9. ΤΗΕΚΝΣ (Diogène).
10. ΙΡΕΝΕ (Irène).
11. ΣΝΤΚΣΣ (Συνταξις).
12. ΟΥΗΝΝ (*Ionien, Grec*).

PAPYRUS DÉMOTIQUE.

13. ΑΛΚΣΝΤΡΟΣ (Alexandre).
14. ΠΤΛΟΜΗΣ (Ptolémée).
15. ΑΡΣΗΝ (Arsinoé).
16. ΒΡΝΗΚ (Bérénice).
17. ΚΛΟΠΤΡ (Cléopâtre).
18. ΑΠΛΟΝΗΣ (Apollonius).
19. ΑΝΤΗΧΟΣ (Antiochus).
20. ΑΝΤΗΚΝΣ (Antigone).

Noms et signes hiéroglyphiques.

21. Signe idéographique du *genre féminin*.
22. ΠΤΟΛΜΗΣ (Ptolémée) *toujours vivant, chéri de Phtha*. (Inscription de Rosette).
23. ΠΤΟΛΜΗΣ (Ptolémée) *toujours vivant, chéri de Phtha*. (Obélisque de Philæ).
23 bis. ΠΤΟΛΜΗΣ (Ptolémée), *toujours vivant, chéri d'Isis*.
24. ΚΛΕΟΠΑΤΡΑ (Cléopâtre). Ce nom est suivi des signes idéographiques du genre féminin ; voyez n° 21. Obélisque de Philæ.
25. ΑΛΚΣΑΝΤΡΣ (Alexandre le grand). Édifices de Karnac.
26. ΑΛΚΣΝΡΕΣ (Alexandre le grand). Karnac. La lettre T manque entre le N et le P ; cette omission peut venir du sculpteur égyptien même.

27. Caractère hiératique répondant au Σ démotique et hiéroglyphique.
28. ΠΤΟΛΜΗΣ (Ptolémée); tiré du texte hiéroglyphique de l'inscription de Rosette.
29. ΠΤΟΛΜΗΣ (Ptolémée), à Dendéra.
30. ΠΤΛΟΜΗΣ (Ptolémée), monolithe de Qous. (Apollinopolis parva.)
31. ΠΤΟΛΜΗΣ (Ptolémée). Le M est exprimé par le nycticorax, espèce de chouette appelée *Mouladj* en langue égyptienne.
32. ΒΡΝΗΚΣ (Bérénice), suivi des marques idéographiques du genre féminin.
33. ΒΡΝΗΚΣ (Bérénice), gravé comme le précédent, sur la porte triomphale du sud, à Karnac.
34. ΚΛΑΠΤΡΑ (Cléopâtre), avec les signes du féminin (voy. n° 21).
35. ΚΛΑΟΠΤΡΑ (Cléopâtre), avec les mêmes signes.
36. ΚΛΕΟΠΑΤΡΑ (Cléopâtre), avec les mêmes signes.
37. ΚΛΟΠΤΡΑ (Cléopâtre). Ce nom est suivi des signes du genre féminin et du titre idéographique *Déesse*, avec une qualification dont les signes sont incomplets.
38 et 39. Groupe hiéroglyphique répondant au mot grec επικαλουμενος et signifiant aussi *surnommé* : il est placé constamment entre les noms et les surnoms des rois Lagides. Voyez les n°s 40, 41 et 42.
40. ΠΤΛΟΜΗΣ (Ptolémée) *surnommé* ΑΡΚΣΝΤΡΣ (Alexandre) *toujours vivant chéri de Phtha.*
41. ΠΤΟΛΜΗΣ (Ptolémée) *qui est surnommé* ΑΡΚΣΝΤΡΣ (Alexandre), *toujours vivant, chéri de Phtha.*
42. ΠΤΟΛΜΗΣ (Ptolémée) *surnommé* ΝΗΟΚΗΣΡΣ (nouveau César), *toujours vivant, chéri d'Isis.* Il faut observer que les deux *plumes* ou *feuilles* du surnom et qui expriment le son H, sont placées de manière à être prononcées à la fois et après le N et après le K; on trouvera d'autres exemples de cette disposition de signes particuliers aux systèmes hiéroglyphiques soit phonétique, soit idéographique. (Voyez n° 71.)
43. ΠΤΟΛΜΗΣ-ΚΗΣΛΣ (Ptolémée-César), à Dendéra.

Planche II.

Titres impériaux romains.

44. ΑΟΤΟΚΡΤΡ (Αυτοκρατωρ, l'empereur.)
45. ΑΟΤΚΡΤΡ (idem).
46. ΑΟΤΑΚΡΤΡ (idem).
47. ΑΟΤΚΡΤΡ (l'empereur), *toujours vivant.*
48. ΑΟΤΟΚΑΤΑ (l'empereur); frise de Dendéra.
49. ΑΟΤΟΚΑΤΑ (l'empereur).
50. ΑΟΤΚΡΤΡ (l'empereur); ce cartouche est sculpté sur le bas-relief qui touchait, vers la droite, le zodiaque circulaire de Dendéra.
51. ΚΗΣΑΣ (César); le Λ étant employé pour le Ρ.
51 a, b, c, d, e, f. Différents exemples de la manière dont le mot Καισαρ, ou plutôt son génitif Καισαρος, est écrit en lettres hiéroglyphiques. Voici la lecture de ces groupes dans le même ordre ΚΗΣΡΣ, ΚΗΣΛΣ, ΚΗΣΡΣ, ΚΗΣΡΣ, ΚΣΡΣ, ΚΗΣΡ.
52. ΚΗΣΡ ΑΤ (pour Καισαρ αυτοκρατωρ) *l'empereur César toujours vivant, chéri d'Isis.*
53. ΚΗΣΡΣ (César), *toujours vivant, chéri d'Isis.*
54. ΚΗΣΛΣ (César), *toujours vivant, chéri d'Isis.*
55. ΚΗΣΡΣ (César), *toujours vivant, chéri d'Isis.*
56. ΑΟΤΟΚΡΤΛ ΚΗΣΡΣ (l'empereur César).
57. ΑΟΤΟΚΡΤΟΡ ΚΕΣΡΣ (l'empereur César). Le Σ final est ici exprimé par une syrinx ou flûte à Pan, instrument nommé CHBI (*sébi*) en langue égyptienne.
58. ΑΟΤΚΡΤΡ ΚΗΣΡ (l'empereur César).
59. ΑΟΤΟΚΡΤΟΡ ΚΣΡΣ (l'empereur César).
60. ΑΟΤΟΚΡΤΡ ΚΗΣΡΣ (l'empereur César).
60 bis. ΑΟΤΚΡΤΡ ΚΗΣΡΣ (l'empereur César).

} à Dendéra

L'empereur Auguste.

61. ΑΟΤΚΡΤΡ-ΚΗΣΡΣ (l'empereur-César), *toujours vivant, chéri d'Isis.* Cartouches accolés.

Tibère.

62. ΑΟΤΚΡΤΡ-ΤΒΛΗΣ ΚΗΣΡΣ (l'empereur Tibère César), *toujours vivant*.

63. ΑΟΤΟΚΡΤΡ-ΤΒΛΗΣ ΚΗΣΡΣ (l'empereur Tibère César), *toujours vivant*.

63 a. ΑΟΤΟΚΡΤΡ-ΤΒΛΗΣ (ΚΗΣΡ) (l'empereur Tibère César) *toujours vivant, chéri d'Isis*.

64. ΑΟΤΟΚΡΤΡ-ΤΒΡΗΣ ΚΗΣΡΣ (l'empereur Tibère César), *toujours vivant*.

Planche III.

Domitien.

65. ΑΟΤΚΡΤΡ (l'empereur), *toujours vivant*, ΤΟΜΤΗΝΣ ΣΒΣΤΣ (Domitien-Auguste).

66. ΑΟΤΟΚΡΤΟΡ ΚΗΣΡΣ-ΤΟΜΤΗΝΣ (l'empereur César-Domitien), *surnommé* ΚΡΜΝΗΚΣ (Germanicus).

67. ΤΟΜΤΗΝΣ (Domitien) *surnommé* ΚΡΜΝΗΚΣ (Germanicus).

68. ΤΟΜΗΤΝΣ (Domitien) *toujours vivant* ΚΡΜΗΝΚΣ (Germanicus).

68 a. Groupe qui, comme le groupe idéographique n° 38, se place entre les noms et les surnoms des souverains. Voyez les n°ˢ 66, 67, 74 ; 78.

68 b. ΑΟΤΚΡΤΡ ΚΗΣΡΣ (l'empereur César), *toujours vivant* ΤΟΜΤΗΝΣ (Domitien), *surnommé* ΚΡΜΝΗΚΣ (Germanicus).

69. ΚΗΣΡΣ ΤΜΗΤΙΗΝΣ (César Domitien), *toujours vivant*. Obélisque Pamphile.

70. ΑΟΤΚΡΤΛ (l'empereur), *enfant du soleil, souverain des couronnes* ΚΗΣΡΣ ΤΜΗΤΕΝΣ ΣΒΣΤΣ (César Domitien-Auguste). Obélisque Pamphile.

70 bis. Cette légende hiéroglyphique pure, sculptée sur l'obélisque Pamphile, et qui contient le cartouche renfermant le nom de Vespasien, père de Domitien, se retrouve, à l'exception du nom propre Impérial, dans la dixième ligne du texte hiéroglyphique de l'inscription de Rosette. Elle signifie : *lequel a reçu la royauté venant de* ΟΥΣΠΣΗΝΣ (Vespasien) *son père*.

Trajan.

71. ΛΟΤΟΚΡΤΡ ΚΗΣΡΣ-ΝΡΟΑ ΤΡΗΝΣ ΣΒΣΤΣ (l'empereur César-Nerva-Trajan-Auguste), *toujours vivant.*
72. ΤΡΗΝΣ ΚΗΣΡ (Trajan-César), *toujours vivant.*
72 a. ΤΡΗΝΣ ΚΗΣΡΣ (Trajan-César), *toujours vivant.*
72 b. ΑΟΤΟΚΡΤΡ ΚΗΣΡΣ (l'empereur César); titres de Trajan dans divers bas-reliefs.
72 c. ΤΒΡΕΣ ΚΡΟΤΗΣ ΚΗΣΡΣ.... - ΚΛΜΝΗΚΣ ΑΟΤΚΡΤΟΡ (. *Tiberius-Claudius-Cæsar..... Germanicus autocrator*). Ces deux cartouches sculptés sur le portique d'Esné, contiennent les titres et les noms de l'empereur Claude. D'autres légendes de ce même empereur, gravées sur les monuments de Dendéra, montrent le nom de *Claude* plus régulièrement écrit ΚΛΟΤΗΣ ; on le trouve aussi orthographié ΚΡΤΙΗΣ. Quant aux trois hiéroglyphes qui terminent le premier cartouche, ils pourraient exprimer idéographiquement le titre *Auguste.*
73. ΑΟΤΟΚΡΤΡ ΚΗΣΡΣ-ΤΡΗΝΣ ΣΒΣΤΣ (l'empereur César-Trajan-Auguste), *toujours vivant, chéri d'Isis.*
74. ΑΟΤΟΚΡΤΡ ΚΗΣ ΝΑΟΛ...ΤΡΗΝΣ (l'empereur-César-Nerva-Trajan) *surnommé* ΚΡΜΝΗΚΣ ΤΗΚΚΣ (Germanicus Dacicus).
75. ΝΡΟα ΤΡΗΝΣ (Nerva-Trajan) *toujours-vivant.* Cartouche central de la frise de l'entre-colonnement de l'édifice de l'Est à Philæ. Les serpents qui flanquent et soutiennent cette espèce d'écusson, sont des *Uréus*, ou serpents royaux.
75. a. ΣΒΣΤΣ (Auguste) *toujours-vivant, chéri d'Isis*; titres qui accompagnent le cartouche n° 75.
75. b. c. Autres manières d'écrire le titre ΣΒΣΤΣ (Auguste) en hiéroglyphes phonétiques.

Hadrien.

76. ΑΤΡΗΝΣ ΚΣΡ (Hadrien-César), de l'obélisque Barbérini. Le premier caractère peut représenter la syllabe aspirée *Ha* ou simplement la voyelle Α. Un autre nom phonétique où ce caractère reparaitrait, peut seul décider la question.

L'impératrice Sabine.

80. Cette légende en hiéroglyphes purs, et renfermant deux cartouches phonétiques, est tirée de l'obélisque Barbérini et signifie : *Pareillement son épouse grandement chérie* ΣΑΒΗΝΑ (Sabine), *déesse vivante, forte* (ou *victorieuse*), ΣΒΣΤΗ (Auguste), *déesse toujours vivante*.

Antonin.

78. ΑΟΤΟΚΡΤΟΡ ΚΗΣΡΣ ΑΝΤΟΝΗΝΣ (l'empereur Cesar-Antonin), *surnommé toujours-vivant.*
79. ΑΤΟΝΗΝΣ, avec un surnom idéographique. On a omis le premier N.

PLANCHE IV.

Cette planche a été divisée en trois colonnes.

La 1re contient les lettres de l'alphabet grec;

La 2e, les caractères *démotiques* qui, dans l'écriture égyptienne populaire, étaient destinés à représenter les sons des mots et des noms étrangers;

La 3e enfin, les divers signes *hiéroglyphiques* qui forment l'alphabet phonétique.

Tous les signes hiéroglyphiques ou démotiques qui répondent aux *consonnes* de l'alphabet grec, prennent une valeur véritablement syllabique, lorsqu'ils sont combinés entr'eux sans mélange d'autres signes de *voyelle*. C'est ainsi, par exemple, que le nom phonétique de Bérénice renfermé dans le cartouche n° 32, devrait se lire et se transcrire Βε-Ρε-ΝΙ-Κε-Σ. Le signe phonétique des articulations B, P, N, ainsi que ceux des autres consonnes Γ, Δ. Λ, M, N. Π . Σ, T, etc., représentent, dans ces occasions très-ordinaires, les syllabes Βε, Γε, Δε, Κε, Λε, Μέ, Νε, Πε . Ρε, Σε, Τε, etc. On a dû remarquer en effet que presque toujours, les Égyptiens n'écrivaient dans les noms phonétiques, que les seules voyelles longues ainsi que les diphthongues. Les voyelles brèves comprises dans le corps des mots, ne sont presque jamais exprimées, parce que le signe de la consonne les emporte en lui-même et doivent, par cela même, un caractère syllabique.

Les signes des voyelles A H E I s'emploient assez indifféremment l'un pour l'autre.

Quant aux signes hiéroglyphiques de la voyelle Υ et des consonnes Z, Ψ, aucun des noms propres phonétiques analysés jusques ici, n'a pu nous les faire connaître.

AN ACCOUNT

OF

SOME RECENT DISCOVERIES

IN

HIEROGLYPHICAL LITERATURE,

AND

EGYPTIAN ANTIQUITIES.

INCLUDING

THE AUTHOR'S ORIGINAL ALPHABET,

AS EXTENDED BY MR. CHAMPOLLION,

WITH A

TRANSLATION OF FIVE UNPUBLISHED GREEK AND
EGYPTIAN MANUSCRIPTS.

BY THOMAS YOUNG, M.D.F.R.S.

FELLOW OF THE ROYAL COLLEGE OF PHYSICIANS.

LONDON:

JOHN MURRAY, ALBEMARLE STREET.

1823.

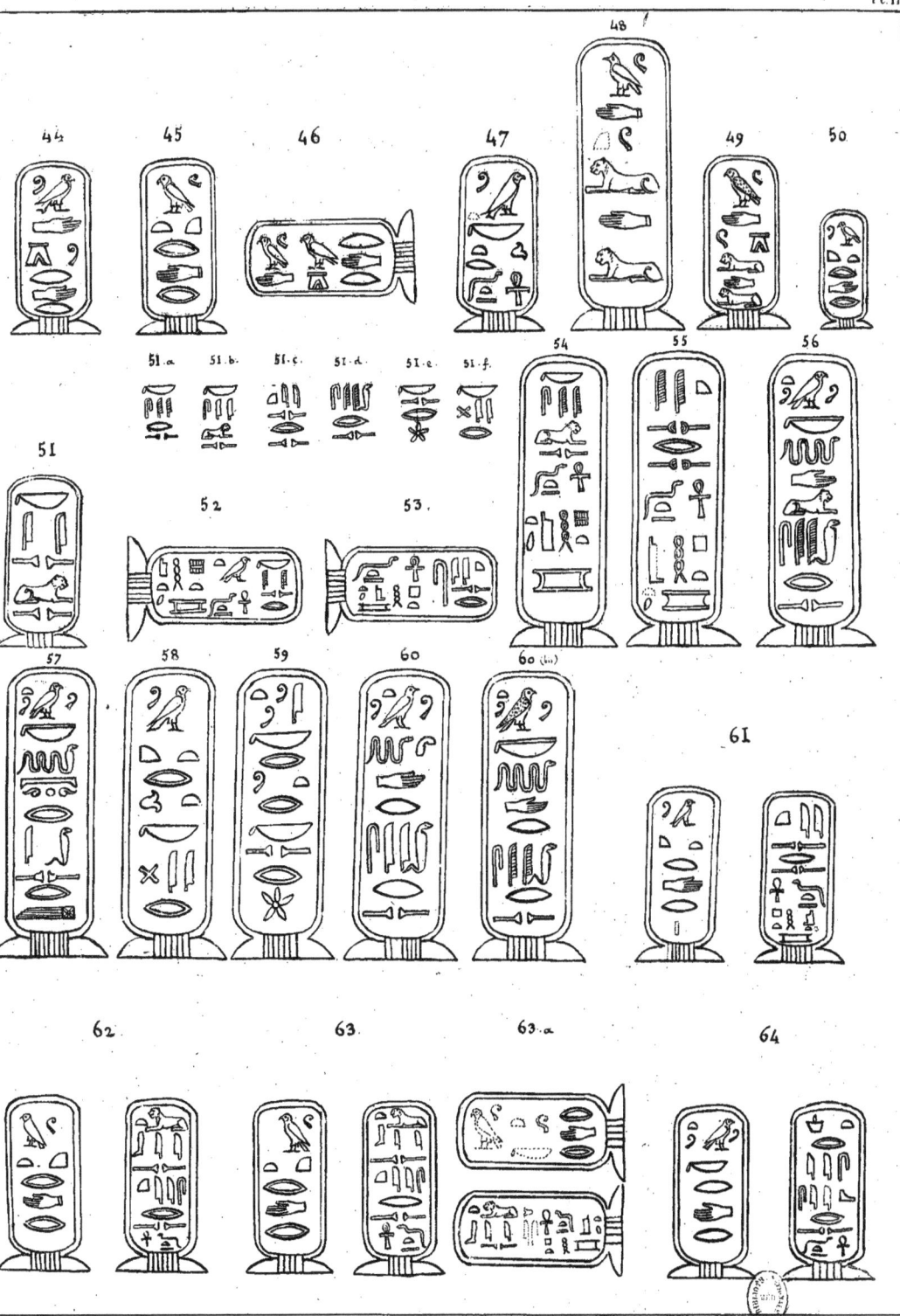

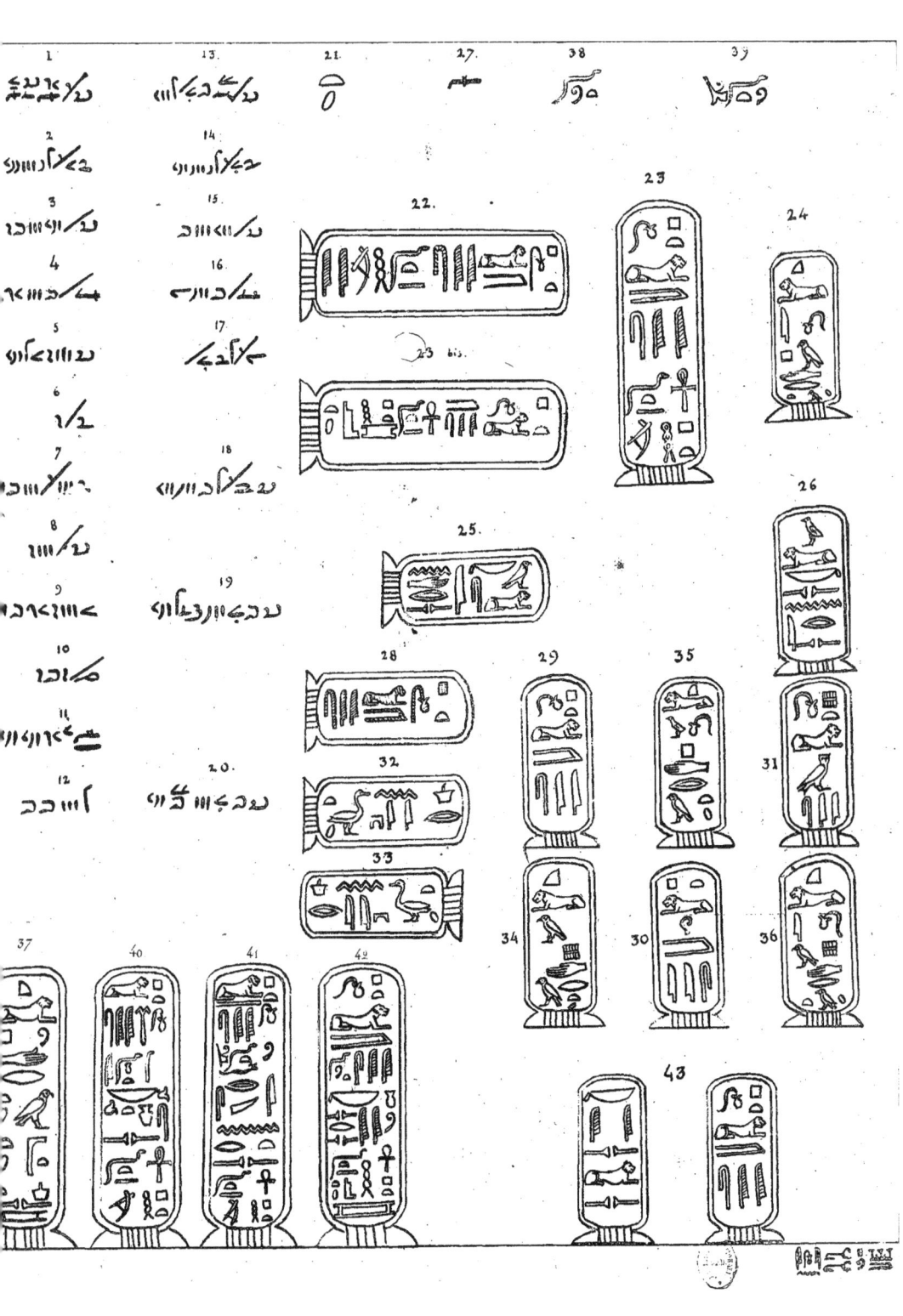

Tableau des Signes Phonétiques
des Écritures Hiéroglyphique et Démotique des anciens Égyptiens

Lettres Grecques	Signes Démotiques	Signes Hiéroglyphiques
A	ⲩ.ⲱ.	
B	ⳑ.ⲍ.	
Γ	κ.⸗	
Δ	⸱⸱	
E	ⲓ.	
Z		
H	III. JH. ⟨II⟩. III.	
Θ		
I	⸱ III.	
K	⸗.⸗.⸗.κ.γ.	
Λ	γ.γ.γ.	
M	).⸱).	
N	⸱.⸱.⸱.⸱	
Ξ	⸱	
O	ʃ.ʃ.ʃ.ʃ.ⲍ.	
Π	⸱.⸱.⸱.⸱.⸱	
P	⸱/⸱/⸱	
Σ	⸱.⸱.⸱.⟨II.ψ⟩.	
T	⸱.⸱.⸱.⸱	
Υ		
Φ	⸱	
Ψ		
X	⸱	
Ω		
ΤΩ. ΤΛ.		

Pl. IV.

TO ALEXANDER BARON VON HUMBOLDT,

AS A MARK OF THE HIGHEST RESPECT,

FOR THE EXTENT OF HIS KNOWLEDGE

AND THE ACCURACY OF HIS RESEARCH,

AS WELL AS

FOR HIS ARDENT ZEAL IN THE PROMOTION OF SCIENCE,

AND FOR HIS CANDOUR AND VIGILANCE

IN THE DISTRIBUTION OF LITERARY JUSTICE,

THIS WORK IS DEDICATED

BY HIS OBLIGED FRIEND,

THE AUTHOR.

VOLVENDA DIES EN ATTULIT ULTRO!

CONTENTS.

	Page
PREFACE	IX

CHAPTER I.
Introductory Sketch of the prevalent Opinions respecting Hieroglyphics 1

CHAPTER II.
Investigations founded on the Pillar of Rosetta . . 8

CHAPTER III.
Additional Inferences, deduced from the Egyptian Manuscripts, and from other Monuments . . 15

CHAPTER IV.
Collections of the French.—Mr. Drovetti.—Mr. Champollion's Discoveries 34

CHAPTER V.
Illustrations of the Manuscripts brought from Egypt by Mr. Grey 55

CHAPTER VI.
Extracts from Diodorus and Herodotus; relating to Mummies 87

CHAPTER VII.
Extracts from Strabo; Alphabet of Champollion; Hieroglyphical and Enchorial Names . . . 116

CHAPTER VIII.
Chronological History of the Ptolemies, extracted from various Authors 130

APPENDIX I.
Greek text of the Manuscripts and Registries . . 145

APPENDIX II.
Specimens of Hieroglyphics. 153

PREFACE.

A complete confirmation of the principal results, which I had some years since deduced, from an examination of the hieroglyphical monuments of ancient Egypt, having been very unexpectedly derived from the ulterior researches of Mr. Champollion, and from the singular good fortune of Mr. George Grey, I cannot resist the natural inclination, to make a public claim to whatever credit may be my due, for the labour that I have bestowed, on an attempt to unveil the mystery, in which Egyptian literature has been involved for nearly twenty centuries.

If, indeed, I have not hitherto wholly withheld from the public the results of my inquiries, it has not been from the love of authorship only, nor from an impatience of being the sole possessor of a secret treasure; but because I was desirous of securing, at least, for my country, what is justly considered as a desirable acquisition to every country, the reputation of having enlarged the boundaries of human knowledge, and of having contributed to extend the dominion of the mind of man over time, and space, and neglect, and obscurity. *Corona in* SACRIS CERTAMINIBUS *non victori datur, sed* PATRIA *ab eo coronari pronuntiatur.* And whatever vanity or enthusiasm there might be in this sentiment, it was at least sincere and unaffected.

In the mean time my Egyptian investigations had been as laborious as they had been persevering: and like many other pursuits, in which I have been engaged, they had been so little enlivened by any fortunate coincidences, or unexpected facilities, that having occasion to adopt a motto for the signatures of some anonymous communications, I had chosen the words FORTUNAM EX ALIIS, as appropriate to my own history. But the new lights, which Mr. Champollion has obtained, and the marvellous accident of the existence of a Greek manuscript, in perfect preservation, which I found, when Mr. Grey had obligingly left it for my examination, to be the translation of a unique hieroglyphic papyrus, lately purchased by the King of France; these circumstances have so far changed the complexion of my literary adventures, that if I remained any longer in masquerade, I should certainly be compelled to adopt the character of POLYCRATES or of ALADDIN.

It would indeed have been a little hard, that the only single step, which leads at once to an extensive result, should have been made by a Foreigner, upon the very ground which I had undergone the drudgery of quietly raising, while he advanced rapidly and firmly, without denying his obligations to his predecessor, but very naturally, under all circumstances, without exaggerating them, or indeed very fully enumerating them. I should not have repined, even if no counterpart to his good fortune had occurred for my own advantage and assistance; but the exhilaration of a success, so unexpected, has brought me more immediately and more openly before the public, than it was previously my intention to appear, in relation to a pursuit so remote from the nature of many other duties which I am bound to fulfil.

It may naturally be expected that I should make some apology, for what is generally considered as a violation of professional decorum; for presuming to appear again before the public, without absolute necessity, in any other capacity than that of a practical physician. I have indeed myself observed, on a former occasion, that the public is inclined to think, and not without something like reason, that the abilities of different individuals are pretty nearly equal; and that if any one has distinguished himself in a particular department of study, he must have bestowed so much the less time and attention on other departments: that, of course, if he excelled in more than one line, out of his profession, the natural inference would be so much the stronger: and that whether this may be fair or not, it is at least fair, that direct evidence should be produced or imagined of a devotion to medical pursuits, before medical confidence can reasonably be expected.

My explanation then is, that I consider myself as having already produced to the public *more than sufficient* " evidence" of my claim to this " medical confidence"; and that, having now acquired the right to celebrate a YEAR of JUBILEE, I think myself fully justified in endeavouring, without further regard to the strict etiquette of my profession, to obtain, while I have yet a few years more to live and to learn, whatever respect may be thought due to the discoveries, which have constituted the amusement of a few of my leisure hours.

In addition to this apology, perhaps already too long, I will venture to state, as a matter of anecdote, the train of occurrences that has accidentally led me to engage in these pursuits. To begin therefore with the beginning, or rather before the beginning, as the subject of a preface may very naturally do: I had been induced by motives both of private friendship, and of professional obligation, to offer, to the editors of a periodical publication, an article, which I thought would be of some advantage to their collection, containing an abstract of Adelung's Mithridates, a work then lately received from the continent. In reading this elaborate compilation, my curiosity was excited by a note of the editor, Professor Vater, in which he asserted that the unknown language of the Stone of

Rosetta, and of the bandages often found with the mummies, was capable of being analysed into an alphabet consisting of little more than thirty letters: but having merely retained this general impression, I thought no more of these inscriptions, until they were recalled to my attention, by the examination of some fragments of a papyrus, which had been brought home from Egypt by my friend Sir William Rouse Boughton, then lately returned from his travels in the East. With this accidental occurrence my Egyptian researches began: their progress and termination will be the subject of the present volume.

T. Y.

Welbeck Street,
1 *March,* 1823.

WORKS OF THE AUTHOR;

TO BE HAD OF THE PUBLISHER.

1. A Course of Lectures on Natural Philosophy and the Mechanical Arts, 2 vols. 4to. 1807.

2. An Introduction to Medical Literature, including a System of Practical Nosology, 8vo. Second edition, 1823.

3. A Practical and Historical Treatise on Consumptive Diseases, 8vo. 1815.

4. Elementary Illustrations of the Celestial Mechanics of Laplace, 8vo. 1821.

DISCOVERIES

IN

HIEROGLYPHICAL LITERATURE.

CHAPTER I.

INTRODUCTORY SKETCH OF THE PREVALENT OPINIONS RESPECTING HIEROGLYPHICS.

THE Greeks and Romans, either from national pride, or from a want of philological talent, were extremely deficient in their knowledge of all such languages as they called barbarous, and they frequently made up for their ignorance by the positiveness of their assertions, with regard to facts which were created by their own imagination. It was very currently believed, on their authority, not only that Egypt was the parent of all arts and sciences, but that the hieroglyphical inscriptions, on its public monuments, contained a summary of the most important mysteries of nature, and of the most sublime inventions of man: but that the interpretation of these characters had been so studiously concealed by the priests, from the knowledge of the vulgar, and had indeed been so imperfectly understood by themselves, that it was wholly lost and forgotten in the days of the later Roman Emperors. The story, however, of a reward, supposed to have been offered in vain by one of the first of the Caesars, for an interpretation of the inscription on an obelisc, then lately brought from Egypt to Rome, appears to rest on no authentic foundation.

Among the works of more modern authors, who had employed themselves in the study of the hieroglyphics, it is difficult to say whether those were the more discouraging, which, like the productions of Father Kircher and the Chevalier Palin, professed to contain explanations of every thing, or which, like the ponderous volume of Zoëga on the Obeliscs, confessed, after collecting all that was really on record, that the sum and substance of the whole amounted absolutely to nothing.

Father Kircher's six folios contain some tolerably faithful, though inelegant, representations of the principal monuments of Egyptian art, which had before his days been brought to Europe: and, according to his interpretation, which succeeded equally well, whether he happened to begin at the beginning, or at the end, of each of the lines, they all contain some mysterious doctrines of religion or of metaphysics. With equal sagacity, but with much less appearance of laborious research, the Chevalier Palin, beginning, in one instance at least, by way of variety, in the middle, has more recently discovered, that Hebrew translations of many of the Egyptian consecrated rolls of papyrus are to be found, in the Bible, under the name of the Psalms of David. Whatever may be thought of the judgment of these antiquaries, their opinions are not particularly discreditable to their talents and ingenuity: for having once allowed themselves to set out with the mistaken notion, that it was possible to determine the sense of the hieroglyphics, by internal evidence and by the force of reasoning only, the imperfections of their superstructures were. the unavoidable consequences of the unsubstantial nature of the foundations, on which they were raised.

There was indeed a traditional record of the true sense of one single character, denoting LIFE, which had been handed down by the ecclesiastical writers, and had been generally received as correct by scholars and antiquaries: although I cannot help suspecting that Sir Archibald Edmonstone's memory deceives him when he remarks, that the same symbol is often substituted, in Christian inscriptions, for the simpler sign of the cross, with which they more commonly begin. We also find some imperfect hints of a partial knowledge of the sense of the hieroglyphics in the puerile work of Horapollo, which is much more like a collection of conceits and enigmas than an explanation of a real system of serious literature: and while such scattered truths were confounded with a multitude of false assertions, it was impossible to profit by any of them, without some clue to assist us in the selection. For my own part, if I had ever read of the true signification of the handled cross, it had entirely escaped my recollection.

The French expedition to Egypt was most liberally provided, by the government of the day, with a select body of antiquaries, and architects, and surveyors, and naturalists, and draughtsmen, whose business it was to investigate all that was interesting to science or to literature in that singular country. Their labours have been made public, with all the advantages of chalcographical and typographical elegance, in the splendid collection, entitled *Déscription de l'Egypte*. But it is scarcely too much to say, that the only real benefit, conferred on Egyptian literature, by that expedition, was the discovery of a huge broken block, of black stone, in digging for the foundations of Fort St. Julian, near Rosetta, which the British army had afterwards the honour of bringing to this country, as a proud trophy of their gallantry and success. It is not to a want of ability, nor of industry, nor of accuracy, nor of fidelity, in the Egyptian Commission, that so total a failure is to be attributed; but partly to the real difficulty of the subject, and still more to the preconceived opinion, which was very generally entertained by their men of letters, of the exorbitant antiquity of the Egyptian works of art, which caused them to neglect the lights, that might have been derived, from a comparison of Greek and Roman inscriptions, with the hieroglyphics in their neighbourhood; and to suppose, that whatever bore the date of less than thirty or forty centuries must necessarily be an interpolation, unconnected with the original architecture and decorations of the edifice, to which it belonged: and when a strong prejudice has once been imbibed, we all know that the senses themselves are perpetually blunted and perverted by it, even without the consent of the reasoning powers. Mr. William Hamilton had, however, very successfully brought forwards a variety of evidence, in favour of the utility of the various inscriptions of the Greeks and Romans, for ascertaining the date of many of the buildings to which they belong; and the question, thus agitated between the French and the English travellers, had already assumed somewhat of a national character.

A cursory inspection of the Greek inscription, contained in the pillar of Rosetta, was sufficient to establish, as incontrovertible, the opinion, which had been very ably maintained by our acute and learned countryman Bishop Warburton, that the hieroglyphics, or sacred characters, were not so denominated, as being exclusively appropriated to sacred subjects, but that they constituted a real written language, applicable to the purposes of history and common life, as well as to those of religion and mythology; since this inscription speaks of the three divisions of the pillar, as containing different versions of the same decree, in the sacred and the vulgar character, and in the Greek language, respectively: and, that there was no fraud in this description, was at once made evident by the just observation of Akerblad, who pointed out, at the end of the hieroglyphical inscription, the three first numerals, indicated by I, II, and III, respectively, where the Greek has " the first and the second ..."; the end being broken off. It was also evident, that the hieroglyphical language continued to be understood and employed in the time of Ptolemy Epiphanes: but here the matter rested for several years; no single representation of an existing object having been so identified, on this or any other monument among the hieroglyphics, as to have its signification determined, even by a probable conjecture.

In the mean time, the enterprising and enlightened Baron Alexander Von Humboldt was contributing to illustrate the nature of hieroglyphical languages, by his account of the Mexican drawings, contained in his Views of the Cordilleras and Monuments of the American nations. The symbols, however, of the Americans appear to have had little or nothing in common with those of the Egyptians. The written language of the Chinese, on the contrary, exhibits, in some cases, a much closer analogy with that of ancient Egypt: and Mr. Barrow, by his clear and concise explanation of the peculiar nature of the Chinese characters, has contributed very materially to assist us in tracing the gradual progress of the Egyptian symbols through their various forms; although the resemblance is certainly far less complete than has been supposed by Mr. Palin, who tells us, that we have only to translate the Psalms of David into Chinese, and to write them in the ancient character of that language, in order to reproduce the Egyptian papyri, that are found with the mummies.

CHAPTER II.

INVESTIGATIONS FOUNDED ON THE PILLAR OF ROSETTA.

THE pillar of Rosetta was now safely and quietly deposited in the British Museum; the Society of Antiquaries had engraved, and very generally circulated, a correct copy of its three inscriptions; and several of the best scholars of the age, in particular Porson and Heyne, had employed themselves in completing and illustrating the Greek text, which constituted the third part of the inscription: and it so happened that, although no person acquainted with both these critics could hesitate to give the general preference, for acuteness of observation, and felicity of conjecture, and soundness of judgment, to the English professor, yet in this instance the superior industry and vigilance of the German had given him decidedly the advantage, with respect to two or three passages, in which their translations happen to differ.

But Greek was already sufficiently understood, both in London and at Gottingen, to make this part of the investigation comparatively insignificant. Mr. Akerblad, a diplomatic gentleman, then at Paris, but afterwards the Swedish resident at Rome, had begun to decipher the middle division of the inscription; after De Sacy had given up the pursuit as hopeless, notwithstanding that he had made out very satisfactorily the names of Ptolemy and Alexander. But both he and Mr. Akerblad proceeded upon the erroneous, or, at least imperfect, evidence of the Greek authors, who have pretended to explain the different modes of writing among the ancient Egyptians, and who have asserted very distinctly that they employed, on many occasions, an alphabetical system, composed of twenty five letters only. The characters of the second part of the inscription being called in the Greek ENCHORIA GRAMMATA, or letters of the country, it was natural to look among these for the alphabet in question: and Mr. Akerblad, having principally deduced his conclusions from the preamble of the decree, which consists in great measure of foreign proper names, persisted, to the time of his death, in believing, that this part of the inscription was throughout alphabetical. I have called these characters enchoric, or rather *enchorial*: Mr. Champollion has chosen to distinguish them by the term *demotic*, or popular; perhaps from having been in the habit of employing it before he was acquainted with the denomination which I had appropriated to them: in my opinion, the priority of my publication ought to have induced him to adopt my term, and to suppress his own, rather than to add another useless synonym, for what the ancients, when speaking with accuracy, would probably have described as the " epistolographic" form of writing employed by the Egyptians: for we have no means of determining the precise nature of the characters called *popular* by Herodotus.

Mr. Akerblad was far from having completed his examination of the whole enchorial inscription, apparently from the want of some collateral encouragement or cooperation, to induce him to continue so laborious an inquiry; and he had made little or no effort to understand the first inscription of the pillar, which is professedly engraved in the sacred character, except the detached observation, respecting the numerals at the end: he was even disposed to acquiesce in the correctness of Mr. Palin's interpretation, which proceeds on the supposition, that parts of the first lines of the hieroglyphics are still remaining on the stone.

It was natural to expect, that, after the possibility of a partial success, in this part of the undertaking, had been almost demonstrated by what Mr. Akerblad had cursorily observed, the critics and chronologists of all civilised countries would have united, heart and hand, in a common effort to obtain a legitimate solution of all the doubts and difficulties, in which the early antiquities of Egypt had long remained involved. But, excepting Mr. Champollion and myself, they have all chosen to amuse themselves with their own speculations and conjectures: the mathematicians of France have continued to calculate, and the metaphysicians of England have continued to argue, upon elements which it was impossible either to prove or disprove; while the fortuitous coincidences of some accidental results, with the collateral testimony of history or of astronomy, have been forced into the service of the delusion, as evidences of the truth of the hypotheses from which they had been deduced. Nor are these amusements even at this moment discontinued, by some persons, who have shown themselves capable of doing better things.

It was early in the year 1814, that I had been examining the fragments of papyrus brought from Egypt by Mr. Boughton; and that, after looking over Mr. Akerblad's pamphlet in a hasty manner, I communicated a few anonymous remarks on them to the Society of Antiquaries. In the summer of that year, I took the triple inscription with me to Worthing, and there proceeded to examine first the enchorial inscription, and afterwards the sacred characters. By an attentive and methodical comparison of the different parts with each other, I had sufficiently deciphered the whole, in the course of a few months, to be able to send, as an appendix to the paper printed in the Archaeologia, a translation of each of the Egyptian inscriptions considered separately, distinguishing the contents of the different lines, with as much precision as my materials would enable me to obtain. It is evident that this division of the translation supposes, in general, a distinction of the significations of the single words; and that any person, with a little attention, might retrace my steps, with regard to the sense that I attributed to each part of the two inscriptions. I was obliged to leave many important passages still subject to some doubt, and I hoped to acquire additional information, before I attempted to determine their signification with accuracy; but, having made the first great step, I concluded that many others might be added with facility and with rapidity. In this conclusion, however, I was somewhat mistaken; and when we reflect that, in the case of the Chinese, the only hieroglyphical language now extant, it is considered as a task requiring the whole labour of a learned life, to become acquainted with the greater part of the words, even among those who are in the habit of employing the same language for the ordinary purposes of life, and who have the assistance of accurate and voluminous grammars and dictionaries: we shall then be at no loss to understand that a hieroglyphical language, to be acquired by means of the precarious aid of a few monuments, which have accidentally escaped the ravages of time and of barbarism, must exhibit a combination of difficulties almost insurmountable to human industry.

I had thought it necessary, in the pursuit of the inquiry, to make myself in some measure familiar with the remains of the old Egyptian language, as they are preserved in the Coptic and Thebaic versions of the Scriptures; and I had hoped, with the assistance of this knowledge, to be able to find an alphabet, which would enable me to read the enchorial inscription at least into a kindred dialect. But, in the progress of the investigation, I had gradually been compelled to abandon this expectation, and to admit the conviction, that no such alphabet would ever be discovered, because it had never been in existence.

I was led to this conclusion, not only by the untractable nature of the inscription itself, which might have depended on my own want of information or of address, but still more decidedly by the manifest occurrence of a multitude of characters, which were obviously imperfect imitations of the more intelligible pictures, that were observable among the distinct hieroglyphics of the first inscription: such as a Priest, a Statue, and a Mattock or Plough, which were evidently, in their primitive state, delineations of the objects intended to be denoted by them, and which were as evidently introduced among the enchorial characters. But whether or no any other significant words were expressed, in the same inscription, by means of the alphabet employed in it for foreign names, I could not very satisfactorily determine.

A cursory examination of the few well identified characters, amounting to about 90 or 100, which the hieroglyphical inscription, in its mutilated state, had enabled me to ascertain, was however sufficient to prove, first, that many simple objects were represented, as might naturally be supposed, by their actual delineations; secondly, that many other objects, represented graphically, were used in a figurative sense only, while a great number of the symbols, in frequent use, could be considered as the pictures of no existing objects whatever; thirdly, that, in order to express a plurality of objects, a dual was denoted by a repetition of the character, but that three characters of the same kind, following each other, implied an indefinite plurality, which was likewise more compendiously represented by means of three lines or bars attached to a single character; fourthly, that definite numbers were expressed by dashes for units, and arches, either round or square, for tens; fifthly, that all hieroglyphical inscriptions were read from front to rear, as the objects naturally follow each other; sixthly, that proper names were included by the oval ring, or border, or *cartouche*, of the sacred characters, and often between two fragments of a similar border in the running hand; and, seventhly, that the name of Ptolemy alone existed on this pillar, having only been completely identified by the assistance of the analysis of the enchorial inscription. And, as far as I have ever heard or read, *not one* of these particulars had ever been established and placed on record, by *any other* person, dead or alive.

CHAPTER III.

ADDITIONAL INFERENCES, DEDUCED FROM THE EGYPTIAN MANUSCRIPTS, AND FROM OTHER MONUMENTS.

MY full conviction respecting the nature and origin of the enchorial character I expressed at the end of a collection of letters, inserted in the MUSEUM CRITICUM, and published in 1815. It was not, however, till the next year, that I obtained the most complete evidence of the truth of my opinion: having been obligingly accommodated, by Mr. William Hamilton, with the use of his copy of the great *Déscription de l'Egypte*, as far as it was then published, I proceeded to study its contents: and I discovered, at length, that several of the manuscripts on papyrus, which had been carefully published in that work, exhibited very frequently the same text in different forms, deviating more or less from the perfect resemblance of the objects intended to be delineated, till they became, in many cases, mere lines and curves, and dashes and flourishes; but still answering, character for character, to the hieroglyphical or hieratic writing of the same chapters, found in other manuscripts, and of which the identity was sufficiently indicated, besides this coincidence, by the similarity of the larger tablets, or pictural representations, at the head of each chapter or column, which are almost universally found on the margins of manuscripts of a mythological nature. And the enchorial inscription of the pillar of Rosetta resembled very accurately, in its general appearance, the most unpicturesque of these manuscripts. It did not, however, by any means agree, character for character, with the "sacred letters" of the first inscription, though in many instances, by means of some intermediate steps derived from the manuscripts on papyrus, the characters could be traced into each other with sufficient accuracy, to supersede every idea of any essential diversity in the principles of representation employed. The want of a more perfect correspondence could only be explained, by considering the sacred characters as the remains of a more ancient and solemn mode of expression, which had been superseded, in common life, by other words and phrases; and, in several cases, it seemed probable, that the forms of the characters had been so far degraded and confused, that the addition of a greater number of distinguishing epithets had become necessary, in order that the sense might be rendered intelligible.

A particular account of this comparison of the different modes of writing, and a detailed reference to the passages of the respective manuscripts from which they were derived, is contained in two letters, printed in 1816, as a part of the seventh number of the Museum Criticum, and of which several copies were immediately sent to Paris, and to other parts of the Continent, although the actual publication of the number was retarded till 1821.

The principal contents of these letters were, however, incorporated with other matter into a more extensive article, which I contributed in 1819 to the Supplement of the Encyclopaedia Britannica. I had made drawings of the plates, which were engraved with great fidelity by Mr. Turrell, about a year before; and having been favoured by the proprietors with a few separate copies, I had sent them to some of my friends, in the summer of 1818, with a cover, on which was printed the title Hieroglyphical Vocabulary: these plates, however, were precisely the same that were afterwards contained in the fourth volume of the Supplement, as belonging to the article Egypt.

The characters explained, with confidence, in this vocabulary, amounted to about 200; the number which had been immediately obtained from the pillar of Rosetta having been somewhat more than doubled by means of a careful examination of other monuments, on which the terms god, and king, and other epithets, already ascertained, were so applied as to furnish either certain or probable conclusions respecting the principal deities of the Egyptians, and respecting several of the latest and the most celebrated of their sovereigns. The higher numerals were readily obtained, by a comparison of some inscriptions, in which they stood combined with units and with tens. The hieratic manuscripts assisted also in this identification, by facilitating the determination of the hieroglyphic corresponding to a given enchorial character. The names of Phthah and of Apis were still left on the pillar: to these I was now enabled to add, with tolerable certainty, those of Ammon, or Jupiter, Phre, or the Sun, Rhea, or Urania, Ioh, or the Moon, Thoth, or Hermes, Osiris, Arueris, or Apollo, Isis, Nephthe, Buto, Horus, and Mneuis; besides a multitude of others, to whom I found it convenient to appropriate fictitious or temporary appellations, for the greater convenience of reference. Thus I have called Cerexochus, a figure whose real name was perhaps Amonrasonther, and my Hyperion and Platypterus are supposed by Mr. Champollion to belong to Horus and to Hercules. Of the kings, I have ascertained, as far as the testimony of the Greek and Latin historians and inscriptions would enable me, the names of Mesphres, Memnon, Sesostris, Nechao, Psammis, and Amasis; and having obtained the distinction of Ptolemy Soter from the pillar, I afterwards determined, by its assistance, the name of his queen Berenice. The termination indicating the female sex was another important result of this comparison of various monuments.

I must acknowledge that my respect for the good sense and accomplishments of my Egyptian allies by no means became more profound as our acquaintance became more intimate: on the contrary, all that Juvenal, in a moment, as might have been supposed, of discontent, had held up to ridicule of their superstitions and their depravity, became, as it were, displayed before my eyes, as the details of their mythology became more intelligible. That Plato professed to have learned much during a long residence in Egypt I can easily believe: he may very probably have derived from thence some hints, that led to his own purer doctrines of the immortality of the soul, although he may have been tempted to exaggerate a little the other advantages of his travels in search of truth; but that Pythagoras ever professed to have acquired any solid knowledge from the Egyptians, appears to me to be very inconsistent with what we know of the history of this illustrious philosopher, speculative and visionary as some of his arithmetical metaphysics seem to have been. I shall enter into some further details of my conclusions, in the words which I have already employed in the article Egypt.

" By means of the knowledge of the hieroglyphical characters, which has been already obtained, we are fully competent to form a general idea of the nature of the inscriptions on the principal Egyptian monuments that are extant. Numerous as they are, there is scarcely one of them which we are not able to refer to the class either of sepulchral or of votive inscriptions; astronomical and chronological there seem to be none, since the numerical characters, which have been perfectly ascertained, have not yet been found to occur in such a form as they necessarily must have assumed in the records of this description: of a historical nature, we can only find the triumphal, which are often sufficiently distinguishable, but they may also always be referred to the votive; since whoever related his own exploits thought it wisest to attribute the glory of them to some deity, and whoever recorded those of another was generally disposed to intermix divine honours with his panegyric. It has, indeed, been asserted, that the Egyptians were not in the habit of deifying any mortal persons; but the inscription of Rosetta is by no means the only one in which the sovereigns of Egypt are inserted in the number of its deities; the custom is observable in monuments of a much earlier age: indeed, in such a country, it might be considered as a kind of dilemma of degradation, whether it was most ridiculous to be made a divinity, or to be excluded from so plebeian an assemblage; but flattery is more prone to err by commission than by omission, and, consequently, we find the terms king and god very generally inseparable. The sepulchral inscriptions, from the attention that was paid in Egypt to the obsequies of the dead, appear, on the whole, to constitute the most considerable part of the Egyptian literature which remains, and they afford us, upon a comparative examination, some very remarkable peculiarities. The general tenor of all these inscriptions appears to be, as might be expected from the testimony of Herodotus, the identification of the deceased with the god Osiris, and probably, if a female, with Isis; and the subject of the most usual representations seems to be the reception of this new personage by the principal deities, to whom he now stands in a relation expressed in the respective inscriptions; the honour of an apotheosis, reserved by the ancient Romans for emperors, and by the modern for saints, having been apparently extended by the old Egyptians to private individuals of all descriptions[; as indeed appears to be partially hinted in the concluding line of the golden verses of the Pythagoreans]. It required an extensive comparison of these inscriptions to recognise their precise nature, since they seldom contain a name surrounded by a ring in its usual form: sometimes, however, as in the green sarcophagus of the British Museum, a distinct name is very often repeated, and preceded by that of Osiris; while, in most other instances, there is a certain combination of characters, bearing evident relation to the personage delineated, which occurs, after the symbols of Osiris, instead of the name; so that either the ring was simply omitted on this occasion, or a new and perhaps a mysterious name was employed, consisting frequently of the appellations of several distinct deities, and probably analogous to the real name[, which will, indeed, hereafter appear to have consisted not uncommonly of a similar combination]. That the characteristic phrase [,or group], so repeated, must have had some relation to the deceased, is proved by its scarcely ever being alike in any two monuments that have been compared, while almost every other part of the manuscripts and inscriptions are the same in many different instances, and some of them in almost all; and this same phrase may be observed in Lord Mountnorris's and Mr. Bankes's manuscripts, placed over the head of the person who is brought up between the two goddesses, to make his appearance before the true Osiris, in his own person, and in his judicial capacity, with his counsellors about him, and the balance of justice before him." ....

" The tablet of the last judgment, which is so well illustrated by the testimony of Diodorus concerning the funerals of the Egyptians, is found near the end of almost all the manuscripts upon papyrus, that are so frequently discovered in the coffins of the mummies, and among others in Lord Mountnorris's hieratic manuscript, printed in the collection of the Egyptian Society. The great deity sits on the left, holding the hook and the whip or fan; his name and titles are generally placed over him; but this part of the present manuscript is a little injured. Before him is a kind of mace, supporting something like the skin of a leopard; then a female Cerberus, and on a shelf over her head, the tetrad of termini, which have been already distinguished by the names " Tetrarcha," Anubis, Macedo, and " Hieracion," each having had his appropriate denomination written over his head. Behind the Cerberis stands Thoth, with his style and tablet, having just begun to write. Over his head, in two columns, we find his name and titles, including his designation as a scribe. The balance follows, with a little baboon as a kind of genius, sitting on it. Under the beam stand " Cteristes" and " Hyperion" [supposed by Mr. Champollion to be Anubis and Horus], who are employed in adjusting the equipoise; but their names in this manuscript are omitted. The five columns over the balance are only remarkable as containing, in this instance, the characteristic phrase, or the name of the deceased, intermixed with other characters. Beyond the balance stands a female, holding the sceptre of Isis, who seems to be called

Rhea, the wife of the Sun. She is looking back at the personage, who holds up his hand as a mark of respect, and who is identified as the deceased by the name simply placed over him, without any exordium. He is followed by a second goddess, who is also holding up her hands, in token of respect; and whose name looks like a personification of honour or glory, unless it is simply intended to signify "a divine priestess," belonging to the order of the Pterophori, mentioned on the Rosetta stone. The forty two assessors, [noticed by Diodorus and by these manuscripts], are wanting in this tablet; and, in many other manuscripts their number is curtailed, to make room for other subjects; but, in several of those which are engraved in the *Déscription de l'Egypte*, they are all represented, sometimes as sitting figures, and sometimes standing as termini, with their feet united."

"The principal part of the text of all these manuscripts appears to consist of a collection of hymns, or rather homages, to certain deities, generally expressed in the name of the deceased, with his title of Osiris, although the true Osiris is not excluded from the groups that are introduced. The upper part of each manuscript is occupied by a series of pictural tablets; under them are vertical columns of distinct hieroglyphics, or, in the epistolographic manuscripts, pages of the text, which are commonly divided into paragraphs, with a tablet at the head of each; the first words being constantly written with red ink, made of a kind of ochre, as the black is of a carbonaceous substance. The beginning of the manuscripts is seldom entire, being always at the outside of the roll; as the *umbilicus* of the Romans was synonymous with the end." ..

" The coffins of the mummies, and the larger sarcophagi of stone, are generally covered with representations extremely similar to some of those which are found in the manuscripts. The judicial tablet is frequently delineated on the middle of the coffins; above it are Isis and Nephthe, at the sides, and apparently Rhea in the middle, with outspread wings. The space below is chiefly occupied by figures of twenty or thirty of the principal deities, to whom the deceased, in his mystical character, is doing homage; each of them being probably designated by the relationship in which he stands to the new representative of Osiris. In the sculptures, the figures are generally less numerous; the same deities are commonly represented as on the painted coffins, but without the repetition of the suppliant; and in an order subject to some little variation. The large sarcophagus of granite, in the British Museum, brought from Cairo, and formerly called the Lover's Fountain, has the name of Apis, as a part of the characteristic denomination. This circumstance, at first sight, seemed to make it evident that it must have been intended to contain the mummy of an Apis, for which its magnitude renders it well calculated; but when the symbols of other deities were found in the mystic names upon various other monuments, this inference could no longer be considered as absolutely conclusive." . .

" Of the triumphal monuments, the most magnificent are the obeliscs, which are reported by Pliny to have been dedicated to the Sun; and there is every reason to suppose, that the translation of one of these inscriptions, preserved by Ammianus Marcellinus, after Hermapion, contains a true representation of a part of its contents, more especially as 'the mighty Apollo' of Hermapion agrees completely with the hawk, the bull, and the arm, which usually occupy the beginning of each inscription. These symbols are generally followed by a number of pompous titles, not always very intimately connected with each other, and among them we often find that of 'Lord of the asp bearing diadems,' with some others, immediately preceding the name and parentage of the sovereign, who is the principal subject of the inscription. The obelisc at Heliopolis is without the bull; and the whole inscription may be supposed to have signified something of this kind.

" THIS APOLLINEAN TROPHY IS CONSECRATED TO THE HONOUR OF KING 'REMESSES,' CROWNED

WITH AN ASP BEARING DIADEM; IT IS CONSECRATED TO THE HONOUR OF THE SON OF 'HERON,' THE ORNAMENT OF HIS COUNTRY, BELOVED BY PHTHAH, LIVING FOR EVER; IT IS CONSECRATED TO THE HONOUR OF THE REVERED AND BENEFICIENT DEITY 'REMESSES,' GREAT IN GLORY, SUPERIOR TO HIS ENEMIES; BY THE DECREE OF AN ASSEMBLY, TO THE POWERFUL AND THE FLOURISHING, WHOSE LIFE SHALL BE WITHOUT END."

"It is true, that some parts of this interpretation are in great measure conjectural; but none of it is altogether arbitrary, or unsupported by some probable analogy: and the spirit and tenor of the inscription is probably unimpaired by the alterations, which this approximation to the sense may unavoidably have introduced.

"Of the obeliscs, still in existence, there are perhaps about thirty, larger and smaller, which may be considered as genuine. Several others are decidedly spurious, having been chiefly sculptured at Rome, in imitation of the Egyptian style, but so negligently and unskilfully, as to have exhibited a striking difference even in the character of the workmanship. Such are the Pamphilian, in explanation of which the laborious Kircher has published a folio volume, and the Barberinian or Veranian: in both of these the emblems are put together in a manner wholly arbitrary; and when an attempt is made to imitate the appearance of a name, the characters are completely different at each repetition The Sallustian obelisc has also been broken, and joined inaccurately, and some modern restitutions have been very awkwardly introduced, as becomes evident upon comparing with each other the figures of Kircher and of Zoëga. [A similar restitution has been rather better executed at one corner of the Lateran obelisc, as I observed in the course of a few weeks that I passed at Rome in the summer of 1821: the block of granite, which has been employed, still exhibits some words of a Latin inscription, turned upside down, but not effaced, although the hieroglyphics belonging to the place have been imitated with tolerable fidelity]. Another very celebrated monument, the Isiac table, which has been the subject of much profound discussion, and has given birth to many refined mythological speculations, is equally incapable of supporting a minute examination upon solid grounds; for the inscriptions neither bear any relation to the figures near which they are placed, nor form any connected sense of their own; and the whole is undoubtedly the work of a Roman sculptor, imitating only the general style and the separate delineations of the Egyptian tablets; as indeed some of the most learned and acute of our critical antiquaries had already asserted, notwithstanding the contrary opinion of several foreigners, of the highest reputation for their intimate acquaintance with the works of Greek and Roman art. We may hope, however, that in future these unprofitable discussions and disputes will become less and less frequent, and that our knowledge of the antiquities of Egypt will gain as much in the solidity and sufficiency of its evidence, as it may probably lose in its hyothetical symmetry and its imaginary extent; and while we allow every latitude to legitimate reasoning and cautious conjecture, in the search after historical truths, we must peremptorily exclude from our investigations an attachment to fanciful systems and presupposed analogies on the one hand, and a too implicit deference to traditional authority on the other."

A few general remarks, that I had taken the liberty of sending out to Mr. William Bankes, for his assistance in his Egyptian researches, had been found of some utility in directing his attention to points of the most material importance for the promotion of the investigation: and even before the actual publication of the Supplement of the Encyclopaedia, I had received from Egypt a very agreeable confirmation of my opinions, in a letter addressed by Mr. Salt to Mr. William Hamilton, of which I shall here insert an extract.

"*Cairo, 1st May,* 1819.

" At Dakki in Nubia there is an inscription of the Ptolemies, over the principal entrance, that occupies a place evidently connected with the architecture; and on each side of this is a tablet of hieroglyphics, nearly similar one to the other. Now it struck me on the spot, that these, being nearly of the same length as the Greek tablet, might possibly contain a translation. I therefore referred to a letter in Mr. Bankes's possession, containing some fifty explanations of hieroglyphics from Dr. Young, and was certainly gratified to find that in the oval [ring], conspicuous on each side, was the name of the "immortal Ptolemy": and immediately afterwards the name of Hermes on one side, and of Isis on the other, to whom, by numerous Greek inscriptions, it is certain that the temple was dedicated. In following up this idea, I found, in other parts of the temple, the name of "Ptolemy" without the "immortal," over offering figures; and also those hieroglyphics which Dr. Young supposes to represent the names of Osiris, Isis, and Horus, as well as Hermes, over their respective figures, invariably, I may say, throughout the numerous representations on the walls...

H. S."

Upon Mr. Bankes's return to England, he had the kindness and liberality to allow me free access to the unequalled treasures of drawings and inscriptions, that he had accumulated and brought home; and I soon obtained a knowledge of several additional characters from the comparison of these valuable documents. The most useful of these was the symbol for BROTHER or SISTER, which appears to be the crook generally seen in the hands of Osiris, and which is closely imitated in the enchorial character that I had already ascertained. I found, also, that the emblem which I had taken for MOTHER could only be translated WIFE, as it was applied to Cleopatra with relation to her husband Ptolemy; and that a FATHER was denoted by a bird with an arm, as I had at first inferred from the pillar of Rosetta, though I afterwards abandoned the opinion, from supposing that I had found another emblem for Ptolemy Philopator. It happened, however, by mere accident, that the advantage which I derived from this source was much less considerable than might have been expected, both from its abundance and from its uncontaminated purity; but I had been rather disposed to defer the ultimate study of Mr. Bankes's collections, till their publication should give me a free right to employ them in any manner that I might think proper. Some remarks, however, that occurred to me in consequence of looking them over, I incorporated in a little essay which I gave to Mr. Belzoni, and which makes the appendix to the second edition of his travels. I have here observed, in speaking of the reference of the supposed Jewish captives, exhibited in the catacomb of my "Psammis," to the expeditions of Necho to Jerusalem, in the time of King Josiah and Jehoahaz, " that there are some difficulties in reconciling the name of Psammis with some other monuments, and in particular with a most important fragment of an enumeration of the kings of Egypt, discovered by Mr. Bankes, at Abydos. In this there are only two kings intervening between this Psammis and the Memnon of the ancients: so that, if Pliny is right in his account of this obelisc, the popular tradition respecting the colossus, supposed to represent Memnon, must be erroneous. This, indeed, it would not be difficult to admit, as very likely to have happened in the case of any popular tradition; but there is a still greater difficulty in the inscription found by Mr. Bankes on the leg of the colossus at Ebsambul, in which Psammetichus is mentioned; and if this was the first Psammetichus, as appears in some respects to be the more probable, it would follow that the king who founded that temple was more ancient than Psammetichus. But it is abundantly certain that our Psammis was prior to the founder of that temple: so that either that Psammetichus must be of much later date, as the employment of the Greek Ψ in the inscription would indeed appear to indicate, or this catacomb was not constructed in honour of the son of Pharaoh Necho. It has also been observed by an accomplished scholar, who is much attached to the pursuit of Egyptian antiquities, that, according to the testimony of Herodotus, all the kings of this dynasty were buried at Saïs, and that we must either reject this evidence, or admit that neither Psammis nor Necho can be the personage here represented. We may, however, hope, that future researches will furnish us with materials, that may enable us to remove this and many other difficulties, which at present envelope the chronology of the kings of Egypt."

CHAPTER IV

COLLECTIONS OF THE FRENCH. MR. DROVETTI.
MR. CHAMPOLLION'S DISCOVERIES.

ALTHOUGH the discovery of the general import of the hieroglyphics has by no means excited any great sensation in this country, yet the activity of the various collectors resident in Egypt seems to have been in some measure stimulated by it. Important additions have been made, or are about to be made, to the Egyptian department of the British Museum; and in France, the magnificent liberality of the Government, together with the insatiable curiosity of some affluent individuals, has held out ample encouragement to the commercial antiquarian.

I thought myself extremely fortunate, in my return from the short excursion to Rome and Naples, that I made in the autumn of 1821, to have discovered at Leghorn, among a multitude of Egyptian antiquities, belonging to Mr. Drovetti, the French consul at Alexandria, which had long lain warehoused there, a stone containing an enchorial and a Greek inscription, which was known to have existed formerly at Menouf, but which had been lost and almost forgotten by European travellers in Egypt, and I believe by Mr. Drovetti himself; for I am informed that it is not mentioned in the catalogue of his Museum, which has been sent to Paris and elsewhere. Although both the inscriptions appeared to be almost illegible, yet I did not despair of being able, in a proper light, and with sufficient patience, to decipher the greater part; and I should have been tempted to remain a few days at Leghorn, in order to make the experiment, if I could have obtained permission from the merchants, to whose care the collection was entrusted. The more, however, that I considered the importance of the only supplement to the pillar of Rosetta, that then appeared to be in existence, the more anxiety I felt to make some effort, to secure it from oblivion or destruction; and with more simplicity, perhaps, than good policy, when I returned to Pisa in the evening, I wrote a letter to MM. Mompurgo, of which I shall here insert a translation.

"*Gentlemen*,

"Having fully reflected on the singular importance of the Greek inscription, which I mentioned to you this morning, and the irreparable misfortune that would be incurred, in case that the pillar containing it should ever be lost by shipwreck, I have determined to make you a proposal, which I hope you will not find any impropriety in accepting.

"I am very desirous of sending an experienced artist from Florence, in order to make two impressions in plaster, and two tracings on paper, of this stone; upon condition, that they be considered as the property of Mr. Drovetti, and remain in your possession, until you have received his answer to the inquiry, whether he will permit them to be sent to London, either for myself or for the British Museum, and what price he would expect to receive for them. And in case that he should not think proper to fix such a price on them, as we might agree to pay, I am willing to consent, that they should remain in his collection, upon condition, however, that if this collection should ever be reembarked, for conveyance by sea, they should be kept at Leghorn, until the original stone should have arrived safely at the place of its destination, in order to avoid the chance of wholly losing this literary treasure by shipwreck.

"Whatever may be Mr. Drovetti's decision, I trust that this application, from one who flatters himself that he is the only person living, that can fully appreciate the value of the object in question, will at least not be disagreeable to him. I will beg of you to send me an early answer, directed to Schneiderff's Hotel at Florence.

T. Y. Sec. R. S. Lond.
Pisa, 5th Sept. 1821."

MM. Mompurgo readily agreed to my proposal, and I engaged a distinguished artist of Florence to undertake the performance of my plan; but I believe he was accidentally prevented from fulfilling his engagement. It appears, however, that his labour, as far as I was concerned, would have been wholly lost; for Mr. Drovetti's cupidity seems to have been roused by the discovery of an unknown treasure, and he has given me to understand, that nothing should induce him to separate it from the remainder of his extensive and truly valuable collection, of which he thinks it so well calculated to enhance the price; and he refuses to allow any kind of copy of it to be taken.

But, as it often happens to those who are too eager to monopolize, he has now outstood his market, and the pearl of great price, which six months ago I would have purchased for much more than its value, is now become scarcely worth my acceptance. I was principally anxious to obtain from it a collateral confirmation of my interpretation of the enchorial inscription of Rosetta; but having fortunately acquired materials, from other sources, which are amply sufficient for this purpose, I can wait, with great patience, for any little extension, which my enchorial vocabulary might receive from this source. I had inferred from a note, that had been sent me several years before, respecting the stone of Menouf, by Mr. Jomard, that the first words of the Greek inscription must have been ΒΑΣΙΛΕΙ ΠΤΟΛΕΜΑΙΩΙ ΝΕΩΙ ΔΙΟΝΥΣΩΙ, but this was all that the gentleman, who described it, had even attempted to copy.

The first circumstance, that repressed my eagerness to obtain a copy of Drovetti's inscriptions, was the arrival of Mr. Casati at Paris, with a parcel of manuscripts, among which Mr. Champollion discovered one that considerably resembled, in its preamble, the enchorial text of the pillar of Rosetta: and the value of this discovery was afterwards almost miraculously multiplied, by the existence of a Greek translation of the same manuscript, which has been brought to London by Mr. Grey.

Having had occasion, in the month of September last, to accompany some friends in a short visit to Paris, I was very agreeably surprised with several literary and scientific novelties of uncommon interest, and all of them such as either had originated, or might have originated, from my own pursuits. I had first the pleasure of hearing, at a meeting of the Academy of Sciences, an optical paper read by Mr. Fresnel; who, though he appears to have rediscovered, by his own efforts, the laws of the interference of light, and though he has applied them, by some very refined calculations, to cases which I had almost despaired of being able to explain by them, has, on all occasions, and particularly in a very luminous statement of the theory, lately inserted in a translation of Thomson's Chemistry, acknowledged, with the most scrupulous justice, and the most liberal candour, the indisputable priority of my investigations. In the course of the same week, I was invited to sit next to Mr. Champollion junior, while he was reading, to the Academy of Belles Lettres, a Memoir on the Analysis of the Inscription of Rosetta: he, also, had been partly anticipated in his results by what had been done in this country: though I could not help fancying, that he had not so completely forgiven the injury, as his countryman Mr. Fresnel appeared to have done. But Mr. Fresnel is the friend of Arago, and nothing more requires to be said of his character and sentiments.

I must, however, at once beg to be understood, that I fully and sincerely acquit Mr. Champollion of any intentions actually dishonourable: and if I have hinted, that I have received an impression of something like a want of liberality in his conduct, I have only thrown out this intimation, as an apology for being obliged to plead my own cause, and not as having any right to complain of his silence, or as having any desire or occasion to profit by his indulgence: at the same time I am far from wishing to renounce his friendship, or to forego the pleasure and advantage of his future correspondence.

At the beginning of my Egyptian researches, I had accidentally received a letter from Mr. Champollion, which accompanied a copy of his work on the state of Egypt under the Pharaohs, sent as a present to the Royal Society: and as he requested some particular information respecting several parts of the enchorial inscription of Rosetta, which were imperfectly represented in the engraved copies, I readily answered his inquiries from a reference to the original monument in the British Museum: and a short time afterwards I sent him a copy of my conjectural translation of the inscriptions, as it was inserted in the Archaeologia.

Of Mr. Champollion's *Egypte sous les Pharaons*, the two volumes, that have hitherto appeared, relate only to the geography of ancient Egypt, and especially to the determination of the old Egyptian names of places, as compared with the Greek and the Arabic, by the assistance of Coptic manuscripts, and other intermediate documents. The work exhibits considerable research, and some ingenuity: the author had devoted his life to one very extensive pursuit, and he proposed to illustrate every part of his subject, by the most minute investigation of every circumstance, that could be brought to bear upon it. The undertaking, commenced on so large a scale, appears to have proceeded but slowly; nor is it probable that the life of any man would be sufficient for its complete execution.

With regard to the enchorial Inscription, Mr. Champollion appeared to me to have done at that time but little. A few of the references, that he made to it, seemed to depend entirely upon Mr. Akerblad's investigations, although, as I have formerly had occasion to remark, it was *tacitly* that he adopted Mr. Akerblad's conclusions. I imagine, however, that he even now retains some erroneous prepossessions, which he had imbibed from Mr. Akerblad, although, very possibly, without recollecting their exact origin; in particular respecting the adoption of some Greek epithets, without translation, into the enchorial inscription: this question, however, I trust is now set at rest, by means of some later discoveries.

Mr. Champollion continued to reside at Grenoble, where he had some employment in the public library, till the beginning of 1821. I had not a convenient opportunity of sending him any of my later papers; and it was not till after he had left Grenoble, that he read the Article EGYPT of the Supplement of the Encyclopaedia, into which their contents were condensed. He had been devoting himself, in the mean time, to the uninterrupted study of the enchorial inscription, and he appears to have discovered, before he came to Paris, the original identity of these characters with the imperfect imitations of the more distinct hieroglyphics. Whether he made this discovery before I had printed my letters in the Museum Criticum, I have no means of ascertaining: I have never asked him the question, nor is it of much consequence, either to the world at large or to ourselves. It may not be strictly just, to say, that a man has no right to claim any discovery as his own, till he has printed and published it: but the rule is at least a very useful one. It is always easy to publish such an account of a discovery, as to establish the right of originality, without affording much facility to the pursuits of a competitor: although it is generally true, that not only honesty, but even liberality, is the best policy.

Passing by, however, what I had already done, by far the most important to me was what I had not done, and there was enough of this to satisfy me, that Mr. Champollion was at least capable of doing many things, with respect to which his claim of actual priority might appear more than doubtful.

He had found, in the first place, among the multitude of Egyptian papyri, which he had taken the trouble to copy at length, with the permission of their various possessors, one in particular, of which a series of the chapters were pretty obviously numbered in the enchorial character, the series extending, with a few interruptions, from 1 to 20. He had already applied this discovery to the illustration of some parts of the pillar of Rosetta: and I have since derived at least equal advantage from it, in the examination of the enchorial papyrus of Casati.

He had also discovered a fragment of a pillar formerly in the possession of the Duc de Choiseul, which exhibited the character for a month, followed by several various groups, together with different numbers, evidently indicative of days; so that to the names of the three months, which I had discovered, he was enabled to add at least four more, though without completely ascertaining to which of the months these new symbols belonged.

Mr. Champollion had ascertained, in the third place, the analogy of one of the manuscripts, purchased of Casati, to the enchorial inscription of Rosetta, and he had obtained from it, without difficulty, the mode of writing the name Cleopatra in that character. He did not, however, then mention to me the important consequences which he had derived from this discovery; these, it seems, were the subject of a short paper read to the Academy the succeeding Friday; and it will be proper to extract a more particular account of them, from his Letter to Mr. Dacier, since printed; in which I did certainly expect to find the chronology of my own researches a little more distinctly stated.

" The hieroglyphical text of the inscription of Rosetta," he observes, (p. 6), " exhibited, on account of its fractures, *only the name of Ptolemy*. The obelisc found in the Isle of Philae, and lately removed to London, contains also the hieroglyphical name of *one of the Ptolemies*, expressed by the same characters that occur in the inscription of Rosetta, surrounded by a ring or border, and it is followed by a second border, which must necessarily contain the proper name of a woman, and of a queen of the family of the Lagidae, since this group is terminated by the hieroglyphics expressive of the *feminine* gender; characters which are found at the end of the names of all the Egyptian goddesses without exception. The obelisc was fixed, it is said, to a basis bearing a Greek inscription, which is a petition of the priests of Isis at Philae, addressed to King Ptolemy, to Cleopatra his sister, and to Cleopatra his wife. Now, if this obelisc, and the hieroglyphical inscription engraved on it, were the result of this petition, which in fact adverts to the consecration of a monument of the kind, the border, with the feminine proper name, can only be that of one of the Cleopatras. This name, and that of Ptolemy, which in the Greek have several letters in common, were capable of being employed for a comparison of the hieroglyphical characters composing them; and if the similar characters in these names expressed in both the same sounds, it followed that their nature must be entirely phonetic."

This course of investigation appears, indeed, to be so simple and so natural, that the reader must naturally be inclined to forget that any preliminary steps were required: and to take it for granted, either that it had long been known and admitted, that the rings on the pillar of Rosetta contained the name of Ptolemy, and that the semicircle and the oval constituted the female termination, or that Mr. Champollion himself had been the author of these discoveries.

It had, however, been one of the greatest difficulties attending the translation of the hieroglyphics of Rosetta, to explain how the groups within the rings, which varied considerably in different parts of the pillar, and which occurred in several places where there was no corresponding name in the Greek, while they were not to be found in others where they ought to have appeared, could possibly represent the name of Ptolemy; and it was not without considerable labour that I had been able to overcome this difficulty. The interpretation of the female termination had never, I believe, been suspected by any but myself: nor had the name of a single god or goddess, out of more than five hundred that I have collected, been clearly pointed out by any person.

But, however Mr. Champollion may have arrived at his conclusions, I admit them, with the greatest pleasure and gratitude, not by any means as superseding my system, but as fully confirming and extending it. And here I am compelled to advert to a note of Mr. Champollion's, which I fear will be thought to go a little beyond a *tacit adoption* of my opinions, and to approach very near to an unintentional misrepresentation. "It must, without doubt, (p. 15,) have been by the form of this symbol, which has some resemblance to the figure of a basket, that Dr. Young was led to recognise the name of Berenice in the border that actually contains it. But he was of opinion that the hieroglyphics constituting proper names were employed as expressing whole syllables, that they were therefore a sort of *rebuses*, and that the first character of the name of Berenice, for example, represented the syllable BIR, which means a *basket* in the Egyptian language. This mistaken supposition has vitiated, in great measure, the phonetic analysis which he has attempted of the names of *Ptolemy* and *Berenice*, in which, notwithstanding, he has recognised the phonetic values of four of the characters: these are the P, one of the forms of the T, one of the forms of the M, and the I; but the whole of his syllabic alphabet, established from these two names only, was completely inapplicable to the great number of proper names phonetically expressed on the various monuments of Egypt...Encyclopaedia Britannica, Supplement, IV. Pt. i. Edinb. Dec. 1819."

Now, if Mr. Champollion had attended to my expressions, he must have perceived that it was *not* by any *resemblance* of an imaginary nature that I was " led to recognise the name of Berenice ; ' but by external evidence only. " The appellation SOTERES," I have observed, Art. 57, " as a dual, is well marked in the inscription of Rosetta, and the character, thus determined, explains a long name in the temple at Edfou..58. The wife of Ptolemy Soter, and mother of Philadelphus, was BERENICE, whose name is found on a ceiling at KARNAK, in the phrase, " Ptolemy and .. Berenice, the *saviour gods*." In this name we appear to have another specimen of syllabic *and alphabetical* writing combined, in a manner not extremely unlike the ludicrous mixtures of words and things with which children are sometimes amused; for however Warburton's indignation might be excited by such a comparison, it is perfectly true that, occasionally, "the sublime differs from the ridiculous by a single step only."...I have then proceeded to state, as conjectural *inferences*, the syllabic analogies: but instead of *four* letters which Mr. Champollion is pleased to allow me, I have marked, in a subsequent chapter of this Essay, *nine*, which I have actually specified in different parts of my paper in the Supplement:

and to these he has certainly added *three* new ones; or *four*, if he chooses to reckon the E as a fourth. I allow that I suspected the B, the L, and the S, to be sometimes used syllabically: but the analogy of these characters with the enchorial alphabet was so well marked, that my attempt to refine upon it could not easily have embarrassed any one in making the application. Mr. Champollion has never been led, in any one instance, from the Egyptian name of an object, to infer the phonetic interpretation, that is, the alphabetical power of its symbol: but the letters having once been ascertained, he has ransacked his memory or his dictionary for some name that he thought capable of being applied to the symbol: and not always, as it appears to me, in the most natural manner: I should prefer, for instance, the word HRERI, a flower, as making the R, to the name of pomegranate, which, it seems, was sometimes called ROMAN or ERMAN. I must also observe that my intention, in placing the Coptic names in my vocabulary of hieroglyphics, was to assist in tracing any such analogies that might suggest themselves: and in the instance of AM or EM, N.123, the reading approaches very near to one of the letters, added by Mr. Champollion to my alphabet.

With respect to the diversity of characters representing the same letter, it will be observed that I have marked *three* forms of the M, *three* of the N, with a fourth that was suggested to me by

Mr. Bankes, *two* of the P or PH, and *two* of the s. Of these last, I cannot omit to observe, that Mr. Champollion has devoted at least a page of his letter (p. 13, 14) to the demonstration of the identity of *these same* forms: and that it would not have been unnatural to refer, in a single line of that page, to the assertion of the same identity, which I had made in the article EGYPT, No. 102. " The bent line is often exchanged in the manuscripts for the divided staff, and both are represented in the running hand by a figure like a 9 or a 4." The remainder of the forms, assigned to the letters, are all due to Mr. Champollion's ingenious and successful investigations.

It so happens, that in the lithographical sketch of the obelisc of Philae, which had been put into my hands by its adventurous and liberal possessor, the artist has expressed the first letter of the name of Cleopatra by a T instead of a K, and as I had not leisure at the time to enter into a very minute comparison of the name with other authorities, I suffered myself to be discouraged with respect to the application of my alphabet to its analysis, and contented myself with observing, that if the steps of the formation of an alphabet were not exactly such as I had pointed out, they must at least have been very nearly of the same nature. In return, I was complimented for my candour, while I ought, perhaps, to have been reproved for my timidity. If, however, I may judge from my late correspondence with Mr Champollion, he does not appear to be altogether so averse to the admission of syllabic characters on some occasions, as his note upon my "false point of departure" appears to imply: and I think he will find, in the evidence now first made public, respecting the enchorial character, some additional grounds for enforcing the opinion. I shall insert a specimen of one variety of each of the names which he has succeeded in deciphering: observing only, that his alphabet could scarcely have agreed so well with the various combinations of these names, as it appears to do, if it had not been in great measure correct: and that I also fully agree with Mr. Champollion in his interpretation of the phrase of the Pamfilian obelisc, which he translates, WHO HAS RECEIVED THE KINGDOM FROM VESPASIAN HIS FATHER: the same phrase occurring on the pillar of Rosetta, as well as on the obelisc of Philae, where it had served to correct my later opinion respecting the symbol for FATHER. It is here evident that the expression cannot relate, as Mr. St. Martin imagines it must have done in the inscriptions of Rosetta, to the immediate installation of a son by *the hands* of his father; but that the right of inheritance only was implied by it. I am not however convinced, by the coherence of this passage, that the greater part of the obelisc was ever intended by the sculptor to convey a connected meaning; and at any rate the explanation confirms the opinion, that I had expressed, respecting the Roman origin of the workmanship. There are a few of the busts, now placed in the magical gallery of the Vatican, which appeared to me, on the contrary, to have been brought from Egypt with their genuine and ancient inscriptions, and to have had their features newly formed, and more highly polished, by Roman artists of the age of Adrian, in whose villa at Tivoli they were principally found.

Mr. Champollion has lately had the goodness to communicate to me, by letter, some suggestions, which, I conclude, he is on the point of making public, and I therefore take the liberty of mentioning them, as far as I think them at all admissible, though, perhaps, a little prematurely. He is disposed to refer the name, which I consider as that of the father of Amasis, to SESOSTRIS, as synonymous with RAMESSES, which he thinks the characters are probably intended to express phonetically. Now I readily allow, that where this name is written fully and accurately, as it is repeatedly found in Mr. Bankes's great catalogue of Abydos, it may without much violence be read nearly as Mr. Champollion proposes, " the approved by Phthah, Ramesses," or " the counterpart of Phthah, Ramesses;" the first part of the group undergoing several synonymous variations, while the end remains unchanged; although, if this reading were established, I should refer the first name to Amenophis or MEMNON, who was the son of Ramesses, or of Armesses called Miamun; and to whom the tomb of my Amasis is said to be attributed in the Greek and Latin inscriptions which are found in it; who is also said to have built the palace of Abydos, on which my Amasis evidently appears as the founder; who is more easily understood than Amasis to be prior to the Psammetichus mentioned at Ebsambul; and, who is more likely than Amasis to have been at Berýtus, or Nahr el Kelb, where Mr. Wyse, as I am informed by Sir William Gell, has distinctly observed this name, accompanied by the nail-headed characters. All these reasons are more than sufficient to counterbalance the single assertion of Pliny; and we should be obliged to change my Psammis, according to his place in Mr. Bankes's table of kings, into the Armais of Manetho; though the *vocal* Memnon of the numerous inscriptions would be converted by this comparison into Queen Rathotis, or we should be obliged to leave out three of Manetho's list, to bring him up to the Amenophis who is called the Trojan Memnon by that author. All this is, indeed, a little alluring, and several suppositions might be introduced to overcome the difficulties: but unfortunately the fundamental supposition appears to be liable to an insurmountable objection; that the circle, which Mr. Champollion considers as equivalent to the RE or RA of Ramesses, is also the first character of each of the seventeen names immediately preceding it, and indeed of every other in the catalogue, that remains unmutilated at the beginning.

I am therefore sorry to say that I cannot hitherto congratulate Mr. Champollion on the success of his attempts to carry his system of phonetic characters into the very remotest antiquity of Egypt: he appears, however, to have a better prospect of elucidating some of the Persian names, having, as he informs me, been able to identify that of XERXES, both in the hieroglyphics, and in the nail-headed characters, by means of a vase of alabaster, on which both are found together. This is, indeed, a wonderful opening for literary enterprise; and I am even inclined to hope, from Mr. Champollion's latest communications, that he will find some means of overcoming the difficulties that I have stated respecting the Pharaohs, for he assures me, that he has identified the names of no less than THIRTY of them, and that they accord with the traditions of Manetho, and, as far as he can judge, with the notes that I had sent him of an attempt that I had formerly made to assign temporary names to the kings enumerated at Abydos, in which those of all the later ones began with the syllable RE. He will easily believe that I wish for a satisfactory answer to my own objections: and, in fact, the further that he advances by the exertion of his own talents and ingenuity, the more easily he will be able to admit, without any exorbitant sacrifice of his fame, the claim that I have advanced to a priority with respect to the first elements of all his researches; and I cannot help thinking that he will ultimately feel it most for his own substantial honour and reputation, to be more anxious to admit the just claims of others than they can be to advance them.

CHAPTER V.

ILLUSTRATIONS OF THE MANUSCRIPTS BROUGHT FROM EGYPT BY MR. GREY.

I AM impatient to turn, from every thing of a polemical or personal nature, to a field that has hitherto been exclusively in my own possession, in consequence of an event, which is the most important, considered as a single occurrence, that has taken place since the commencement of my Egyptian researches. It was very soon after my return from France, that George Francis Grey, Esq. of University College, Oxford, having been at Naples upon his return from Egypt, was so good as to bring me a few lines from my old friend Sir William Gell, himself a very successful traveller, and who has always pursued with ardour, the last vestiges of the interesting remains of antiquity, both by his personal exertions, and by assisting and directing the enterprises of others.

Mr. Grey had the kindness, on the 22d of November last, to leave with me a box, containing several fine specimens of writing and drawing on papyrus; they were chiefly in hieroglyphics, and of a mythological nature: but the two which he had before described to me, as particularly deserving attention, and which were brought, through his judicious precautions, in excellent preservation, both contained some Greek characters, written apparently in a pretty legible hand. He had purchased them of an Arab at Thebes, in January 1820; and that which was most intelligible had appeared, at first sight, to contain some words relating to the service of the Christian church. Mr. Grey was so good as to give me leave to make any use of these manuscripts that I pleased; and he readily consented to their insertion among the lithographic copies of the " Hieroglyphics, collected by the Egyptian Society," which I had undertaken to superintend from time to time, in great measure for the private use of an association of my own friends, not sufficiently numerous to insure any permanent stability to its continuance.

Mr. Champollion had done me the favour, while I was at Paris, to copy for me some parts of the very important papyrus, which I have before mentioned as having given him the name of Cleopatra; and of which the discovery was certainly a great event in Egyptian literature, since it was the first time that any intelligible characters, of the enchorial form, had been discovered among the many manuscripts and inscriptions that had been examined, and since it furnished Mr. Champollion at the same time with a name, which materially advanced, if I understood him rightly, the steps that have led him to his very important extension of the hieroglyphical alphabet. He had mentioned to me, in conversation, the names of Apollonius, "Antiochus," and Antigonus, as occurring among the witnesses; and I easily recognised the groups which he had deciphered: although, instead of *Antiochus*, I read *Antimachus*; and I did not recollect at the time that he had omitted the M.

In the evening of the day that Mr. Grey had brought me his manuscripts, I proceeded impatiently to examine that which was in Greek only: and I could scarcely believe that I was awake, and in my sober senses, when I observed, among the names of the witnesses, ANTIMACHUS ANTIGENIS: and, a few lines further back, PORTIS APOLLONII; although the last word could not have been very easily deciphered, without the assistance of the conjecture, which immediately occurred to me, that this manuscript might perhaps be a translation of the enchorial manuscript of Casati: I found that its beginning was, " A copy of an Egyptian writing...;" and I proceeded to ascertain, that there were the same number of names, intervening between the Greek, and the Egyptian signatures, that I had identified, and that the same number followed the last of them; and the whole number of witnesses appeared to be sixteen in each. The last paragraph in the Greek began with the words, " Copy of the Registry;" for such must be the signification of the word ΠΤΩΜΑΤΟΣ, employed in this papyrus, though it does not appear to occur any where else in a similar signification. I could not, therefore, but conclude, that a most extraordinary chance had brought into my possession a document which was not very likely, in the first place, ever to have existed, still less to have been preserved uninjured, for my information, through a period of near two thousand years: but that this very extraordinary translation should have been brought safely to Europe, to England, and to me, at the very moment when it was most of all desirable to me to possess it, as the illustration of an original which I was then studying, but without any other reasonable hope of being able fully to comprehend it; this combination would, in other times, have been considered as affording ample evidence of my having become an Egyptian sorcerer.

Mr. Champollion had not thought it worth while to give me a transcript of the original Greek endorsement: he seemed to consider it as not fully agreeing with the Egyptian text, or, at any rate, as not materially assisting in its interpretation: perhaps, also, he thought it best for me to try my strength upon the original, without any little assistance that might have been derived from it with respect to two or three of the names: or, as I am more disposed to believe, he was fearful of offending some of his countrymen, by making too public what he had no right to communicate without their leave: for after an accidental delay of a month, the answer that I received from Paris was only such as to enable me to state, that my opinion of the identity of the two endorsements is fully confirmed. I have lost, however, no time in sending to the Conservators of the King's cabinet a copy of my registry; with a request to be favoured with theirs in return, in order that I might have the same advantage from the comparison, which I voluntarily afforded the Parisian critics, without any reserve or delay; and in order that the duplicates may stand side by side in the lithographical copy, which has only waited for their answer, to have a vacant space filled up, and to be sent to them entire. In the mean time, I have only to wish, that the philologists of Paris may do as ample justice to these papyri, as one of the most distinguished of their number, Mr. Letronne, has lately done to the inscriptions of the Oasis, of which I had made a very hasty translation from a single copy only, not having had the means of comparing it properly with the second.

My application for the copy of the Registry has been received with the liberality which was to be expected from the directors of a great institution, and I have to return my best thanks to Mr. Raoul Rochette, for a correct copy of the whole of this highly important manuscript, which I am happy to find that it is his intention to publish in a short time.

I am most anxious to avoid anticipating him, in the gratification of the public curiosity, with regard to this interesting relic: but as I find that some account of the Registry has already been made public by Mr. St. Martin, I conceive myself at liberty to make use, at least, of this part of the manuscript: and I do not imagine that Mr. Raoul Rochette means to employ himself on the enchorial conveyance.

The contents of Mr. Grey's Greek manuscript are of a nature scarcely less remarkable than its preservation and discovery: it relates to the sale, not of a house or a field, but of a portion of the Collections and Offerings made from time to time on account, or for the benefit, of a certain number of MUMMIES, of persons described at length, in very bad Greek, with their children and all their households. The price is not very clearly expressed; but as the portion sold is only a moiety of a third part of the whole, and as the testimony of sixteen witnesses was thought necessary on the occasion, it is probable that the revenue, thus obtained by the priests, was by no means inconsiderable.

The result, derived at once from this comparison, is the identification of more than thirty proper names as they were written in the running hand of the country. It might appear, upon a superficial consideration, that a mere catalogue of proper names would be of little comparative value in assisting us to recover the lost elements of a language. But, in fact, they possess a considerable advantage, in the early stages of such an investigation, from the greater facility and certainty with which they are identified, and from their independence of any grammatical inflexions, at least in the present case; by means of which they lead us immediately to a full understanding of the orthographical system of the language, where any such system can be traced.

The general inference, to be derived from an examination of the names now discovered, is somewhat more in favour of an extensive employment of an alphabetical mode of writing, than any that could have been deduced from the pillar of Rosetta, which exhibits, indeed, only foreign names, and affords us therefore little or no information respecting the mode of writing the original Egyptian names of the inhabitants. Several of the words, which occur in these documents, and more especially in those which are hereafter to be mentioned, might be read pretty correctly, by means of the alphabet originally made out by Mr. Akerblad from the foreign names of the enchorial inscription; but there are many more which appear to be rather syllabically than alphabetically constituted: and the names of the different deities seem to be very commonly employed in writing them; for instance, those of Horus, Ammon, and Isis; and perhaps in the same way that they are often composed, in the mythological manuscripts, found with the mummies: in which, for want of the occurrence of a ring or border, or of the corresponding enchorial marks, I had concluded that the groups could not be intended to represent the ordinary names of the individuals. But these marks are, in fact, by no means constantly employed in the enchorial papyri; and they seem only to have been inserted when either great precision, or some distinguished mark of respect was required.

Important, however, as are the additions that are likely to be made to our knowledge by means of this "Antigraph", it is by no means the only valuable acquisition for which we are indebted to the enterprise and the diligence of Mr. Grey: a second papyrus, of considerably greater magnitude, contains three Egyptian conveyances in the enchorial character, with separate registries on the margin, in very legible Greek. These are not only of use for the illustration of other similar documents, but they afford us also many additional examples of enchorial proper names, besides a general idea of the subjects of the respective manuscripts, all of which relate to the sale of lands in the neighbourhood of Thebes. It will be most convenient to consider them as parts of a series, of which those are the first to be examined, that are the most capable of affording an independent testimony; beginning with the Greek papyrus in the possession of Mr. Anastasy, the Swedish consul at Alexandria, and proceeding to the Antigraph and its original, and thence to the three enchorial manuscripts, which are also the property of Mr. Grey. It is scarcely conceivable, by a person who has not made the experiment; how much the difficulty of reading a depraved character is almost universally diminished by the comparison of two or three copies of the same or of similar passages; the words, which would be wholly unintelligible in either taken singly, being often very easily legible when both are at once under the eye; and, still more commonly, a word which is confused or contracted in one, being written clearly or at length in another.

It is in this manner, that several of the deficiencies of the manuscript of Anastasy, as edited by the learned and ingenious Professor Böckh of Berlin, have been in some measure supplied, in the late republication at Paris, by the care of Mr. Jomard, from a comparison with the Greek manuscripts purchased of Mr. Casati, in order to be added to the unrivalled treasures of literature contained in the King's library and cabinet. Several more of the obscurities of this manuscript, if not the whole, I flatter myself are now removed, by the further comparison, which I have attempted to make, by means of Mr. Grey's indulgence in allowing me the use of his manuscripts; and by means of the duplicate which I have received from Paris in exchange for the registry of his Antigraph.

The manuscript of Anastasy, besides its curiosity as a subject of antiquarian and historical research, becomes of great importance, in this inquiry, as affording a more complete specimen, than the Antigraph, of the usual form of a contract in Egypt under the Ptolemies; and as assisting in the investigation of the sense of the preamble of the enchorial manuscript, which is omitted in the Antigraph. I shall therefore insert here a translation of this document, and shall reprint the original in an appendix, with such corrections as I have thought it appeared to require; in order to restore it to the form intended by the writer. The registries, in their original language, I shall print side by side, and in the order of time which I attribute to them.

TRANSLATION OF THE GREEK PAPYRUS OF
ANASTASY.

See Appendix I.

(1) In the reign of Cleopatra and Ptolemy her son surnamed Alexander, the Gods Philometores Soteres, in the year XII, otherwise IX; in the priesthood of the existing priests (2) in Alexandria, [the priest] of Alexander and of the Gods Soteres, and of the Gods Adelphi, and of the Gods Evergetae, and of the Gods Philopatores, and of the Gods Epiphanes, and of the God (3) Philometor, and of the God Eupator, and of the Gods Evergetae: the Prize bearer of Berenice Evergetis, the Basket bearer of Arsinoe Philadelphus and the priestess of Arsinoe (4) Eupator at present in Alexandria: and, in the Thebaic Ptolemais, in the priesthood of the existing priests and priestesses of Ptolemy Soter, [and of ...] (5) in Ptolemais; on the 29th of the month Tybi [v; February]: Apollonius being President of the Exchange of the Memnonians, and of the lower government of the Pathyritic nome.

(6) There was sold by Pamonthes, aged about 45, of middle size, dark complexion, and handsome figure, bald, round faced, and straight nosed; and by Snachomneus, aged about 20, of middle size, sallow complexion, (7) likewise round faced

and straight nosed; and by Semmuthis Persineï, aged about 22, of middle size, sallow complexion, round faced, flat nosed, and of quiet demeanour; and by Tathlyt (8) Persineï, aged about 30, of middle size, sallow complexion, round face, and straight nose, with their principal Pamonthes, a party in the sale; the four (9) being of the children of Petepsais of the leather cutters of the Memnonia; out of the piece of level ground which belongs to them in the southern part of the Memnonia, (10) eight thousand cubits of open field, one fourth [of the whole?] bounded on the south by the Royal Street; on the north and east by the land of Pamonthes and Boconsiemis, who is his brother, (11) and the common land [or wall] of the city; on the west by the house of Tages the son of Chalome: a canal running through the middle, leading from the river: these are the neighbours on all sides. It was bought by Nechutes the less, (12) the son of Asos, aged about 40, of middle size, sallow complexion, cheerful countenance, long face, and straight nose, with a scar upon the middle of his forehead; for 601 pieces of brass: the sellers standing as (13) brokers, and as securities for the validity of the sale. It was accepted by Nechutes the purchaser.

APOLLONIUS Pr. Exch?

[REGISTRY.]

In the year XII, otherwise IX; the 20th of Pharmuthi [VIII; May], [transacted] at the table in Hermopolis, at which Dionysius presides, over the 20th department; in the account of the partners receiving the duties on sales, of which Heraclides is the subscribing clerk, the acceptor in in the sale is Nechutes the less, the son of Asos; an open field of eight thousand cubits, one fourth portion; in the southern part of the Memnonia: which he bought of Pamonthes and Snachomneus, the sons of Petepsais, with their sisters: 601 pieces? The end ...

Dionysius subscribes.

The beginning of this preamble may be illustrated by that of the inscription of ROSETTA, which runs nearly thus:

In the reign of the young king..Ptolemy Epiphanes the munificent..the son of Ptolemy and Arsinoe, the gods Philopatores..in the year IX; the priest of Alexander and of the gods Soteres, and of the gods Adelphi, and of the gods Evergetae, and of the gods Philopatores, and of the god Epiphanes the munificent being Aëtus, the son of Aëtus: the prize bearer of Berenice Evergetis being Pyrrha the daughter of Philinus: the basket bearer of Arsinoe Philadelphus being Areia daughter of Diogenes; and the priestess of Arsinoe Philopator, Irene the daughter of Ptolemy: on the 4th day of Xanthicus, or the 18th of Mechir: it was decreed...

In comparing the preamble of the deed of sale with this monument, we have first to observe the successive addition of the names of Philometor, Eupator, and the Evergetae, to the titles of the priests of Alexander and his successors. Eupator, it seems, according to other authorities, cited by Böckh, was Ptolemy Evergetes II, the successor of Philometor, called also Cacergetes and Physcon; and the Evergetae, named after him, can only have been the reigning sovereigns, before called Philometores Soteres: and Cleopatra, at least, had some right to the name Evergetis, as having derived it from her husband, so that she may easily be supposed to have shared it occasionally with her son. The remaining part of the preamble varies but little, except that Arsinoe, instead of Philopator, is called Eupator: but this diversity is not more material than the substitution of Adelphi for Philadelphi, which frequently occurs. The double date is well known to have been adopted by Cleopatra and Alexander, and its origin is sufficiently explained by Eusebius and Porphyry. Professor Böckh makes the year, 104 B. C.; but from a comparison of different authorities it seems rather more probable that it was 106 B. C., at least so I have been obliged to arrange it in a table, formed from a comparison of the chronologies of Porphyry, Champollion Figeac, and St. Martin, which I have inserted in an Appendix.

TRANSLATION OF MR. GREY'S GREEK ANTIGRAPH.

(1) *Copy of an Egyptian Writing respecting the Dead Bodies in Thyn. having been* (2) *ratif* . . .

(3) In the XXXVIth year; Athyr [III] 20, after the usual preamble, this writing witnesses: that the ¿ Dresser? (4) among the servants of the great goddess [Isis?] Onnophris the son of Horus and of Senpoeris ,[aged about] forty, lively, tall, of a sallow complexion, hollow eyed, (5) and bald, has ceded voluntarily for the price of .. to Horus the son of Horus and of Senpoeris, (6) one moiety of the third part of the Collection for the dead (7) lying in Thynabunun, on the Libyan side of the Theban suburb, (8) in the Memnonia : likewise one moiety of the third part of the Services or Liturgies (9) and so forth : their names being | Muthes the son of Spotus, with (10) his children (10) and all his household ; Chapocrates the son of Nechthmonthes, with his children and all; Arsiesis the son of Nechthmonthes ; likewise Petemestus the son of (11) Nechthmonthes; likewise Arsiesis the son of Zminis; likewise (12) Osoroeris the son of [Horus]; likewise Spotus the

son of Chapochonsis; likewise (13) Zoglyphus: from which there belongs to Asos the son of Horus and of Senpoeris (14) " thy" younger brother, one of [or, the younger brother of] the same ¿ Dressers? a moiety of the (15) aforesaid third part of the services and fruits and (16) so forth. He has sold it to him in the year XXXVI; 20 Athyr, in the reign of the everlasting (17) king, for the completion of the third part. Also a moiety of the fruits (18)¿ and so forth? of the ¿ other? dead bodies in Thy. that is to say, Pateutemis with his children and (19) all; and a moiety of the fruits belonging to me from the property of (20) Petechonsis the milk bearer, and from a place on the Asiatic side, called (21) Phrecages, with the dead bodies in it; of which a moiety belongs to the (22) same Asos: all these things I have sold to him. They are thine, (23) and I have received their price from thee, and I make no demand upon thee (24) for them from this day: and if any person disturb thee (25) in the possession of them, I will withstand the attempt, and if I do not [otherwise] repel it (26) I will use compulsory means. Written by Horus the son of Phabis, the writer of the (27) [priests] of Amonrasonther, and the other gods of the temple. (28) Witnesses: Erieus the son of Phanres. Peteartres the son of Pateutemis. (29) Petearpocrates the son of [Horus]. Snachomneus the son of Peteuris. Snachomes (30) the son of Psenchonsis. Totoes the son of Phibis. Portis the son of

APOLLONIUS. Zminis (31) the son of Petemestus. Peteutemis the son of Arsiesis. Amonorytius (32) the son of Pacemis. Horus the son of Chimnaraus. Armenis the son of Zthenaetis (33). Maësis the son of Mirsis. ANTIMACHUS the son of ANTIGENES. Petophois the son of Phibis. (34) Panas the son of Petosiris. Witnesses 16.

Copy of the Registry. In the year XXXVI; the ninth of Choeak [IV]. Transacted at the table in Diospolis, at which Lysimachus is the President of the 20th department; in the account of Asclepiades and Zminis, farmers of the tax, in which the subscribing clerk is Ptolemaeus: the purchaser Horus the son of Horus the ¿ Dresser? a part of the sum, collected by them, on account of the dead bodies lying in Thynabunun, in the Memnonian tombs of the Libyan suburb of Thebes, for the services which are performed. Bought of Onnophris the son of Horus, Pieces of brass 400 . Z . . The end.

Lysimach. subscribes.

TRANSLATION OF THE ENCHORIAL PAPYRUS OF PARIS, CONTAINING THE ORIGINAL DEED RELATING TO THE MUMMIES.

(1) This writing, dated in the year XXXVI; Athyr 20, in the reign of our Sovereigns Ptolemy and Cleopatra his sister, the children of Ptolemy and Cleopatra, the divine, (2) the Gods Illustrious: and the Priest of Alexander, and of the Saviour Gods, of the Brother Gods, of the [Beneficent Gods], of the Father loving Gods, of the Illustrious Gods, of the Paternal God, and (3) of the Mother loving Gods being [as by law appointed]: and the Prize bearer of Berenice the Beneficent, and the Basket bearer of Arsinoe the Brother loving, and the Priestess of (4) Arsinoe the Father loving, being as appointed in the metropolis [of Alexandria]; and in [Ptolemaïs] the Royal City ¿ of the Thebaid? the Guardian Priest ¿ for the year? of Ptolemy Soter, and the Priest of King Ptolemy the Father loving, (5) and the Priest of Ptolemy the Brother loving, and the Priest of Ptolemy the Beneficent, and the Priest of Ptolemy the Mother loving; and the Priestess of Queen Cleopatra, and the Priestess (6) of the Princess Cleopatra, and the Priestess of Cleopatra the [Queen] Mother, deceased, the Illustrious; and the Basket bearer of Arsinoe the Brother loving, [being as

appointed]: declares: The ¿Dresser? in the temple (7) of the Goddess, Onnophris the son of Horus, and of Senpoeris ¿ daughter of Spotus? [" aged about forty, lively"], tall, [" of a sallow complexion, hollow eyed, and bald"]: in the temple of the goddess (8) to [Horus] ¿ his brother? the son of Horus and of Senpoeris, has sold, for a price in money, half of one third of the Collections for the dead, " Priests of Osiris?" lying (9) in Thynabunun ... in the Libyan suburb of Thebes, in the Memnonia ... likewise half of one third of the Liturgies: their names being, Muthes the son of Spotus, with his children and his household; Chapocrates (10) the son of Nechthmonthes, with his children and his household; Arsiesis the son of Nechthmonthes, with his children and his household; Petemestus the son of Nechthmonthes, Arsiesis the son of Zminis, with his children and his household; Osoroeris (11) the son of Horus, with his children and his household; Spotus the son of Chapochonsis ¿ surnamed? Zoglyphus [the Sculptor,] with his children and his household: while there belonged also to Asos the son of Horus and of Senpoeris ¿ daughter of Spotus? (12) in the same manner one half of a third of the collections for the dead, and of the fruits and so forth .. : he sold it on the 20th of Athyr, in the reign of the king everliving, to [complete] the third part: likewise the half ¿ of one third? of the collections relating to (13) Peteutemis, with his household and .. : likewise the half ¿ of one third? of the collections and fruits for Petechonsis the bearer of milk, and of the .. place on the Asian side called Phrecages (14), and .. and the dead bodies in it: there having belonged to Asos the son of Horus one half of the same: he has sold to him in the month of .. the half of one third of the collections (15) for the Priests ¿ of Osiris? lying in Thynabunun, with their children and their households: likewise the half of one third of the collections for Peteutemis, and also for (16) Petechonsis the bearer of milk, in the place Phrecages on the Asian side: I have received for them their price in silver: .. and gold: .. and I make no further demand on thee for them from the present day, .. (17) .. before the authorities .. [and if any one shall disturb thee in the possession of them, I will resist him, and if I do not succeed, I will indemnify thee?] .. (18) Executed and confirmed : Written by Horus the son of Phabis, clerk to the chief priests of Amonrasonther and of the ¿ contemplar? Gods, of the Beneficent Gods, of the Father loving Gods, of the Paternal God, and of the (19) Mother loving Gods. Amen. (20) Names of the witnesses present. ..

[*Column at the edge of the paper.*] (1) Names of the authorities. (2) Erieus the son of Phanres ¿ Erieus? (3) Peteartres the son of Peteutemis. (4) Petearpocrates the son of Horus. (5) Snachomneus the son of Peteuris. (6) Snachomes the son of Psenchonsis. (7) Totoes the son of Phibis. (8) Portis the son of APOLLONIUS. (9) Zminis the son of Petemestus. (10) Peteutemis the son of Arsiesis. (11) Amonorytius the son of Pacemis. (12) Horus the son of Chimnaraus. (13) Armenis [rather Arbais,] the son of Zthenaetis. (14) Maesis the son of Mirsis. (15) ANTIMACHUS the son of ANTIGENES. (16) Petophois the son of Phibis. (17) Panas the son of Petosiris. (18) Were present [as witnesses.]

The additions to the Sovereigns, named in the preamble of the stone of Rosetta, are here the Paternal God and the Mother loving Gods, or Eupator and the Philometores, and we want only the Evergetae of the papyrus of Anastasy. We can, therefore, only refer the date to one of the two preceding reigns, of Philometor or Evergetes Eupator, which it is very difficult to distinguish from each other with precision. We have, however, no evidence that Philometor's dates extended beyond 35, and we must naturally consider this 36 as belonging to Eupator, corresponding to 135 B. C. which was 11 years after the death of Philometor. If we judged from this manuscript alone, we should infer that Eupator was canonized, by some accident, during his temporary reign, before his brother, and that the order of the names remained undisturbed through the different changes of their governments. The epithet "Illustrious" in this preamble is not easily recognised; but it is distinguished by the termination from "Beneficent," for which I had in the first instance mistaken it: an epithet so placed is almost always referred to the person last mentioned. The enchorial name of the divinity here called Amonrasonther considerably resembles that of the "Cerexochus" of the Article Egypt. The epithet, which I have conjecturally translated "Dresser", was at first supposed to mean Brazier, and was read Chalchytes: but the Parisian Registry has distinctly Cholchytes: which may possibly be a derivative of DCHOLH or JOLH, to dress, to put on, and may have been applied to some of the Hierostolists, or Tire men, of the temple.

TRANSLATION OF MR. GREY'S ENCHORIAL PAPYRUS.
REGISTRY IN GREEK (A).

In the year XXVIII; the 28 Mesore [XII]. Transacted at the table in Hermopolis, at which Dio.[nysius] is President of the 20th department, in the Account of Asclepiades [contractor for the tax] on sales; of which Ptolemaeus is the subscribing clerk: the purchaser being Teephbis the son of Amenothes ¿ for 300 pieces of brass? ¿ of 7000? cubits, at the southern end of the whole open field, which is at the south of Diospolis the Great; of which the boundaries are given in the annexed agreement: which he bought of Alecis and Lubais and Tbaeais the sons of Erieus, and of Senerieus the daughter of Petenephotes, and Erieus the son of Amenothes, and Senosorphibis the daughter of Amenothes, and of Spois also ¿ the son? of Erieus the son of Amenothes. In the XXVIIIth year, Pachon [IX] 20. ¿ Pieces?.. End of the record.

Dionysius has subscribed.

ENCHORIAL AGREEMENT (A).

Year XXVIII; Month ... In the reign of Ptolemy and Cleopatra his sister, the children of Ptolemy and Cleopatra, the Illustrious Gods: and the Priest of Alexander, of the Saviour Gods, of the ¿ Maternal? [Brother] Gods, of the Beneficent Gods, of the Father loving Gods, of the Illustrious Gods, of the Mother loving Gods: and the Prize bearer of Berenice the Beneficent, and the Basket bearer of Arsinoe the Brother loving, and the Priest of Arsinoe the Father loving, being as appointed in the metropolis [of Alexandria; and in Ptolemais], the Royal City ¿ of the Thebaid ? the Guardian Priest ¿ for the year? of Ptolemy Soter, and the Priest of Ptolemy the Mother loving, and the Priest of Ptolemy the Brother loving, and the Priest of Ptolemy the Beneficent, and the Priest of Ptolemy the Father loving, and the Priest of Ptolemy the Illustrious and Munificent, and the

Priest of Queen Cleopatra, and the Priest of Cleopatra the Mother, the late Goddess Illustrious; and the Basket bearer of Arsinoe the Brother loving, being [all as by law appointed]: The brothers, Alecis the son of Erieus, Lubais the son of Erieus, and Tbaeais the son of Erieus, their mother being Senerieus the daughter of Petenephotes son of Lubais; Erieus the son of Amenothes, and Senosorphibis daughter of Amenothes, whose mother was Senamunis, and Spois the son of Erieus, the son of Amenothes, his mother being ¿ Senchonsis? coming into the temple of ¿ Thebes? agreed with Teephbis son of Amenothes, to sell for a sum of money .. α .. α .. α .. α .. of the city .. in the year and month and day [above mentioned] of the King everliving .. α .. ¿ Alecis Phaïne? . α .. (16) α .. Asos the son of Horus and of Senpoeris .. the Royal Street (HIR=ῥύμη) .. ¿ vineyard? .. α .. α .. (19) .. (20) .. place .. (21) given up .. month .. time .. (22) .. (23) .. (24) .. Executed and confirmed. Written by Erieus the son of Phanres, clerk to the chief Priests of Amonrasonther and the contemplar Gods .. Amen.

It is sufficiently obvious that this deed must belong to the same period as the sale of the collections for the mummies, and that it must consequently have been at least eight years earlier. The "God Eupator" is here omitted, perhaps accidentally, or perhaps because he had not been canonized at the time. The date 28 is equally applicable to the reigns of Philometor and of Eupator: and several names occur in this deed which are also found in the preceding: for example, Erieus the son of Phanres, who is the first witness in that deed, is the clerk that drew up the present. Asos the son of Horus and Senpoeris, who is one of the "Dressers" of the temple, appears here as the possessor, probably of a neighbouring piece of land, and in the next deed as a purchaser. The question remains whether we should assign to this deed a date 19 years earlier than the former, or only 8; that is, whether 154 B.C. or 143; and there appears to be no evidence at present existing that is sufficient to decide it: except that the omission of the name of Eupator was less likely to happen in his own reign than in his predecessor's. The priesthoods of Ptolemaïs are somewhat negligently arranged at the end of this preamble, but they present no essential discordances. The Registry affords us a remarkable instance of a double contraction for the word ΠΟΛΙΣ or city, it is first represented by a semicircle with a central point, ⊙, and then by a figure of 2, in the names of Hermopolis, and Diospolis, or Thebes. The contraction for Hermopolis, in the papyrus of Anastasy, would not easily have been explained without the aid of these manuscripts. The Dionysius of the reign of Ptolemy Alexander, being near fifty years later, may perhaps have been a son of this Dionysius, and may have succeeded him in his office.

TRANSLATION OF THE SECOND DEED (B).

REGISTRY, IN GREEK.

In the year XXIX; Phamenoth [VII] 9. Transacted at the table in Hermopolis, at which Dionysius is president of the 20th department; in the account of Asclepiades and Crates [contractors for the duties] on sales, of which Ptolemaeus is the subscribing clerk: Asus, the son of Horus, purchaser of an open field of ¿ 2000? [square cubits], lying in the southern part of Diospolis the Great; of which the boundaries are given in the present agreement: which he bought of Alecis the son of Erieus, and Lubais and Tbaeais the sons of Erieus, and Senerieus the daughter of Petenephotes, and Erieus the son of Amenothes, and Senosorphibis the daughter of Amenothes, and Spois [or Spoetus] also the son of Erieus the son of Amenothes . .
¿ Pieces . . 1004? The end . . .

                Diony[sius] has subscribed.

ENCHORIAL AGREEMENT (B).

Year XXIX. In the reign of Ptolemy and Cleopatra, the children of Ptolemy and Cleopatra the Gods Illustrious and Munificent: living for ever.

The brothers, Alecis the son of Erieus, Lubais the son of Erieus, and Tbaeais the son of Erieus, their mother being Senerieus the daughter of Petenephotes, son of Lubais; Erieus the son of Amenothes, and Senosorphibis daughter of Amenothes, her mother being Senamunis, and ¿ Spois ? the son of Erieus, the son of Amenothes, his mother being ¿ Senchonsis ? coming into the temple of ¿ Thebes ? agreed with Asus the son of Horus to sell for a sum of money .. α .. α .. α .. α .. of the city .. in the year and month and day [above mentioned] of the king everliving .. α .. ¿ Phaine ? .. α .. the Royal Street; ¿ the sister of Alecis, Phaine ? .. α .. α .. place .. has released .. months .. time .. Executed and confirmed. Written by Erieus the son of Phanres, clerk to the chief priests of Amonrasonther and the contemplar Gods.... Amen.

The preamble is here abridged, which was perhaps the safer, as the deed stands by the side of the preceding on the same papyrus. The phrase "α" is the same in both deeds, and probably means "a piece of open field bounded by," or something of a similar nature: for forms of this kind appear to be repeated without limit in the old Egyptian language.

TRANSLATION OF THE THIRD DEED (C).

REGISTRY IN GREEK.

In the year XXXV; Pharmuthi [VIII] 20. Transacted at the table in Diospolis the Great, at which Lysim[achus] [is president]; in the account of Sarapion and his partners [contractors for the duties] on sales, in which the subscribing clerks are Hermophilus and Sarapion: the purchaser being Pechytes the son of Arsiesis; of the fourth part of an open field of ¿ 3000 square cubits? in the southern part of Diospolis the Great; on the western side of the canal of Her[cules], leading to the river; of which the boundaries are given in the present agreement; which he bought of Ammonius the son of Pyrrhius, and Psenamunis the son of Pyrrhius. ¿ Pieces 3000? The end. Of which . .

                Lysimach. has subscribed.

ENCHORIAL AGREEMENT (C).

¿ XXXV ? Month .. In the reign of Ptolemy and Cleopatra his sister, the children of Ptolemy and Cleopatra the Gods Illustrious; and the Priest of Alexander and of the Saviour Gods, of the Brother Gods, of the Beneficent Gods, of the Father loving Gods, of the Illustrious Gods, of the ¿ hostile ? Paternal God, and of the Mother loving Gods : and the Prize bearer of Berenice the Beneficent, and the [Gold and Silver] Basket bearer of Arsinoe the Brother loving, and the Priest of Arsinoe the Father loving, being [as appointed in the metropolis]: the bargain was made by the men of the family of Alecis: Ammonius the son of Pyrrhius, and Psenamunis the son of Pyrrhius, coming into the temple .. agreed with Pechytes the son of Arsiesis and ¿ Oenone ? to sell for a sum of money ..   .. (14) Royal Street .. month .. time ..   . Executed and confirmed . Written by .. clerk to the chief priests of Amonrasonther and the contemplar Gods, the Gods ¿ Beneficent ? the Father loving Gods and the Gods Illustrious, the ¿ hostile ? Paternal God, and the Mother loving Gods. Amen.

The name of Eupator appears here to contain, in two different places, the characters which in the

Rosetta inscription denote hostile or turbulent; and this circumstance would incline us to prefer the date of the last year of the reign of Philometor: but it is possible that the same epithets may have been intended to mean warlike, in a favourable sense.

There remains a fourth enchorial manuscript, of some importance, at present in the British Museum, but still belonging to Mr. Salt, without whose permission it would be improper to make public its whole contents, even if they were perfectly intelligible. But, in fact, the preamble of this manuscript has been lost, and the registry is nearly illegible, except that the date is clearly XLVII, and the signature of the President at the table of Hermopolis appears to be Dionysius. The names of Horus and Erieus and Arsiesis are also distinguishable in the body of the deed, and the word " two thousand" is written at length, at the end of the registry. Now the year 47 can only belong to the reign of Philadelphus, or to that of Eupator, and the style of the registry too much resembles that of all the other deeds, including Anastasy's, to allow us to assign it to the former reign: it must, therefore, belong, not to 277, but to 124 B. C. This date will not indeed give us any certain evidence respecting that of Mr. Grey's deeds; though it might rather incline us to take the later than the earlier, of two periods, equally probable in other respects. On the whole, we can only leave the alternative open for future decision between the dates, as thus contrasted:

Mr. Grey's enchorial deed	(A), XXVIII	154 or	143 B.C.
	(B), XXIX	153	142
	(C), XXXV	147	136
Mr. Grey's Greek Antigraph, or rather the enchorial deed of Paris		XXXVI 146	135
Mr. Salt's enchorial deed		XLVII	124
Anastasy's Greek conveyance		XII-IX	106.

The registry of Mr. Grey's first deed is therefore at least 37, and, on the whole, most probably 48 years more ancient, than any other writing with a pen and ink that exists; and it still remains in the most perfect preservation. Mr. Jomard has compared the manuscript of Anastasy, for its importance, to the pillar of Rosetta: but it can in no respect whatever be put in competition with the Antigraph of Mr. Grey.

SPECIMEN OF MR. GREY'S ENCHORIAL PAPYRUS.

CHAPTER VI.

EXTRACTS FROM DIODORUS AND HERODOTUS; RELATING TO MUMMIES.

IT is rather as being illustrated by the discovery of Mr. Grey's Greek papyrus, than as contributing much to its illustration, that I shall here introduce such passages of Diodorus Siculus and of Herodotus, as tend to explain the customs of the Egyptians respecting the honours shown to the dead bodies of their relations.

" The inhabitants of this country," says Diodorus, Book I. § 51, Wess., in the language of Booth, p. 26, " little value the short time of this present life; but put a high esteem upon the name and reputation of a virtuous life after death; and they call the houses of the living, *Inns*, because they stay in them but a little while ; but the sepulchres of the dead they call *Everlasting habitations*, because they abide in the graves to infinite generations. Therefore they are not very curious in the building of their houses; but in beautifying their sepulchres they leave nothing undone that [the excess of magnificence can suggest]."

§. 72. W. " What the Egyptians performed, after the deaths of every one of their kings, clearly evidences the great love they bore to them. For honour done to him that cannot possibly know it, in a grateful return of a former benefit, carries along with it a testimony of sincerity, without the least colour of dissimulation." Booth, p. 37.

§ 73. W. The whole of Egypt being divided into a number of parts, called Nomes by the Greeks, each of these is governed by a Nomarcha, to whom the care of all its public concerns is entrusted. The land being every where divided into three portions, the first is occupied by the priesthood, who are held in the greatest respect by the inhabitants, as being devoted to the worship of the gods, and as possessing the greatest power of understanding, from the superiority of their education: and from the revenues of these lands they perform all sacrifices throughout Egypt, and support the servants of the temples as well as their own families: for they hold that the administration of the honours of the gods ought not to be fluctuating, but to be conducted always by the same persons, and in the same manner: and that those, who are above all their fellow citizens in wisdom and knowledge, ought not to be below any of them in the comforts and conveniences of life: and the priests are in the habit of associating very generally with the kings, partly as counsellors, partly as assistants, and partly as expounders and instructors: foretelling future events by means of astronomy and of augury, and reading the most useful lessons from the past, out of the records of their sacred volumes: for it is not the custom, as in Greece, for one man, or one woman, to be appointed to each priesthood, but there are many who are employed together in the sacrifices and in other ceremonies; and these transmit the same professional occupation to their descendants. The whole of the families of the priests are exempt from taxes, and they come immediately after the king in rank and authority. The second portion of the land is retained in the power of the king for his own revenue, out of which he has to provide for all military expenses, and for the support of his own splendour and dignity, as well as for the liberal remuneration of those who have distinguished themselves by their virtues and their valour: so that being amply supplied from this territory, they are not obliged to burden their subjects with oppressive taxes. The last of the three portions is assigned to the military population, who are subject to the duties attending on a state of warfare: in order that those, who are exposed to danger in battle, may be the more ready to undergo the hazards of the field, from the interest that they feel in the country as occupiers of the soil: for it would be thought absurd to commit the common safety to the care of those, who possessed nothing in the country that was worthy of preservation: and this system had the still greater advantage of acting as an encouragement to population, in order that the country might not be in want of foreign auxiliaries: and their descendants, in like manner, receiving the constitution thus transmitted to them from their forefathers, are excited by the emulation of the valiant deeds of their ancestors, and become invincible by the courage and experience which they acquire.

§ 74. There are also three other classes that enter into the political system of Egypt; those of the Shepherds, the Husbandmen, and the Artisans. The husbandmen, occupying, at a low rent, the arable land belonging to the king, and the priests, and the military, employ their whole time in cultivating it: and being educated from their infancy in agricultural pursuits, they are superior, from their experience, to the husbandmen of other countries: for they are perfectly well acquainted, partly from the knowledge derived from their ancestors, and partly from their own observation, with the nature of the soil, and its irrigation, and with the times and seasons for sowing and reaping, and for collecting all kinds of fruits. The same advantages are possessed by the shepherds, who receive the charge of the flocks from their forefathers as by inheritance, and pass their whole lives in the care of their cattle: and having derived much information from their ancestors, respecting the best modes of treatment and fattening of the different animals, they also add not a little from their own zeal and industry in their occupations: and, what is most remarkable, from their excessive refinement in these pursuits, the poulterers and geese feeders, besides the natural modes of breeding birds, which are common in other countries, have procured an infinite multitude of poultry by their own ingenuity: for they do not hatch their eggs by the incubation of the hens, but, by means of an artificial operation, derived from their own talents and invention, they are enabled to rival, if not to exceed, the activity of nature: and the arts in general are carried to a very elaborate degree of perfection by the Egyptians; for in this country no artist is allowed to meddle either with political affairs, or with any other employment, besides that which he has received from his parents, and to which he is confined by the law: so that neither the jealousy of a master, nor any public business, can ever divert him from the exclusive study of his profession: for in other countries we often observe that an artist is diverted by a variety of pursuits, and is too avaricious to confine himself to his own work; some employing themselves in husbandry, some in commerce, and some in two or three different arts at once; and in democratical countries, many are constantly frequenting popular assemblies, and doing mischief to the government, while they are receiving bribes from the leaders of parties : but among the Egyptians, if any artisan should meddle with politics, or should employ himself in any other concerns besides that in which he has been educated, a severe punishment would be inflicted on him. Such then were the institutions of the ancient Egyptians with regard to their public and private occupations.

§ 75. For the regulation of judicial proceedings, they also took no common pains: since they held that the sentences, pronounced by the legal tribunals, had the greatest possible influence, whether beneficial or injurious, on the concerns of common life: and they saw that the punishment of offenders, and the relief of oppressed persons, were the most effectual remedies for the evils of a state: and that if the terror, that arises from the condemnation of the guilty, were to be superseded by money or by favour, there would be nothing but confusion in all ranks of society: and they attained the end they desired, by the selection of the best men out of the most considerable cities as Common Judges: taking ten from Heliopolis, and the same number from Thebes and from Memphis: and the Bench, thus assembled, did not appear to be inferior either to the Areopagites at Athens, or to the Elders among the Lacedaemonins. When these thirty had met, they proceeded to elect the most distinguished of their number as their President, with the title of Arch judge: and his place among themselves was supplied by another person, sent by the same city. The judges all received allowances from the king, sufficient for their support, and the arch judge received a manifold portion. He was distinguished by wearing round his neck a golden chain, suspending a figure adorned with precious stones, which was called Alethía, or Truth: and the trial began when the arch judge put on this image of Truth. Now the whole of the laws of the country being written in eight books, and these books being placed near the judges, it was the custom for the accuser to write down in detail the offense to be proved, and the manner in which the action was committed, and the estimated amount of the damage or the injury: the accused party then, taking the depositions of his opponents, wrote his answer to each of them, either denying the facts, or maintaining that they were not illegal; or, if they were illegal, that the damages were appreciated too highly: the accuser replied again in writing, and the accused party rejoined: and both having given in their writings to the judges, the thirty proceeded to declare their opinions among themselves; and lastly, the arch judge touched one of the contending parties, who was to be successful, with the figure of Truth which he wore .. And this was done, in order to supersede the influence of artificial eloquence, and the fascination of personal appearance, which too often pervert the distribution of justice..

§ 80. The Priests of the Egyptians are allowed to marry but one wife: other persons marry as many as they please: but they are obliged to rear all their children, since a numerous population is esteemed highly conducive to the happiness of every country and state: and none of their children are accounted illegitimate, even if the mother has been purchased as a slave: for the children are supposed to belong more particularly to the father, the mother being considered as little more than a nurse. They feed their children very lightly, and at an incredibly small expense: giving them a little meal of the coarsest and cheapest kind, the pith of the papyrus, baked under the ashes, with the roots and stalks of some marsh weeds, either raw, or boiled, or roasted: and since most of them are brought up, on account of the mildness of the climate, without shoes, and indeed without any other clothing; the whole of the expense, incurred by the parents, till they come to years of maturity, does not exceed about 20 drachmas, or 13 shillings, each. This frugality is the true reason of the great populousness of Egypt, and of the magnificence of the public works, with which the country is adorned.

§ 81. The children of the priests, however, are instructed in two descriptions of literature; the sacred and the more general: and they apply themselves with diligence to geometry and arithmetic: for the river, changing the appearance of the country very materially every year, is the cause of many and various discussions among the neighbouring proprietors : and these it would be difficult for any person to decide, without geometrical reasoning, founded upon actual observation : and for arithmetic they have frequent occasion both in their domestic economy, and in the application of geometrical theorems, besides its utility in the cultivation of astronomical studies: for the orders and motions of the stars are observed at least as industriously by the Egyptians as by any other people whatever: and they keep records of the motions of each for an incredible number of years; the study of this science having been, from the remotest times, an object of national ambition with them: they have also most punctually observed the motions and periods and stations of the planets, as well as the powers which they possess, with respect to the nativities of animals, and what good or evil influences they exert: and they frequently foretel what is to happen to a man throughout his life, and not uncommonly predict a failure of crops, or an abundance, and the occurrence of epidemic diseases among men or beasts: they foresee also earthquakes and floods, and the appearances of comets, and a variety of other things which appear impossible to the multitude. It is said also that the Chaldaeans in Babylon are derived from an Egyptian colony, and have acquired their reputation for astrology by means of the information obtained from the priests in Egypt: but the generality of the common people in Egypt learn only, from their parents or relations, that which is required for the exercise of their peculiar professions, as we have already seen: a few of them only teach them something of literature, especially those who cultivate the more refined of the arts: wrestling and music it is not their custom to practice: for they conceive that, by exercise in the palaestra, young men acquire not solid health, but a temporary increase of strength, which is by no means free from danger; and music they esteem not only useless, but even injurious, as rendering the minds of men effeminate ...

§. 83. W. The customs of the Egyptians with regard to their sacred animals are exceedingly surprising, and worthy to be examined; for they venerate some of these animals in an extraordinary degree, not only while they are living, but even after their death: for example, cats, and ichneumons, and dogs; and besides these, the hawk and the ibis; furthermore, wolves and crocodiles, and other beasts of prey .. Now each kind of the animals, that are held sacred, has a piece of ground appropriated to them, affording a rent sufficient for the care and the food that they require: the Egyptians are also in the habit of making vows to some of their divinities on behalf of their children; and if they recover from the disease, they shave off their hair, and counterpoising it with silver or with gold, they give the money to the priests, who have the care of these animals: the priests expend this money in articles of food; and cutting up the meat for the hawks, call out to them with a loud voice, and throw it to them as they fly near: and for the cats and the ichneumons they soften the bread in milk, and lay it before them with the proper calls and signals; or give them some of the fishes of the Nile cut in pieces : and in the same manner they furnish to every other kind of animal its appropriate food: nor do they attempt to perform these services with any degree of privacy, or to avoid the sight of the multitude; but on the contrary they value themselves, as being the ministers of the highest honours of the Gods, and travel through the cities and the country with their appropriate standards : showing obviously at a distance to what deities they are attached; and receiving the universal respect and homage of those who meet them: and when any one of these animals dies, they roll it up in fine linen, and bewail themselves, and beat their breasts, as they carry it to be embalmed : and then they embalm it with resins, and with substances fit to perfume and to preserve it, and bury it in the sacred vaults: and if any one voluntarily destroys one of these animals, he suffers death : with the exception of the cat and the ibis; for if a person kills either of these, even involuntarily, he infallibly loses his life, a multitude immediately collecting and tearing him in pieces, often without any form of trial; so that, for fear of such a calamity, if any one finds one of these animals dead, he stands at a distance, and calls out with a loud voice, lamenting, and protesting that the animal has been found dead. This superstitious regard to the sacred animals is so thoroughly rooted in their minds, and every one of them has his passions so strongly bent upon their honour, that at the time when Ptolemy had not yet been called a king by the Romans, and the people were using every possible effort to flatter the Italians, who were visiting the country as strangers, and studious to avoid every thing that could excite disputes, or lead to war, on account of their dread of the consequences; a Roman having killed a cat, and a crowd being collected about his residence, neither the magistrates, who were sent by the king to appease their rage, nor the general terror of the Roman name, were able to save the offender from vengeance, although he had done it unintentionally: and this we relate, not from the testimony of others, but from what we ourselves had an opportunity of seeing, upon our journey to Egypt.

§. 84. If these things appear to many incredible and almost fabulous, what remains to be told will be thought still more extraordinary. In the time of a great famine in Egypt, it is related that many of the inhabitants were compelled by hunger to devour each other, but that nobody was even accused of having touched the flesh of any of the sacred animals. Indeed whenever a dog has died in a house, the whole of the persons, residing in it, shave their whole bodies, and go into mourning: and what is still more remarkable, if there was either wine or corn, or any other provisions, in the house, in which the animal died, they would not dare to make any use of it whatever: and if they lose these animals, while they are absent upon any military expedition, they carry back their cats and their hawks in sorrow to Egypt: this they will do even if they are themselves in want of the means of returning with convenience. The manner in which they treat their Apis in Memphis, and Mneuis in Heliopolis, and the Goat in Mendes, and the Crocodile in the Lake Moeris, and the Lion that is kept at Leontopolis, with many other things of the same kind, is easily narrated, but not easily credited, except by an eye witness: for all these animals are kept in sacred inclosures, and attended by many of the most respectable persons, who supply them with the most delicate food; fine flour or prepared corn, boiled in milk, and all kinds of cakes mixed with honey, and geese, either boiled or roasted, are continually provided for them; and for those which are carnivorous, various birds are caught, and given to them alive: and their whole establishments are arranged on a very expensive scale, for they are furnished with warm baths, and anointed with the finest ointments, and the choicest perfumes are burned before them: they have also rich carpets and ornamented furniture, and care is taken to provide them with female companions of the greatest beauty, who are also fed in the most luxurious manner: and when they die, they are lamented like favourite children, and are buried not according to the means of their attendants only, but often much more magnificently: for after the death of Alexander, when Ptolemy the son of Lagus had lately become King of Egypt, the Apis at Memphis happened to die of old age; and the person, who had the care of him, not only spent the whole of the allowances, which were very considerable, upon the funeral, but borrowed also fifty talents, or twelve thousand pounds, more of Ptolemy, to defray the expense: and within our own memory it has happened, that the guardians of these animals have spent not less than a hundred talents at their funeral.

§. 85. Besides these ceremonies, there are many other customs at the death of the sacred bull named Apis; for after he has been splendidly interred, the priests seek for a calf who is marked as nearly as possible in the same manner: and having found him, they release the public from their mourning, and the appointed persons carry the calf first to Nilopolis, where they feed him for forty days; and then embarking him on board of a yacht with a gilded cabin, they conduct him as a god to the sacred grove of Vulcan, at Memphis. In these forty days only, he is allowed to be seen by women, who perform certain evolutions before him, which are probably more amusing to his attendants than to himself: and at no other time are women allowed to see him. The reason of the honours paid to him is said to be, that at the death of Osiris, his soul transmigrated into this animal, and that it is continually transferred to his successors, when he dies: others however inform us, that when Osiris was killed by Typhon, his limbs were collected by Isis, and thrown into a wooden cow, covered with cotton cloths, and that the city was thence called Busiris. [It seems however that this must have been a Grecian fiction, for in Egyptian BUSIRIS must have meant the *tomb* of Osiris, and not the *cow*.] For the deification of the other animals, as well as of their kings, a variety of reasons are assigned [; all as uninteresting as they are absurd; except the story of a hawk having brought, to the priest at Thebes, a book of laws and religious observances, tied up with purple; and that hence the Hierogrammates, or sacred scribes, were distinguished by a purple sash, and by wearing a hawk's feather on their heads: that the crocodile is said to be venerated as the watchman of the Nile, preventing the predatory excursions, which would be undertaken, if the thieves could swim across the river in safety; and that the diversity of deities, worshipped in neighbouring parts of the country, is supposed by some to have originated in a political contrivance of the government, to keep the people in subjection, by preventing their too intimate union].

§. 91. The customs of the Egyptians, with regard to their funerals, are not the least wonderful of their peculiar institutions. For when any one dies among them, the whole of his family and all his friends cover their heads with clay, and go about the city lamenting, until the body is buried; partaking neither of baths, nor of wine, nor of any abundant food, nor putting on rich clothing. The funerals are conducted upon three different scales, the most expensive, the moderate, and the humblest: the first costs a talent of silver [£250]; the second twenty minae [£60]; the third is extremely cheap. Now the persons, that undertake this office, are artists, who exercise the profession from generation to generation: and they bring to the friends of the deceased an estimate of the expenses of the funeral, and ask them in what manner they wish that it should be performed. When the agreement is made, the operations are commenced by the proper persons: and first the scribe marks out how the dissection is to be performed, upon the left side of the body; the dissector then cuts it with a sharp Ethiopian stone, and immediately betakes himself to flight, and is pursued and beaten, as if he had committed an inhuman action; the embalmers, on the contrary, are held in all honour and respect, associating with the priests, and having free access to the temples, as sacred persons: these embalmers commence their office by removing such parts as are most susceptible of decay, and, washing the rest with palm wine, and spices, apply various kinds of resins for more than thirty days, and then impregnate the whole with myrrh and cinnamon, and other substances calculated not only to preserve it, but to communicate to it an agreeable smell: and finally they return the body to the relations, so perfectly preserved in every part, that even the hairs of the eyelids and eyebrows remain undisturbed, and the whole appearance of the person is unchanged, and the features are capable of being recognised: so that the Egyptians, very commonly, keeping the bodies of their ancestors in magnificent apartments, are able to see the very faces of those, who have died several generations before them: each of whom being distinguishable, not only by his height, and the outline of his figure, but even by the character of his countenance, they enjoy a wonderful gratification, as if they lived in the society of those whom they see before them. [It is indeed related by Damascenus, Orat. 1, that they placed them on seats at their tables, as if they wished to eat and drink in their society: and Lucian, in his Essay on Grief, declares, that he has been an eye witness of the custom. Wessel. It is not however probable that such a practice should have been continued in the times of the Ptolemies: although Lucian, who had an appointment in Egypt under Marcus Aurelius, may be considered as pretty good authority, when he speaks seriously.]

§. 92. But when the body is about to be finally buried, the relations announce the appointed day to the judges, and to all the friends of the deceased, declaring that he is about to pass the lake of the Nome: and forty two judges being collected, and placed in a semicircle, which is prepared beyond the lake, a boat is brought up, which had been provided for the purpose, conducted by a boatman who is called, in their language, Charon, [the Silent]: whence they say that Orpheus, in former times, having travelled into Egypt, and seen this custom, invented the fable of Hades, partly from imitating what he saw, and partly from his own imagination: but when the boat was brought into the lake, before the coffin with the dead body was put on board, it was lawful, for any person who thought proper, to bring forwards his accusation against the deceased: and if he showed that the deceased had led an evil life, the judges declared accordingly, and the body was deprived of the accustomed sepulture: but if the accuser failed of establishing what he advanced, he was subject to very heavy penalties. When there had been no accuser, or when the accusation had been repelled as unjust, the relations, laying aside their mourning, pronounced encomiums on the deceased: not enlarging upon his descent, as is usual among the Greeks, for they hold that all the Egyptians are equally noble: but relating his earliest education and the course of his studies, and then his piety and justice in manhood, and his temperance, and the other virtues that he possessed, they supplicated the infernal deities to receive him as a companion of the pious: the multitude in the mean time applauded, and joined in extolling the glory of the deceased, as being about to remain to eternity with the virtuous in the regions of Hades. The body is then placed, by those who have family catacombs already prepared, in the compartment allotted to it: those who are not possessed of catacombs construct a new apartment for the purpose, in their own houses, and set the coffin upright against the firmest of the walls. Those who are debarred of the rites of burial, on account of the accusation which has been brought forwards against them, or on account of debts which they have contracted, are placed in their own houses: and then, if their children's children happen to be prosperous, they are frequently released from the impediments of their creditors and their accusers, and at length obtain the ceremony of a magnificent funeral.

§. 93. It is most solemnly established in Egypt, to pay a more marked respect to their parents and their ancestors, when they are removed to their everlasting habitations. It is also usual among them to deposit the bodies of their deceased parents, as pledges for the payment of money that they borrow: and those who do not redeem these pledges are subject to the heaviest disgrace, and are deprived of burial after their death...

§. 96. We must now enumerate such of the Greeks as have visited Egypt in ancient times, for the acquirement of knowledge and wisdom. The priests of the Egyptians relate, from the records preserved in their sacred volumes, that they were visited by Orpheus and Musaeus, and Melampus and Daedalus; by Homer, the poet, and Lycurgus, the Spartan: by Solon, the Athenian, and Plato, the philosopher: and that Pythagoras, of Samos, also came there, and the mathematician Eudoxus: and Democritus of Abdera, and Oenopides of Chius. All these they identify by some distinct marks, either portraits, or appellations derived from their residences or their works: and they produce evidence from the branches of knowledge, which they respectively cultivated, that they had only borrowed, from the Egyptians, all that acquired them the admiration of their countrymen. That Orpheus had learned of them the greatest part of his mystical ceremonies, and the orgies that celebrate the wanderings [of Ceres], and the mythology of the shades below: for that the rites of Osiris and of Bacchus are the same: and those of Isis extremely resemble those of Ceres, with the change of name only: and the punishments of the impious in Tartarus, and the Elysian plains of the virtuous, and the common imagery of fiction, were all copied from the ceremonies of the Egyptian funerals: that Hermes, the conductor of souls, was, according to the old institution of Egypt, to convey the body of Apis to an appointed place, where it was received by a man wearing the mask of Cerberus, [probably the *Cteristes* of the temporary nomenclature;] and that Orpheus having related this among the Greeks, the fable was adopted by Homer, who makes the Cyllenian Hermes call forth the souls of the suitors, holding his staff in his hand:

Cyllenius now to Pluto's dreary reign
Conveys the dead, a lamentable train!
The golden wand that causes sleep to fly,
Or in soft slumber seals the wakeful eye,
That drives the ghosts to realms of night or day,
Points out the long, uncomfortable way.
Trembling the spectres glide, and plaintive vent
Thin, hollow screams, along the deep descent..

And now they reached the Earth's remotest ends,
And now the gates where evening Sol descends,
And Leucas' rock, and Ocean's utmost streams,
And now pervade the dusky land of dreams;
And rest at last where souls unbodied dwell
In ever flowery meads of Asphodel,
The empty forms of men inhabit there,
Impassive semblance, images of air!

POPE.

The river he calls Ocean, as they say, because the Egyptians call the Nile Oceanus in their own language [? ?]: the gates of the Sun are derived from Heliopolis: and the meadow is so called, from the lake which is named Acherusian, and which is near Memphis, being surrounded by beautiful meadows, and canals, with lotus and flowering rushes: and that it is consistent with the imitation to make the deceased inhabit these places: because the greater number and the most considerable of the Egyptian catacombs are there, the bodies being ferried over the river and the Acherusian lake, and the mummies being deposited in the catacombs there situated. And the rest of the Grecian mythology respecting Hades agrees also with the present practice in Egypt: the boat which carries over the bodies, and is called BARIS; and the penny that is given for the fare to the boatman, who is called CHARON in the language of the country. They say there is also, in the neighbourhood of the same place, a temple of the nocturnal Hecate, with the gates of Cocytus and of Lethe, fastened with brazen bars; and that there are, besides, other gates of Truth; and near them a figure of Justice without a head.

§. 97. In the city of Acanthae, on the Libyan side of the Nile, 120 stadia from Memphis, they say there is a barrel pierced with holes, to which 360 of the priests carry water from the Nile: and that a mystery is acted in an assembly in that neighbourhood, in which a man is made to twist one end of a long rope, while other persons untwist the other end; an allusion to which has become proverbial in Greece. Melampus, they say, brought from Egypt the mysteries of Bacchus, and the stories of Saturn, and the battles of the Titans: and Daedalus imitated the Egyptian labyrinth, in that which he built for king Minos: the Egyptian labyrinth having been constructed by Mendes, or by Marus, an ancient king, many years before his time; and that the style of the ancient statues in Egypt is the same with that of the statues sculptured in Greece: but that the very fine Propylon of Vulcan in Memphis was the work of Daedalus as an architect: and that being admired for this work, he had the honour of obtaining a place, in the same temple, for a wooden statue of himself, which was the work of his own hands : that his talents and inventive faculties at last acquired him even divine honours, and that there is to this day a temple of Daedalus, on one of the islands near Memphis, which is honoured by the neighbouring inhabitants. That Homer had been in Egypt, they argue, among other reasons, from the administration of the Nepenthes by Helen to Telemachus, which occasioned a forgetfulness of the evils that had befallen him: for he seems to have perfectly understood the nature of this remedy, which he says Helen received in the Egyptian Thebes, of Polydamne the wife of Thon, for that the women of the same place still make use of it, for a similar purpose, and it is only among the Diospolitan women, that it is known as a remedy for anger and for sorrow, and that Diospolis is the Thebes of the ancients; and that Venus is called golden by its inhabitants from an old tradition, and that there is a field belonging to the golden Venus in the neighbourhood of Momemphis: and that he has copied from them the history of the embraces of Jupiter and Juno, and of Jove's absence in Ethiopia: for that they have an annual ceremony, in which the temple or shrine of Jupiter is carried across the river into Libya, and is brought back in a few days, as if the deity returned from Ethiopia: and that the embraces of the deities are found

(§. 346) in their assemblies, when both of their shrines are carried to a mountain which is strewed by the priest with flowers. [Analogies all too slight to be admitted as any thing like evidence.]

§. 98. They say also that Lycurgus and Plato and Solon transferred many of the customs of the Egyptians into their own establishments. And that Pythagoras learned in Egypt both his divinity and his geometrical theorems, and his arithmetic, and the transmigration of the soul into all kinds of animals. They believe too that Democritus spent five years among them, and was taught by them many things relating to astronomy. And that Oenopides [of Chius] in the same way, by living with their priests and astronomers, learned of them, among many other things, the position of the sun's orbit, that it moved obliquely, and in a direction contrary to that of the other stars. And that Eudoxus, in the same manner, gained great reputation among his countrymen, by having studied astronomy among them, and made known many of their useful discoveries among the Greeks: and the most celebrated of the ancient statuaries had lived among them, Telecles and Theodorus, the sons of Rhoecus, who made for the Samians the image of the Pythian Apollo: for it is said that one half of the image was executed in Samos by Telecles, and the other half at Ephesus by his brother Theodorus; and that both parts, when put together, agreed so well with each other, as to appear precisely as if they had been the work of one person: and that this kind of workmanship was never practised by the Greeks, but was very common among the Egyptians: for that with them it was not usual to judge of the symmetry of a figure by the sight of the whole, as with the Greeks; but that when the stones were quarried and properly cut out, they then proceeded by proportion from the smallest to the greatest; and dividing the whole fabric of the body into one and twenty parts, and a quarter, they arranged the whole symmetry accordingly: and hence, when their artists consult with each other about the magnitude of any figure, although separated from each other, they still make the results agree so well, that this peculiarity of their practice excites the greatest astonishment: and that the image in Samos, according to this refinement of the Egyptians, being divided from the summit of the head, and as far as the middle, is still perfectly consistent with itself, and in all parts alike: they also observe that it extremely resembles the Egyptian figures as having the hands stretched out, and the legs separated, as in walking. And enough has now been said of what is most celebrated and remarkable in the country and customs of the Egyptians: [the greater part of which is of much more value, as occasionally furnishing anecdotes from the arguments that were advanced by the priests in there discussions, than as by any means rendered fully credible by the application of these anecdotes.]

The process of embalming is described very nearly in the same manner by Herodotus. "Their customs," he says, Book II, § 85, " relating to mourning and to funerals are these. When any person of consequence dies, the females of his family cover their heads and faces with clay, and leaving the dead body at home, wander through the city, beating themselves, wearing a close girdle, and having their bosoms bare, accompanied by all their intimate friends : the men also make similar lamentations in a separate company : they then proceed to embalm the body.

(86). This service is performed by persons appointed to exercise the art, as their business : and when a dead body is brought to them, they show their patterns of mummies in wood, imitated by sculpture : and the most elaborate of these they say belongs to the character of [Osiris] one, whose name I do not think it pious to mention on such an occasion : the second, that they show, is simpler and less costly: the third, the cheapest of all : and having shown them these, they inquire in which way the service shall be performed : the parties then make their agreement, and the body is left for preparation. The interior soft parts being removed both from the head and from the trunk, the cavities are washed with palm wine and fragrant gums, and partly filled up with myrrh and cassia and other spices; the whole is then steeped in a solution of soda for seventy days, which is the longest time permitted; and then, having been washed, the body is rolled up with bandages of cotton cloth, being first smeared with gum, instead of glue. The relations then, receiving the body, procure a wooden case for it in a human shape, and inclose the dead body in it: and when thus inclosed, they treasure it up in an appropriate building or apartment, placing it upright against the wall. And this is the most expensive mode of preparation.

(87). For those who prefer the middle class, in order to avoid expense, the process is simplified by omitting the actual removal of the interior parts, and introducing a corrosive liquid to melt them down: the soda consumes the flesh, so that skin and bone only is left, when the body is restored to the friends.

(88). The third and simplest process is merely to cleanse the body well, within and without, by means of some vegetable decoctions, and to keep it in the alkaline solution for the seventy days, without further precautions."

It is difficult to say, according to these statements, what part of the ceremony might be considered as actually constituting the burial. But we find in a Greek inscription on the coffin of a mummy, found by Mr. Grey, which he has had the goodness to communicate to me, "The tomb of Tphuto (or Tphus) the daughter of Heracléus Soter and Sarapus. She was born in the Vth year of Adrian our Lord, the 2d Athyr [III], and died in the XIth year, Tybi [v] the 10th. Aged six years, two months, and eight days. She was buried in the XIIth year, the 12th of Athyr." So that here the burial took place a full year after the death; and there was time enough for every imaginable luxury of the embalmer's art. The coffin is not, in this instance, made in imitation " of the human form," as the coffins of the more ancient mummies, but it is merely an oblong trunk, with an arched cover, and a pillar rising a little at each angle. We have no precise account of the liturgies, or services, performed to these canonized personages, but they were probably some forms of adoration, combined with offerings of flowers and fruit, which were placed before or beside them, and it is well known that some corn and some cakes have been found still standing in baskets, in some of the catacombs lately opened; and that specimens of them have been brought to the British Museum.

CHAPTER VII.

EXTRACTS FROM STRABO; ALPHABET OF CHAMPOLLION; HIEROGLYPHICAL AND ENCHORIAL NAMES.

THE manner in which the Hieroglyphical alphabet was employed, in the time of the Roman emperors, may be understood from the examination of the specimens inserted in this chapter; they comprehend an example of each of the names and titles, which Mr. Champollion has included in his catalogue. In order to illustrate the veneration paid to the Roman emperors in Egypt, I shall subjoin an extract from Strabo, relating to the administration of that country, in the days of the earlier Caesars, for he was a contemporary and a subject of Tiberius.

Book xvii. " The whole of Egypt was divided into Nomes, the Thebaid containing ten, the Delta ten, and the intermediate parts sixteen, making in all 36 .. The nomes were generally divided into Toparchiae, or local governments: and these again into other portions .. At Alexandria, the Necropolis is a separate suburb, containing gardens, and sepulchres, and subterraneous passages, employed for preserving the dead."

"After the death of Julius Caesar, and after the battle of Philippi, Antony went into Asia, and paid extravagant honours to Cleopatra, even making her his wife, and having several children by her. He carried on, in concert with her, the war that was terminated at Actium, and accompanied her, as is well known, in her flight. Augustus following them, destroyed them both, and set Egypt at rest from the revels of a drunkard. It is now governed as a province, or an Eparchia, paying considerable taxes, but being always administered by moderate men, who are sent as Governors, and who hold the rank of a king. Under the governor is the Dicaeodotes, that is the lawgiver, or chancellor: another officer is called the Privy purse, or private accountant, whose business it is to take charge of every thing which is left without an owner, and which falls of right to the Emperor. These two are also attended by Freedmen and Stewards of Caesar, who are intrusted with affairs of greater or less magnitude. There are also three battalions of soldiers, one in the city of Alexandria, the others in the country. Besides these, there are nine companies of Romans; three in the city, three in garrison at Syene, upon the frontiers of Ethiopia, and three in other parts of the country. There are also three regiments of cavalry, similarly distributed, among the fittest places. But of the natives, who are employed in the government of the different cities, the principal are the Exegétes, or Expounder, who is dressed in purple, and is honoured according to the usages of the country, and takes care of what is necessary for the welfare of the city; and the Register, or writer of commentaries; and the Archidicastes, or chief judge; and. fourthly, the Captain of the Night. These same magistracies existed in the time of the kings: but the kings governed so ill, that the welfare of the state was disturbed by all kinds of irregularities. Polybius, who was in Egypt, expresses his horror of the condition of the country at that time: he says there were three kinds of inhabitants in Alexandria; the Egyptians, or the people of the country, a keen and civilised race, and the mercenary troops, who were numerous and turbulent; for it was the custom to keep foreign soldiers in their pay, who, having arms in their hands, were more ready to govern than to obey: the third description of people were the Alexandrians, not very decidedly tractable, for similar reasons, but still, better than the last: for those, who had mixed with them, were originally Greeks, and remembered the habits of their country. This part of the population was however then dwindling-away, more especially through Evergetes Physcon, in whose reign Polybius came to Alexandria: for on several occasions, when there had been some seditious proceedings he attacked this plebeian multitude with his troops, and destroyed great numbers of them. Polybius could not therefore help exclaiming, that he had " To Egypt come, a long and weary way," with but little pleasure or comfort. The subsequent sovereigns administered their governments as ill, or still worse. The Romans may be said to have effected a great reformation in many respects, and to have regulated the city very effectually; and in the country they appointed persons as Commanders, and Monarchae, and Ethnarchae, that is, masters of single places, and of districts, without very extensive powers .. With respect to the revenues of the country, we may judge of them from Cicero, who mentions, in one of his orations, that Auletes, the father of Cleopatra, had an income, from the taxes, of twelve thousand five hundred talents, [between three and four millions sterling]. If then a king, who administered his government in the worst and most negligent manner possible, received so large a revenue, what are we to suppose it must be at present, when it is managed with so much care, and when it has been so much increased by the enlargement of the Indian and African commerce? In former times, there were not twenty vessels, that ventured to navigate the Red Sea, so as to pass out of the Straights: but now there are great fleets, that make the voyage to India, and to the remotest parts of Ethiopia, returning, laden with very valuable cargos, to Egypt, whence they are distributed to other parts; so that they are subjected to a double duty, first upon importation, and then upon exportation: and the customs upon these valuable articles are themselves proportionally valuable; besides that they have the advantages of a monopoly: since Alexandria alone is so situated, as to afford, in general, the only warehouse for receiving them, and for supplying other places with them."

From a comparison of the Enchorial names, which are here inserted, we may confidently add to the alphabet a semicircle, open above, as a form of the P; we have also several variations of the T, and perhaps of the TH; and the character, which is sometimes represented by Z, and sometimes by S, must, in all probability, be the Coptic SH; so that ZMINIS ought rather to be written SHMINIS, meaning OCTAVIUS, from SHMEN, *eight*. The same character is found in the phrase of the Pillar of Rosetta, "who has *received* the kingdom from his father;" and may probably have belonged to the word SHEP, if it is allowable to pursue the analogy so far: it is also remarkable, that the hieroglyphic, which corresponds to this character, has very nearly the same form with that, to which Mr. Champollion attributes the power of SH or X in the name of Xerxes. His Enchorial form of the CH is wholly unsupported by any of these names.

ALPHABET OF CHAMPOLLION.

*Y: †B.

HIEROGLYPHICAL NAMES.

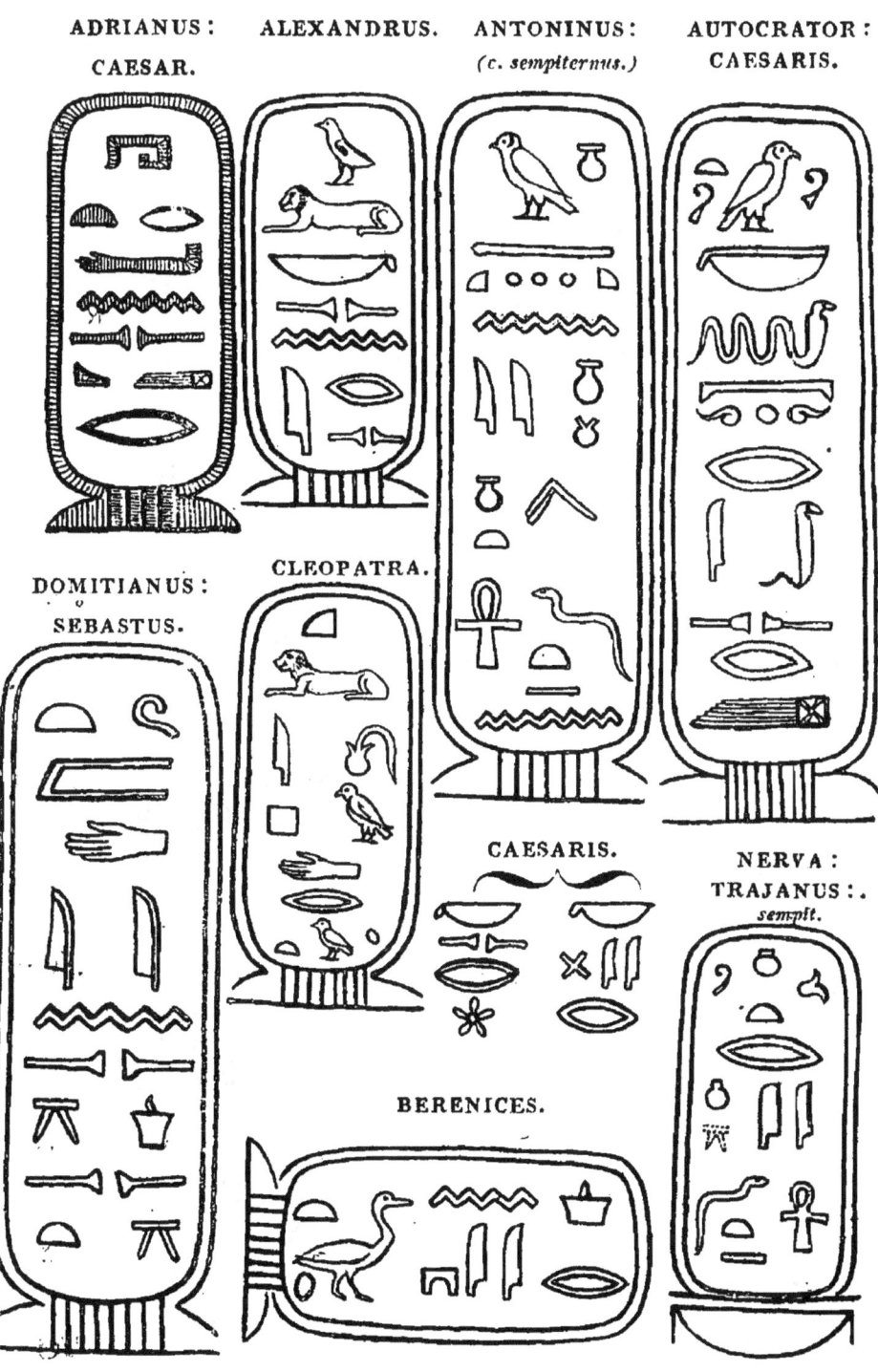

HIEROGLYPHICAL NAMES. 123

PTOLEMAEUS:
c. NEOCAESARIS:
semp: dit: Is. Phth.

SABINA.

SEBASTE:
sempiterna.

SEBASTUS:
semp. Is. Phth.

TIBERIUS:
CAESARIS: *semp*

TRAJANUS:
CAESARIS: *semp.*

TRAJANUS: C.
GERMANICUS:
DACICUS.

VESPASIANUS:
PIUS?

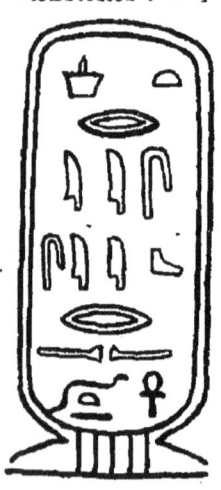
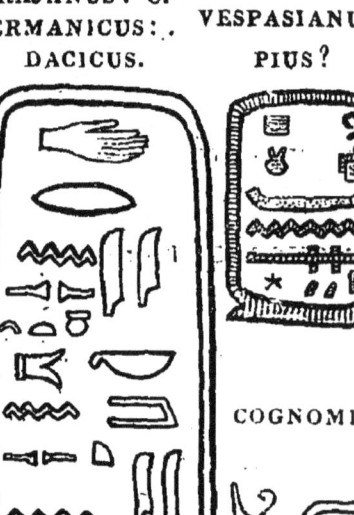

COGNOMINE.

ENCHORIAL PROPER NAMES.

Aëtus	
Alecis, Lecis?	
Alexander	
Alexandria	
Amenothes	
Ammon, Jupiter	
Ammonius	
Amonorytius	
Amonrasonther	
Antigenes	
Antimachus	
Apollonius	
Areia	
Arm"enis"	
Arsiesis	

ENCHORIAL PROPER NAMES.

ARSINOE	
ASUS, ASYS, ASOS	
ATHYR	
BERENICE	
BUSIRITES	
CHAPOCHONSIS	
CHAPOCRATES	
CHIMNARAUS	
CLEOPATRA	
DIOGENES	
EIRENE, IRENE	
ERIEUS	
HORUS	
ISIS	
LUBAIS	
LYCOPOLIS	

126 ENCHORIAL PROPER NAMES.

Maësis	
Mechir	
Mesore	
Mirsis	
Muthes	
Nechthmonthes	
Onnophris	
Osiris	
Osoroeris	
Pacemis	
Panas	
Pateutemis	} {
Peteutemis	
Pechytes	
Petearpocrates	
Peteartres	

ENCHORIAL PROPER NAMES. 127

PETECHONSIS

PETEMESTUS

PETENEPHOTES

PETEURIS

PETOPHOIS

PETOSIRIS

PHABIS

PHANRES

PHIBIS

PHILINUS

PORTIS

PSENAMUNIS

PSENCHONSIS

PTOLEMAEUS

PYRRHA

PYRRHIUS

ENCHORIAL PROPER NAMES.

SENERIEUS	
SENOSOR	
SENPOERIS	
SNACHOMES	
SNACHOMNEUS	
SOTER	
SPOTUS	
TBAEAIS	
TEEPHBIS	
THOTH, HERMES	
THOYTH	
THYNABUNUN	
TOTOES	
ZMINIS	
ZTHENAËTES	
ZOGLYPHUS	

From these specimens, we are also enabled to make some further inferences respecting the "popular" system of writing among the Egyptians. They show incontestably, that the employment of the alphabet, discovered by Akerblad, is not altogether confined to foreign, or at least to Grecian names: it is applicable, for example, very readily, to the words Lubais, Tbaeais, Phabis, and perhaps to some others. But they exhibit also unequivocal traces of a kind of syllabic writing, in which the names of some of the deities seem to have been principally employed, in order to compose that of the individual concerned: thus it appears, that wherever both M and N occur, either together, or separated by a vowel, the symbol of the god Ammon or Amun is almost uniformly employed: for example in AMENOthes, AMONOrytius, AMONrasonther, CHIMNaraus, PsenAMUNis, and SnachoMNeus, in which we find neither M nor N, but the symbol for AMMON, or Jupiter. It follows therefore, that such must have been the original pronunciation of the word, and that this deity was not called either HO or NO, as Akerblad was disposed to imagine. In the same manner we have traces of Osiris, Arueris, Isis, and Re; in *Osoroeris, Petosiris, Senpoeris, Arsiesis, Maesis,* and *Peteartres.* The SE, in PSEnamunis and SEnerieus, is the symbol for a child, and is probably a contraction of SHERI: the gender seems to be distinguished in the enchorial name, while the distinction is lost in the alphabetical mode of writing.

CHAPTER VIII.

CHRONOLOGICAL HISTORY OF THE PTOLEMIES, EXTRACTED FROM VARIOUS AUTHORS.

i. *EXTRACT from* PORPHYRY, *an author of the age of Diocletian, as quoted in Scaliger's* EUSEBIUS, *and probably* thence *in the Armenian translation.*

Alexander, the Macedonian, died in the CXIVth Olympiad, after a reign of 12 years in the whole: and was succeeded in his kingdom by Aridaeus, whose name was changed to Philip, being brother to Alexander, by another mother; for he was the son of Philip by Philinna of Larissa: and after a reign of seven years, he was killed in Macedonia, by Polysperchon the son of Antipater.

Now Ptolemy the son of Arsinoe and of Lagus, after one year of this reign, by an appointment derived from Philip, was sent as a Satrap into Egypt; which he governed in this capacity for 17 years, and afterwards, with Royal authority, for 23; so that the number of all the years of his government, to the time of his death, became 40; but since he retired from the government two years before, in favour of his son Ptolemy Philadelphus, and considered himself as a subject of his son, who had been crowned in his place, the years of this first Ptolemy, called Soter, are reckoned not 40, but 38 only.

He was succeeded by his son, surnamed, as

already mentioned, Philadelphus, who reigned two years during his fathers' life, and thirty [six] afterwards, so that his whole reign occupied, like his father's, 38 years.

In the third place, the throne was ascended by Ptolemy surnamed Evergetes, who reigned 25 years.

In the fourth by Ptolemy called Philopator, whose reign was in the whole 17 years.

After him, the fifth Ptolemy was surnamed Epiphanes, and reigned 24 years.

Epiphanes had two sons, both named Ptolemy, who reigned after him; the elder was surnamed Philometor, and the younger Evergetes the second; their reigns together occupy a period of 64 years. We have placed this as a single number, because, as they were at variance with each other, and reigned alternately, the dates were necessarily confounded. For Philometor first reigned eleven years alone; but when Antiochus made war upon Egypt, and deprived him of his crown, the Alexandrians committed the government to the charge of his younger brother; and, having driven back Antiochus, set Philometor at liberty. They then numbered the year the [twelfth] of Philometor and the first of Evergetes; and this system was continued till the seventeenth: but from the eighteenth forwards, the years are attributed to Philometor alone.

For the elder, having been expelled from his kingdom by the younger, was restored by the

Romans; and he retained the crown of Egypt, leaving his brother the dominion of Libya, and continued to reign alone for 18 years. He died in Syria, having conquered that country: Evergetes being then recalled from Cyrene, and proclaimed King, continued to number the years of his reign from his first accession to the crown; so that having reigned [29] years after the death of his brother, he extended his dates to 54: for the 36th year of Philometor, which should have been called his 1st, he determined to make the 25th. In the whole therefore we have 64: first 35 of Philometor, and the remainder of Evergetes: but the subdivision may lead to confusion.

Now Ptolemy Evergetes the second had two sons, called Ptolemy, by Cleopatra; the elder Soter, and the younger [Alexander]. The elder was proclaimed king by his mother: and appearing to be obsequious to her wishes, he was beloved for a certain time: but when, in the tenth year of his reign, he put to death the friends of his parents, he was deposed by his mother for his cruelty, and driven as a fugitive into Cyprus.

The mother then sent for her younger son from Pelusium, and proclaimed him sovereign together with herself; so that they reigned in common, the dates of public acts being referred to both: and the year was called the eleventh of Cleopatra, and the eighth of Ptolemy Alexander: comprehending the time as a part of his reign, which began with the fourth year of his brother; during which he reigned in Cyprus: and this custom continued during the whole of the life of Cleopatra: but after her death the epoch of Alexander alone was employed; and, though he actually held the sceptre for eighteen years only, from the time of his return to Alexandria, he appears, in his public records, as having reigned twenty six. In his nineteenth year, having quarrelled with his troops, he went out into the country in order to raise a force to control them; but they pursuing him, under the command of Tyrrhus, a relation of the royal family, engaged him by sea, and compelled him to fly, with his wife and daughter, to Myrae, a city of Lycia: whence crossing over to Cyprus, and being attacked by Chaereas, who had the command of the hostile fleet, he was killed in battle.

The Alexandrians, after his flight, sent an embassy to the elder Ptolemy, Soter [or Lathurus], inviting him back from Cyprus, to take possession of the kingdom. During the seven years and six months that he survived, after his return, the whole time that had elapsed since the death of his father was attributed to his reign: so that the number of years became 35, and six months, of which, however, only 17 and six months properly belonged to him, in the two separate portions of his reign: while the second brother, Alexander, had reigned 18 in the intermediate time: and although these could not be effaced from the annals, they suppressed them as far as it was in their power;

since he had offended them by some alliance with the Jews. They do not therefore reckon these years separately, but attribute the whole 36 to the elder brother, omitting again to assign to Cleopatra, the daughter of the elder, and wife of the younger brother, who took possession of the government after her father's death, the six months that she reigned, which were a part of the 36th year. Nor did they distinguish by the name of the Alexander, that succeeded her, the nineteen days that he retained the crown.

This Alexander was the son of the younger brother, Ptolemy Alexander, and the step son of Cleopatra; he was residing at Rome, and the Egyptian dynasty failing of male heirs, he came by invitation to Alexandria, and married this same Cleopatra [his step mother]; and having deprived her by force of her authority, he put her to death after 19 days, and was himself killed in the Gymnasium, by the guards, whom his barbarity had disgusted.

Alexander the second was succeeded by Ptolemy, who was called Neus Dionysus, or the young Bacchus, the son of Ptolemy Soter, and the brother of the Cleopatra last mentioned: his reign continued for 29 years.

His daughter Cleopatra was the last of the family of the Lagidae, and the years assigned to her reign are 22.

Neither did these different reigns fill up the whole series of years from beginning to end in a regular order, but several of them were intermixed with the others. For, in the time of Dionysus, three years are attributed to his two daughters, Cleopatra Tryphaena, and Berenice; a year conjointly, and two years, after the death of Cleopatra Tryphaena, to Berenice alone; because in this interval Ptolemy was gone to Rome, and was spending his time there, while his daughters, as if he were not about to return, took possession of the government for themselves; Berenice having also called in to a share of her dominion some men who were her relations: until Ptolemy, returning from Rome, and forgetting the indulgence due to a daughter, took offence at her conduct, and deprived her of life.

The first years of the reign of his successor Cleopatra were also referred to her in common with her elder brother Ptolemy; and the following to other persons, for this reason: Ptolemy Neus Dionysus, [or Auletes], left at his death four children, two Ptolemies, and Cleopatra, and Arsinoe; appointing as his successors his two elder children, Ptolemy and Cleopatra; they were considered as joint sovereigns for four years, and would have remained so; but that Ptolemy, having departed from his father's commands, and resolved to keep the whole power in his own hands, it was his fate to be slain in a sea fight near the coasts of Egypt, by Julius Caesar, who took part with Cleopatra.

After the destruction of this Ptolemy, Cleopatra's younger brother, also named Ptolemy, was placed on the throne with his sister, by Caesar's decree, and the year was called the fifth of Cleopatra, and the first of Ptolemy: and this custom continued till his death, for two more years. But when he had been destroyed by the arts of Cleopatra, in his fourth year and in the eighth of his sister, the subsequent years were distinguished by the name of Cleopatra alone, as far as fifteen. The sixteenth was named also the first, since, after the death of Lysimachus, king of Chalcis in Syria, the "Autocrator" Marc Antony gave Chalcis and all the neighbouring country to Cleopatra; and from this time the remaining years of her reign, as far as the 22nd, which was the last, were reckoned in the same manner, with an additional number, the 22nd having been called also the 7th, [as the Armenian has very properly read, for the 27th].

From Cleopatra the government devolved to Octavius Caesar, called also Augustus, who overcame the power of Egypt in the battle of Actium, the second year of the CLXXXIVth Olympiad. And from the first year of the CXIth Olympiad, when Aridaeus Philippus [or rather Alexander], the son of Philip, took possession of the government, to the second of the CLXXXIVth, there are 73 Olympiads and a year, or 293 years. And so many are the years of the sovereigns that reigned in Alexandria, to the time of the death of Cleopatra.

ii. *Blair's Chronology of the Ptolemies.*

Year of Nab.	Olympiad.		B. C.		
413	CXI, year	1	336		Aug. Alexander succeeds Philip.
426	CXIV,	2	323		Apr. 21; Alexander dies: Ptolemy S. 1.
464	CXXIII,	4	285	39	Ptolemy Soter.
465	CXXIV,	1	284	1	} Ptolemy Philadelphus.
502	CXXXIII,	2	247	38	
503		3	246	1	} Ptolemy Evergetes.
527	CXXXIX,	3	222	25	
528		4	221	1	} Ptolemy Philopator.
544	CXLIII,	4	205	17	
545	CXLIV,	1	204	1	} Ptolemy Epiphanes.
568	CXLIX,	4	181	24	
569	CL,	1	180	1	} Ptolemy Philometor.
579	CLII,	3	170	11	
580		4	169	12	Ptolemy [Eupator.]
600	CLVII,	4	149	35	Ptolemy Philometor.
604	CLVIII,	4	145	1	} Ptolemy [Eupator.]
632	CLXV,	4	117	21	
633	CLXVI,	1	116	9	} Ptolemy Lathurus and Cleopatra.
642	CLXVIII,	2	107	10	
643		2	106	1	} Cleopatra and Alexander.
660	CLXXII,	4	89	18	
661	CLXXIII,	1	88	1	} Ptolemy Lathurus.
667	CLXXIV,	3	82	7	
668		4	81	[1]	Cleopatra II, 6 months: Alexander II, 19 days.
669	CLXXV,	1	80	1	} Ptolemy Alexander III.
683	CLXXVIII,	3	66	15	
684		4	65	1	} Ptolemy Auletes.
697	CLXXXII,	1	52	14	
698		2	51	1	} Ptolemy Dionysius II, and Cleopatra III.
702	CLXXXIII,	2	47	5	
703		3	46	1	} Cleopatra III, Ptolemy, jun.
704		4	45	2	
705	CLXXXIV,	1	44	3	Ptolemy dies, leaving Cleopatra III.
719	CLXXXVII,	3	30	17	Sept. 2. Battle of Actium. Augustus makes Egypt a Roman Province.

iii. *Chronology of the Ptolemies, according to Champollion Figeac.* Annales des Lagides, 2 v. 8. Par. 1819.

B. C.

323 May 30,   Death of Alexander, Nab. 424 Ol. CXIII, 4.
323 Oct.   Ptolemy Soter arrives in Egypt.
285 End.   39 Ptolemy places Philadelphus on the throne.
284 Nov. 2 1 Philadelphus.
246 Sum.   38 : 1 of Evergetes.
221 Sum.   25 : 1 of Philopator.
204 March 29, 17 : 1 of Epiphanes.
180 March   24 : 1 of Philometor.
146 Aut.   35 : 1 of Evergetes II. [Eupator.]
117 Oct.   29 : 1 of Lathurus.
107 Sum.   10 Lathurus expelled; Alexander reigns.
 88 Sum.   29 Lathurus restored; Alexander dies.
 81 Middle 36 : 1 Lathurus dies, Berenice reigns 6 months : Alexander II.
 72 Beg.   8 : 1 Ptolemy Auletes, "22 years" only.
 51 Spr. "22": 1 Cleopatra with her brother Ptolemy.
 47 July   5   of Cleopatra : 1 of Ptolemy the younger.
 44 July   8 Ptolemy poisoned early in the year.
 41 July   11 Caesarion takes the title of king; [the Neocaesar of the Hieroglyphical alphabet.]
 30 Sept. 2 22 Battle of Actium.
 29 Aug. 1 22 Cleopatra kills herself. Egypt a Roman Province.

iv. *Mr. St. Martin's Chronology of the Ptolemies.* Recherches sur la Mort d'Alexandre, 8 Par. 1820.

Nabon. B. C.
424   324 June 22 Death of Alexander Ol. CXIII, 4.
      323 Nov. 8 Ptolemy Soter governor of Egypt, 17 years.
      306 Nov. 1 Ptolemy Soter king; reigns 21 years.
      285 Nov. 7 Soter and his son Philadelphus reign, 2 years.
      283 Oct. 17 Philadelphus; reigns alone 36 years.
      247 Nov. 8 Ptolemy Evergetes; reigns 25 years.
      222 Nov. 2 Ptolemy Philopator; reigns 17 years.

ST. MARTIN'S CHRONOLOGY. 139

" 210 Oct.   9 Ptolemy Epiphanes associated in the crown."
" 208 Oct.   28 First year named after Epiphanes with his father."
  205 Oct.   13 Epiphanes reigns alone, 24 years
  199 March 28 Anticipated coronation of Epiphanes.
  181 Oct.   28 Ptolemy Philometor reigns alone 11 years.
  170 Oct.   29 With Evergetes II. [Eupator] 6 years.
  164 Oct.   21 Alone again, 18 years; Evergetes at Cyrene.
  146 Nov.   2 Evergetes II. alone 29 years.
  117 Nov.   10 Soter II. [Lathurus] with Cleopatra 10 years.
  114 Nov.   8 Alexander I. reigns 7 years in Cyprus.
  107 Oct.   21 Alexander reigns 18 years: Soter in Cyprus
   89 Nov.   1 Soter II. restored, reigns 8 years.
   82 Oct.   17 Last of Soter: Berenice reigns 6 months; Alexander II. 19 days.
   81 Nov.   4 Ptolemy Auletes; reigns 29 years.
   59 Feb.   24 In the Roman year beginning this day, Auletes was acknowledged king by the Senate.
   58 Feb.   14 He was driven out of Egypt after this day, which was the beginning of a Roman year.
   58 Oct.   21 Cleopatra Tryphaena and Berenice; 1 year.
   57 Nov.   7 Berenice; 2 years with Cybiosactes and Archelaus.
   55 May   2 Auletes had been re-established.
   52 Nov.   12 Cleopatra with the elder Ptolemy; 4 years.
   48 June   29 Battle of Pharsalia.
   47 Feb.   6 Alexandria taken by Caesar; death of Ptolemy.
   47 Oct.   18 Cleopatra with the younger Ptolemy.
   44 Oct.   15 Cleopatra alone; 14 years.
   31 Sept.   2 Battle of Actium.
      Oct.   21 Last year of Cleopatra begins.
   30 Aug.   1 Alexandria taken by Augustus: end of the Lagidae.

Mr. St. Martin being the latest chronologist, that has examined these dates, I have thought it right to insert his table, which I suppose to be correct in the principal part of its foundation, although I cannot readily believe that he is right in attributing to the Ptolemies the observance of the Macedonian year rather than of the Egyptian. He says that in Egypt, as all the world knows, the years of the sovereigns were reckoned from the first day of the year, in which they took the reins of government: meaning by this the first day of the Macedonian year: it appears, however, unquestionable from almost every inscription and manuscript found in Egypt, which exhibits a date, that the Egyptian months and years were employed almost exclusively in that country. It happens, however, that about the time in question, the beginning of these years did not vary very exorbitantly from each other: the Egyptian year having begun in September, October, November or December: and the Macedonian, according to Mr. St. Martin, in October or November.

v. *Genealogy of the Ptolemies, from Champollion Figeac I, p. 231.*

Reigns.	Names and Descriptions.	Reigned.	Death.	Wives.	Children.
I.	SOTER, Son of Lagus and Arsinoe, first governor, then King.	39 y. 5 m.	Natural.	1. 2. 3. Eurydice, d. of Antipater. 4. Berenice: died old.	[Arsinoe.] Ceraunus: seized the crown of Macedonia. Philadelphus: succeeded him.
II.	PHILADELPHUS. Son of Soter and Berenice.	37 y. 11 m.	Natural.	1. Arsinoe d. of Lysimachus, and of his sister. 2. Arsinoe, her mother.	Evergetes. None.
III.	EVERGETES: Tryphon; son of Philadelphus and Arsinoe.	25 y.	Poisoned by his son.	Berenice, daughter of Magas.	Philopator. Magas: put to death by his brother. Arsinoe.
IV.	PHILOPATOR: Gallus; son of Evergetes and Berenice.	16 y. 5 m.	Natural.	Arsinoe his sister: killed by her husband.	Epiphanes.
V.	EPIPHANES. Son of Philopator and Arsinoe.	24 y.	Poisoned.	Cleopatra, d. of the king of Syria, survived him 8 y.	Philometor. Cacergetes. Cleopatra.
VI.	PHILOMETOR. Son of Epiphanes and Cleopatra.	11 y.			
VII.	EVERGETES II: Physcon. Cacergetes. Philologus. [Eupator.] Brother of Philometor.	4 y.			
VIII.	PHILOMETOR and EVERGETES.	2 y.			
IX.	PHILOMETOR.	18 y.	Fall from his horse.	Cleopatra his sister.	A son: killed by his uncle. Cleop. Cocce.
X.	EVERGETES II.	29 y.	Natural.	1. Cleopatra, his brother's widow, repudiated. 2. Cleopatra Cocce, her daughter.	Memphites killed by his father. Lathurus. Alexander Tryphaena: married Antiochus. Cleopatra: m. Lathurus, k. by Tryph. Selene: m. Lathurus; afterwards Antiochus.

Reigns.	Names and Descriptions.	Reigned.	Death.	Wives.	Children.
XI.	SOTER II: Lathurus: Pothinus. With Cleopatra Cocce, his mother.	10 y.	(Deposed.)	1. Cleopatra, his sister. repudiated. 2. Selene: repudiated, and given to Antiochus. 3. A concubine.	Berenice. Auletes. Another son, who reigned in Cyprus, and killed himself. Cleopatra.
XII.	ALEXANDER. Parisactes; his brother. With Cleopatra Cocce.	17 y. 6 m.	Killed in battle, after killing his mother.	Uncertain.	Alexander II. A daughter: killed with him.
XIII.	SOTER II, again.	8 y.	Natural.		
XIV.	BERENICE, daughter of Soter.	6 m.	Killed by Alexander II.		
XV.	ALEXANDER II. Son of Alexander.	"8 y. 3 m." [19 d.]	"Dies at Tyre."	Berenice; whom he killed.	
XVI.	NEUS DIONYSUS: Auletes. Natural son of Lathurus.	"16 y."		Cleopatra.	Berenice. Cleopatra. Ptolemy: dr. Ptolemy: pois. Arsinoe, left Egypt.
XVII.	BERENICE, daughter of Auletes.	2 y.	Killed by her father.		
XVIII.	AULETES.	2 y.	Natural.		
XIX.	PTOLEMY the elder and Cleopatra, children of Auletes.	3 y.	Drowned after a battle.	Cleopatra his sister.	
XX.	PTOLEMY the younger and Cleopatra.	4 y. 6 m.	Poisoned by his wife.	Cleopatra his sister.	
XXI.	CLEOPATRA, alone.	14 y. 3 m.	Killed herself.	By Julius Caesar. By Antony.	Caesarion. A son. A son. A daughter: carried in triumph by Augustus.

CHRONOLOGY OF THE PTOLEMIES. 143

vi. *Approximate dates of the various Reigns; according to Porphyry and to the Medals.*

B.C.	Ptolemy Soter.	B.C.	Philadelphus.	B.C.	Evergetes.	B.C.	Epiphanes.	B.C.	Philometor.
323	1	280	44	236	12	195	11	155	27
322	2	279	45	235	13	194	12	154	28
321	3	278	46	234	14	193	13	153	29
320	4	277	47	233	15	192	14	152	30
319	5	276	48	232	16	191	15	151	31
318	6	275	49	231	17	190	16	150	32
317	7	274	50	230	18	189	17	149	33
316	8	273	51	229	19	188	18	148	34
315	9	272	52	228	20	187	19	147	35
314	10	271	53	227	21	186	20	146	36
313	11	270	54	226	22	185	21		Evergetes II.
312	12	269	55	225	23	184	22	146	25
311	13	268	56	224	24	183	23	145	26
310	14		57?	223	25	182	24	144	27
309	15	267	19?		Philopator.		Philometor.	143	28
308	16	266	20	222	1	181	1	142	29
307	17	265	21	221	2	180	2	141	30
306	18	264	22	220	3	179	3	140	31
305	19	263	23	219	4	178	4	139	32
304	20	262	24	218	5	177	5	138	33
303	21	261	25	217	6	176	6	137	34
302	22	260	26	216	7	175	7	136	35
301	23	259	27	215	8	174	8	135	36
300	24	258	28	214	9	173	9	134	37
299	25	257	29	213	10	172	10	133	38
298	26	256	30	212	11	171	11	132	39
297	27	255	31	211	12		Philometor and Evergetes II.	131	40
296	28	254	32	210	13			130	41
295	29	253	33	209	14			129	42
294	30	252	34		Philopator and Epiphanes.	170	12—1	128	43
293	31	251	35			169	13—2	127	44
292	32	250	36	208	15	168	14—3	126	45
291	33	249	37	207	16	167	15—4	125	46
290	34	248	38	206	17	166	16—5	124	47
289	35		Evergetes.			165	17—6	123	48
288	36				Epiphanes			122	49
287	37	247	1				Philometor.	121	50
286	38	246	2	205	1			120	51
	Soter and Philadelphus.	245	3	204	2	164	18	179	52
		244	4	203	3	163	19	118	53
		243	5	202	4	162	20	117	54
285	39	242	6	201	5	161	21		
284	40	241	7	200	6	160	22		Lathurus and Cleopatra.
	Philadelphus.	240	8	199	7	159	23		
283	41	239	9	198	8	158	24	117	1
282	42	238	11	197	9	157	25	116	2
281	43	237	10	196	10	156	26	115	3

CHRONOLOGY OF THE PTOLEMIES.

B.C.	Lathurus and Cleopatra.	B.C.	Cleopatra and Alexander.	B.C.	Alexander II.	B.C.	Auletes.	B.C.	Cleopatra and Ptolemy, jun.
114	4	96	22—19	81	1	63	19	48	5—1
113	5	95	23—20			62	20	47	6—2
112	6	94	24—21		Auletes.	61	21	46	7—3
111	7	93	25—22	81	1	60	22	45	8—4
110	8	92	26—23	80	2	59	23	44	9
109	9	91	27—24	79	3	58	24	43	10
108	10	90	28—25	78	4		Cleopatra and Berenice.	42	11
			Alexander.	77	5			41	12
	Cleopatra and Alexander.	89	26	76	6	57	1	40	13
		88	27	75	7		Berenice.	39	14
107	11— 8		Lathurus.	74	8	56	1	38	15
106	12— 9	88	30	73	9	55	2	37	16—1
105	13—10	87	31	72	10		Auletes.	36	17—2
104	14—11	86	32	71	11	54	28	35	18—3
103	15—12	85	33	70	12	53	29	34	19—4
102	16—13	84	34	69	13		Cleopatra and Ptolemy.	33	20—5
101	17—14	83	35	68	14			32	21—6
100	18—15	82	36	67	15	52	1	31	22—7
99	19—16	81	37 ?	66	16	51	2		
98	20—17		Berenice.	65	17	50	3		
97	21—18	81	1	64	18	49	4		

OMISSION IN CHAPTER VI.

Page 115. *At the end, add.* To administer these rites, and to renew these offerings, at least as often as could be required, was apparently the duty of the priests, and they were no doubt amply remunerated for their attentions, by the families of the deceased, in the form of the " collections," which are the objects of sale in Mr. Grey's papyrus. The deed was registered 19 days after its execution.

APPENDIX I.

I. GREEK PAPYRUS OF MR. GREY.

(1) ΑΝΤΙΓΡΑΦον συΝΓΡΑΦΗΣ ΑΙΓΥΠΤΙΑΣ περι νεκΡΩΝ εν ΘΥν̄. γενοΜΕΝΗΣ (2) ΚΑΤΑΔ Υ...
(3) ΕΤΟΥΣ Λς αϑυΡ|Κ̄ ΜΕΤΑ ΤΑ ΚΟΙΝΑ ΤΑΔΕ ΛΕΓΕΙ ΧΟΛΧΥΤΗΣ (4) ΤΩΝ Δουλων ισιδος ΤΗΣ ΜΕΓΑΛΗΣ ΟΝΝΩΦΡΙΣ ΩΡΟΥ ΜΗΤΡΟΣ (5) ΣΕΝΠΟΗΡις ως ∟ Μ ΕΥΠΕΤΕΣΙΟΣ ΜΕΓας μεΛΙΧΡΩΣ ΚΟΙΛΟΦΘΑΛΜΟΣ (6) ΑΝΑΦΑΛΑΝτος ΩΡΩΙ ΩΡΟΥ ΜΗΤΡΟΣ ΣΕΝΠΟΗΡΙΣ ΗΥΔΟΚΗσΕ ΑΣΜΕ [νως?] (7) ΤΗΣ ΤΙΜης του ΗΜΙΣΟΥΣ ΤΟΥ ΤΡΙΤΟΥ της ΛΟΓΕΙΑΣ ΤΩΝ ΚΕΙΜΕΝΩΝ (8) ΝΕΚΡΩΝ εν ΘΥΝΑΒΟΥΝΟΥΝ ΕΝ τηι ΛΙΒΥΗΙ ΤΟΥ ΠΕΡΙΘΗΒΑΣ (9) ΕΝ ΤΟΙΣ ΜΕΜΝΟΝΕΙΟΙΣ ΟΜΟΙΩΣ ΚΑΙ ΤΟΥ ΗΜΙΣΟΥΣ ΤΟΥ ΤΡΙΤΟΥ ΛΕΙΤΟΥΡΓΙΩΝ (10) ΚΑΙ ΤΩΝ ΑΛΛΩΝ ΩΝ ΤΑ ΟΝΟΜΑΤΑ | ΜΟΥϑΗΣ ΣΠΟΤΟΥΤΟΣ ΣΥΝ (11) ΤΕΚΝΟΙΣ ΚΑΙ πΑΝΤΩΝ ΧΑΠΟΧΡΑΤΗΣ ΝΕΧΘΜΩΝΘΟΥ ΣΥΝ ΤΕΚΝΟΙΣ (12) ΚΑΙ ΠΑΝΤΩν αΡΣΙΗΣΙΣ ΝΕΧΘΜΩΝΘΟΥ ΟΜΟΙΩΣ ΠΕΤΕΜΕΣΤΟΥΣ (13) ΝΕΧΘΜωνϑου ΩΣΑΥΤΩΣ ΑΡΣΙΗΣΙΣ ΖΜΙΝΙΟΣ ΟΜΟΙΩΣ (14) ΟΣΟΡΟΗΡΙΣ ωρου οΜΟΙΩΣ ΣΠΟΤΟΥΣ ΧΑΠΟΧΩΝΣΙΟΣ ΩΣΑΥΤΩΣ (15) ΖΩΓΛΥΦΟΣ ΑΦ ΩΝ ΕΠΙΒΑΛΛΕΙ ΑΣΩΤΙ ΩΡΟΥ ΜΗΤΡΟΣ ΣΕΝΠΟΗΡΙΣ (16) ΤΩΙ ΝΕωτΕΡΟΥ ΣΟΥ ΑΔΕΛΦΩΙ ΤΩΝ ΑΥΤΩΝ ΧΟΛΧΥΤωΝ ΤΟ ΗΜΙΣΥ (17) ΤΟΥ ΠΡΟΕΙρηΜΕνΟΥ ΤΡΙΤΟΥ ΜΕΡΟΥΣ ΛΕΙΤΟΥΡΓΙΩΝ ΚΑΙ ΚΑΡΠΕΙΩΝ ΚΑΙ (18) ΤΩΝ ΑΛΛΩν αΠΕΔΟΤΟ ΑΥΤΩΙ ΕΝ ΤΩΙ λς ¯.¯. αϑΥΡ ΕΠΙ ΒΑΣΙΛΕΩΣ (19) ΑΙΩΝΟΒιΟΥ εις ΠΛΗΡΩΣΙΝ ΤΟΥ ΤΡΙΤΟΥ ΚΑΙ ΤΟΥ ΗΜΙΣΟΥΣ ΚΑΡΠΕΙΩΝ (20) ΚΑΙ ΤΩΝ ΑΛΛΩν νεΚΡΩΝ ΕΝ ΘΥ. ΠΑΤΕΥΤΗΜΕΙ ΣΥΝ ΤΕΚΝΟΙΣ ΚΑΙ (21) ΠΑΝΤΩΝ Και ηΜΙΣΟΥΣ

ΚΑΡΠΕΙΩΝ ΕΠΙΒΑΛΛΟΝΤΩΝ ΜΟΙ ΕΝ ΤΟΙΣ (22) ΠΕΤΕΧΩνσΙΟΣ ΓΑΛΑΚΤΟΦΟΡΟΥ ΚΑΙ ΤΟΠΟΥ ΑΣΙΗΤΟΣ ΚΑΛΟΥΜΕΝΟΥ (23) ΦΡΕΚΑΓΗΣ ΣΥΝ ΤΩΝ ΕΝ ΑΥΤωι ΝΕΚΡΩΝ ΑΦ ΩΝ ΕΠΙΒΑΛΛΕΙ (24) ΤΩΙ ΑΥΤΩΙ ασΩΤΙ ΤΟ ΗΜΙΣΥ ΑΠΕΔΟΜΗΝ ΑΥΤΩΙ ΣΑ ΕΙΣΙΝ (25) ΚΑΙ ΕΧΩ ΑΥΤΩΝ ΠΑΡΑ ΣΟΥ ΤΗΝ ΤΙΜΗΝ ΚΟΥΘΕΝ ΣΟΙ ΕΓΚΑΛΩ (26) ΠΕΡΙ ΑΥΤΩΝ αΠΟ ΤΗΣΗΜΕΡΟΝ ΕΑΝ ΔΕ ΤΙΣ ΣΟΙ ΕΠΕΛΘΗΙ (27) ΠΕΡΙ ΑΥΤΩΝ υΠΟΣΤΗΣΩ ΑΥΤΟΝ ΕΑΝ ΔΕ ΜΗ ΑΠΟΣΤΗΣΩΙ (28) ΑΠΟΣΤΗΣΩ ΕΠΑΝΑΓΚΟΝ ΕΓΡΑΨΕΝ ΩΡΟΣ ΦΑΒΙΤΟΣ Ο ΠΑΡΑ ΤΩΝ (29) ΙΕΡΕΙΩΝ του ΑμοΝΡΑΣΟΝΘΗΡ ΚΑΙ ΤΩΝ ΣΥΝΝΑΩΝ ΘΕΩΝ ΜΟΝΟ(30)ΓΡΑΦΟΣ ΜαρτυΡΕΣ ΕΡΙΕΥΣ ΦΑΝΡΕΟΥΣ ΠΕΤΕΑΡΤΡΗΣ ΠΑΤΕΥΤΗΜΙΟΣ (31) ΠΕΤΕΑΡΠΟΧΡΑΤΗΣ ωροΥ ΣΝΑΧΟΜΝΕΥΣ ΠΕΤΕΥΡΙΟΣ ΣΝΑΧΟΜΗΣ (32) ΨΕΝΧΩΝΣΙΟΣ ΤΟΤΟΗΣ ΦΙΒΙΟΣ ΠΟΡΤΙΣ ΑΠΟΛΛΩΝΙΟΥ ΖΜΙΝΙΣ (33) ΠΕΤΕΜΕΣΤΟΥΤΟΣ ΠΕΤΕΥΤΗΜΙΣ ΑΡΣΙΗΣΙΟΣ ΑΜΟΝΟΡΥΤΙΟΣ (34) ΠΑΚΗΜΙΟΣ ΩΡΟΣ ΧΙΜΝΑΡΑΥΤΟΣ ΑΡΜΗΝΙΣ ΖΘΕΝΑΗΤΙΟΣ (35) ΜΑΗΣΙΣ ΜΙΡΣΙΟΣ ΑΝΤΙΜΑΧΟΣ ΑΝΤΙΓΕΝΟΥΣ ΠΕΤΟΦΩΙΣ ΦΙΒΙΟΣ (36) ΠΑΝΑΣ ΠΕΤΟΣΙΡΙΟΣ ΜΑΡΤΥΡΕΣ Ις

(37) ΑΝΤΙΓΡΑΦΟΝ ΠΤΩΜΑΤΟΣ/ ΕΤΟΥΣ Λς ΧΟΙΑΧ $\bar{9}$ τ ΕΠΙ ΤΗΝ ΕΝ ΔΙΟΣ☉ (38) ΤΡΑΠΕΖΑΝ ΕΦ ΗΣ ΛΥΣΙΜΑΧΟΣ Κ ΕΓΚ ΚΑΤΑ ΔΙΑΓΡΑΦηΝ ΑΣΚΛΗΠΙΑΔΟΥ (19) ΚΑΙ ΖΜΙΝΙΟΣ ΤΕΛΩΝΩΝ ΕΦ ΗΝ ΥΠΟΓΡ ΠΤΟΛΕΜΑΙΟΣ ΑΝΤΙΓΡ ΩΡΟΣ ΩΡΟΥ (40) ΧΟΛΧΥΤΗΣ ο π. ΤΩΝ ΛΟΓΕΙΟΜΕΝΩΝ Δι αυΤΩΝ ΧΑΡΙΝ ΤΩΝ ΚΕΙΜΕΝΩΝ (41) ΝΕΚΡΩΝ ΕΝ ΘΥΝΑΒΟΥΝΟΥΝ ΕΝ ΤΟΙΣ ΜΕΜΝΟΝΕΙΟΙΣ ΤΗΣ λιβνΗΣ (42) Της ΠΕΡΙΘ͂ ΤΑΦΟΙΣ ΑΝΘ ΗΣ ΠΟΙΟΥΝΤΑΙ ΛΕΙΤΟΥΡΓΙΑΣ Α ΕΩΝΗΣΑΤΟ (43) ΠΑΡΑ ΟΝΝΩΦΡΙΟΣ ΤΟΥ ΩΡΟΥ ΧΑΛΚοΥ ΖΓ T̄ Τ,Τ

(44) ΛΥΣΙΜΑΧ . ΥΓ͞Ρ

II. PAPYRUS OF ANASTASY AND BÖCKH.

(1) ΒΑΣΙΛΕΥΟΝΤΩΝ ΚΛΕΟΠΑΤΡΑΣ ΚΑΙ ΠΤΟΛΕΜΑΙ-
ΟΥ ΥΙΟΥ ΤΟΥ ΕΠΙΚΑΛΟΥΜΕΝΟΥ ΑΛΕΞΑΝΔΡΟΥ ΘΕΩΝ
ΦΙΛΟΜΗΤΟΡΩΝ ΣΩΤΗΡΩΝ ΕΤΟΥΣ ΙΒ ΤΟΥ ΚΑΙ Θ ΕΦ
ΙΕΡΕΩΣ ΤΟΥ ΟΝΤΟΣ (2) ΕΝ ΑΛΕΧΑΝΔΡΕΙΑΙ ΑΛΕΞΑΝΔΡΟΥ
ΚΑΙ ΘΕΩΝ ΣΩΤΗΡΩΝ ΚΑΙ ΘΕΩΝ ΑΔΕΛΦΩΝ ΚΑΙ ΘΕΩΝ
ΕΥΕΡΓΕΤΩΝ ΚΑΙ ΘΕΩΝ ΦΙΛΟΠΑΤΟΡΩΝ ΚΑΙ ΘΕΩΝ ΕΠΙ-
ΦΑΝΩΝ ΚΑΙ ΘΕΟΥ (3) ΦΙΛΟΜΗΤΟΡΟΣ ΚΑΙ ΘΕΟΥ ΕΥΠΑ-
ΤΟΡΟΣ ΚΑΙ ΘΕΩΝ ΕΥΕΡΓΕΤΩΝ ΑΘΛΟΦΟΡΟΥ ΒΕΡΕΝΙΚΗΣ
ΕΥΕΡΓΕΤΙΔΟΣ ΚΑΝΗΦΟΡΟΥ ΑΡΣΙΝΟΗΣ ΦΙΛΑΔΕΛΦΟΥ
ΚΑΙ [ΙΕΡΕΙ]ΑΣ ΑΡΣΙΝΟΗΣ (4) ΕΥΠΑΤΟΡΟΣ ΤΩΝ ΟΝΤΩΝ
ΕΝ ΑΛΕΞΑΝΔΡΕΙΑΙ ΕΝ ΔΕ ΠΤΟΛΕΜΑΙΔΙ ΤΗΣ ΘΗΒΑΙΔΟΣ
ΕΦ ΙΕΡΕΩΝ ΠΤΟΛΕΜΑΙΟΥ ΤΟΥ ΜΕΝ ΣΩΤΗΡΟΣ ΤΩΝ ΟΝ-
ΤΩΝ ΚΑΙ ΟΥΣΩΝ (5) ΕΝ ΠΤΟΛΕΜΑΙΔΙ ΜΗΝΟΣ ΤΥΒΙ Κ̄Θ̄
ΕΠ ΑΠΟΛΛΩΝΙΟΥ ΤΟΥ ΠΡΟΣ ΤΗΙ ΑΓΟΡΑΝΟΜΙΑΙ ΤΩΝ ΜΕ
ΚΑΙ ΤΗΣ ΚΑΤΩ ΤΟΠΑΡΧΙΑΣ ΤΟΥ ΠΑΘΥΡΙΤΟΥ
(6) ΑΠΕΔΟΤΟ ΠΑΜΩΝΘΗΣ ΩΣ L ΜΕ ΜΕΣΟΣ ΜΕΛΑΝΧΡΩΣ
ΚΑΛΟΣ ΤΟ ΣΩΜΑ ΦΑΛΑΚΡΟΣ ΣΤΡΟΓΓΥΛΟΠΡΟΣΩΠΟΣ
ΕΥΘΥΡΙΝ ΚΑΙ ΣΝΑΧΟΜΝΕΥΣ ΩΣ L Κ ΜΕΣΟΣ ΜΕΛΙΧΡΩΣ
(7) ΚΑΙ ΟΥΤΟΣ ΣΤΡΟΓΓΥΛΟΠΡΟΣΩΠΟΣ ΕΥΘΥΡΙΝ ΚΑΙ ΣΕΜ-
ΜΟΥΘΙΣ ΠΕΡΣΙΝΗΙ ΩΣ L ΚΒ ΜΕΣΗΙ ΜΕΛΙΧΡΩΣ ΣΤΡΟΓΓΥ-
ΛΟΠΡΟΣΩΠΟΣ ΕΝΣΙΜΟΣ ΗΣΥΧΗ ΚΑΙ ΤΑΘΛΥΤ (8) ΠΕΡ-
ΣΙΝΗΙ ΩΣ L̇ Λ ΜΕΣΗΙ ΜΕΛΙΧΡΩΣ ΣΤΡΟΓΓΥΛΟΠΡΟΣΩΠΟΣ
ΕΥΘΥΡΙΝ ΜΕΤΑ ΚΥΡΙΟΥ ΤΟΥ ΕΑΥΤΩΝ ΠΑΜΩΝΘΟΥ ΤΟΥ
ΣΥΝΑΠΟΔΟΜΕΝΟΥ ΟΙ ΤΕΣΣΑΡΕΣ (9) ΤΩΝ ΠΕΤΕΨΑΙΤΟΣ
ΤΩΝ ΕΚ ΤΩΝ ΜΕΜΝΟΝΕΙΩΝ ΣΚΥΤΕΩΝ ΑΠΟ ΤΟΥ ΥΠΑΡ-

ΧΟΝΤΟΣ ΑΥΤΟΙΣ ΕΝ ΤΩΙ ΑΠΟ ΝΟΤΟΥ ΜΕΡΕΙ ΜΕΜΝΟΝΕΩΝ ΠΛΑΚΟ"Υ"Σ (10) ΨΙΛΟΥ ΤΟΠΟΥ ΠΗΧΕΙΣ ΕΝ ΤΕΤΑΡΤΟΝ Η ΓΕΙΤΟΝΕΣ ΝΟΤΟΥ ΡΥΜΗ ΒΑΣΙΛΙΚΗ ΒΟΡΡΑ ΚΑΙ ΑΠΗΛΙΩΤΟΥ ΠΑΜΩΝΘΟΥ ΚΑΙ ΒΟΚΟΝΣΙΗΜΙΟΣ ΑΔΕΛΦΟΣ (11) ΚΑΙ ΚΟΙΝΟΣ ΠΟΛΕΩΣ [or ΤΟΙΧΟΣ] ΛΙΒΟΣ ΟΙΚΙΑ ΤΑΓΗΤΟΣ ΤΟΥ ΧΑΛΟΜΗ ΡΕΟΥΣΗΣ ΑΝΑ ΜΕΣΟΝ ΔῙ ΦΕρΟΥΣΗΣ ΑΠΟ ΤΟΥ ΠΟ͞ ΓΕΙΤΟΝΕΣ ΠΑΝΤΟΘΕΝ ΕΠΡΙΑΤΟ ΝΕΧΟΥΤΗΣ ΜΙΚΡΟΣ (12) ΑΣΩΤΟΣ ΩΣ L Μ ΜΕΣΟΣ ΜΕΛΙΧΡΩΣ ΤΕΡΠΝΟΣ ΜΑΚΡΟΠΡΟΣΩΠΟΣ ΕΥΘΥΡΙΝ ΟΥΑΗ ΜΕΤΩΠΩΙ ΜΕΣΩΙ ΧΑΛΚΟΥ ΝΟΜΙΣΜΑΤΟΣ Χ͞Λ ΠΡΟΠΩΛΗΤΑΙ ΚΑΙ (13) ΒΕΒΑΙΩΤΑΙ ΤΩΝ ΚΑΤΑ ΤΗΝ ΩΝΗΝ ΤΑΥΤΗΝ ΟΙ ΑΠΟΔΟΜΕΝΟΙ ΕΝΕΔΕΞΑΤΟ ΝΕΧΟΥΤΗΣ Ο ΠΡΙΑΜΕΝΟΣ .

ΑΠΟΛ . Κ . Αγ͞ρ .

L. 9. ΠΛΑΚΟΥΣ for ΠΛΑΚΟΣ. L. 10. ΑΔΕΛΦΟΣ seems inserted parenthetically. L. 11. ΔΙ for ΔΙΩΡΥΓΟΣ.

L. 13. Possibly Ο ΕΔΕΞΑΤΟ, but not ΟΝ. L. 14. The signature somewhat resembles the Κ' ΕΓΚν, which occurs in almost all the registers; but from the interpretation of that contraction, afforded by the Parisian manuscript, it would be unapplicable here; and these characters may probably be part of κατ' ἀγοράν. The term λόγεια, or λογία, of the former manuscript, was afterwards applied to the collections made for the poor, in the Christian Churches.

III. VARIOUS REGISTRIES COMPARED.

1. GREY. A.   ΕΤΟΥΣ ΚΗ ΜΕΣΟΡΗ ΚΗ̄
2.   B.   ΕΤΟΥΣ ΚΘ ΦΑΜ^ε Θ̄
3.   C.   ΕΤΟΥΣ ΛΕ ΦΑΡΜΟ^υ Κ̄
4. PARIS. ENCH. ΕΤΟΥΣ Λς ΧΟΙΑΧ Θ̄
5. GREY ANT.   ΕΤΟΥΣ Λς ΧΟΙΑΧ Θ̄
6. ANASTASY.   ΕΤΟΥΣ ΙΒ ΤΟΥ ΚΑΙ Θ ΦΑΡΜΟΥΘΙ Κ̄

1. ΓΕΓ̄   ΕΠΙ ΤΗΝ   ΕΝ ΕΡΜΩ2ΕΙ
2. ΓΕΓ̄   ΕΠΙ ΤΗΝ   ΕΝ ΕΡΜ^ω
3. ΤΕΤ̄   ΕΠΙ ΤΗΝ   ΕΝ ΔΙΟΣ⊙ ΤΗΙ Μ^ε
4. ΤΕΤΑΚΤΑΙ   ΕΠΙ ΤΗΝ   ΕΝ ΔΙΟΣΠΟΛΕΙ ΤΗΙ ΜΕΓΑΛΗΙ
5. Τ   ΕΠΙ ΤΗΝ   ΕΝ ΔΙΟΣ⊙
6. ...   ΕΠΙ ΤΗΝ   ΕΝ ΕΡ̄2

1. ΤΡ̄   ΕΦ ΗΣ ΔΙΌ   Κ́   ΕΓΚ́^{υ}
2. ΤΡ̄   ΕΦ ΗΣ ΔΙ̣ΟΝ̄   Κ́   ΕΓΚ́^{υ}
3. ΤΡ̄   ΕΦ ΗΣ ΛΥ̇ΣΙΜ
4. ΤΡΑΠΕΖΑΝ ΕΦ ΗΣ ΛΥΣΙΜΑΧΟΣ ΕΙΚΟΣΤΗΣ ΕΓΚΥΚΛΙΟΥ
5. ΤΡΑΠΕΖΑΝ ΕΦ ΗΣ ΛΥΣΙΜΑΧΟΣ Κ́   ΕΓΚ́^{υ}
6. ΤΡ̄   ΕΦ ΗΣ ΔΙΟΝ́^{υ} Κ̄   ΕΓΚ́^{υ}

150 VARIOUS REGISTRIES COMPARED.

1. ΚΑΤΑ ΤΗΝ ΠΑΡ ΑΣΚΛ^Η
2. ΚΑΤΑ ΤΗΝ ΠΑΡ ΑΣΚ$\overline{Α}$ ΚΑΙ ΚΡΑΤΟΥ
3. ΚΑΤΑ ΤΗΝ ΠΑΡΑ ΣΑΡΑΠΙΩΝΟΣ ΚΑΙ ΤΩΝ ΜΕΤΟΧΩΝ
4. ΚΑΤΑ ΔΙΑΓΡΑΦΗΝ ΑΣΚΛΗΠΙΑΔΟΥ ΚΑΙ ΖΜΙΝΙΟΣ
5. ΚΑΤΑ ΔΙΑΓΡΑΦ$η$Ν ΑΣΚΛΗΠΙΑΔΟΥ ΚΑΙ ΖΜΙΝΙΟΣ
6. ΚΑΤΑ ΔΙΑΓ$\overline{Ρ}$ $μετοχ^ω$

1. ΤΟΥ ΠΡΟΣ ΤΗΙ ΩΝΗΙ ΔΙΑΓ$\overline{Ρ}$ ΥΦ ΗΝ ΥΠΟΓΡ ΠΤΟΛ^ε
2. ΤΩΝ ΠΡΟΣ ΤΗΙ ΩΝΗ ΔΙΑΓ$\overline{Ρ}$ ΥΦ ΗΝ ΥΠΟΓ$\overline{Ρ}$ ΠΤΟΛΕΜΑΙΟΣ
3. ΤΩΝ ΠΡΟΣ ΤΗΙ ΩΝΗΙ ΔΙΑΓ$\overline{Ρ}$ ΥΦ ΗΝ ΥΠΟΓ$\overline{Ρ}$ ΕΡΜΟΦΙΛΟΣ
4. ΤΕΛΩΝΩΝ ΥΦ ΗΝ ΥΠΟΓ$\overline{Ρ}$ ΠΤΟΛΕΜΑΙΟΣ
5. ΤΕΛΩΝΩΝ ΥΦ ΗΝ ΥΠΟΓ$\overline{Ρ}$ ΠΤΟΛΕΜΑΙΟΣ
6. ΤΕ^λ ΥΦ ΗΝ ΥΠΟΓ$\overline{Ρ}$ Η$\overline{Ρ}$ΚΛΕΙΔΗΣ

1. ΑΝΤΙΓ$\overline{Ρ}$ ΩΝΗΣ ΤΕΕΦΒΙΣ ΑΜΕΝ^ω
2. Ο ΑΝΤΙΓ$\overline{Ρ}$ ΑΣΥΣ ΩΡΟΥ ΩΝΗΣ
3. ΚΑΙΣΑ$\overline{Ρ}$ ΟΙ ΑΝΤΙΓ$\overline{Ρ}$ ΩΝΗΣ ΠΕΧΥΤΗΣ ΑΡΣΙΗΣΙΟΣ
4. Ο ΑΝΤΙΓ$\overline{Ρ}$ $ασω$Σ ΩΡΟΥ ΧΟΛΧΥΤΟΥ
5. ΑΝΤΙΓ$\overline{Ρ}$ ΩΡΟΣ ΩΡΟΥ Χ$ο$ΛΧΥΤΗΣ
6. Ο ΑΝΤΙΓ$\overline{Ρ}$ ΤΗ^Λ ΩΝΗΣ ΝΕΧΟΥΤΗΣ ΜΙΚΡΟΣ ΑΣΩΤΟΣ

1. ΤΧΧ | ΑΠΟ Π$^{2'}$ ⊥ $\widehat{Ζ}$ ΑΠΟ $\overset{o}{Ν}$ ΤΟΥ ΟΛΟΥ ΨΙΛΟΥ $\overset{o}{Τ}$
2. ΨΙΛΟΥ $\overset{o}{Τ}$ $\widehat{Β}$
3. Δ' ΜΕΡΟΥΣ ΨΙΛΟΥ $\overset{o}{Τ}$ $\widehat{Γ}$ ∠
4. ΕΝ Η: ΤΩΝ ΛΟΓΕΙΟΜΕΝΩΝ ΔΙ ΑΥΤΩΝ ΧΑΡΙΝ ΤΩΝ
5. $εΝ$ $η$. ΤΩΝ ΛΟΓΕΙΟΜΕΝΩΝ ΔΙ ΑΥΤΩΝ ΧΑΡΙΝ ΤΩΝ
6. ΨΙΛΟΝ ΤΟΠΟΝ $\overline{Η}$ ΕΝ ΤΕΤΑΡΤ$ον$

VARIOUS REGISTRIES COMPARED.

1. ΤΟΥ ΟΝΤΟΣ ΑΠΟ ΝΟΤΟΥ ΔΙΟΣ(Γ) ΤΗΣ Μ^ε
2. ΤΟΥ ΟΝΤΟΣ ΑΠΟ Ν̊   ΔΙΟΣ(Γ) ΤΗΣ Μ^ε
3. ΕΝ ΤΩΙ ΑΠΟ Ν̊ Μ^ε ΔΙΟΣ(Γ) ΤΗΣ Μ̄ ΑΠΟ ΛΙΒΟΣ
4. ΚΕΙΜΕΝΩΝ ΝΕΚΡΩΝ ΕΝ ΟΙΣ ΕΧΟΥΣΙΝ   ΕΝ ΤΟΙΣ
5. ΚΕΙΜΕΝΩΝ ΝΕΚΡΩΝ ΕΝ ΘΥΝΑΒΟΥΝΟΥΝ ΕΝ ΤΟΙΣ
6. ΕΝ ΤΩΙ ΑΠΟ ΝΟΤΟΥ ΜΕΡΕΙ ΜΕΜΝΟΝΕΩΝ

3. ΤΟΥ ωΡ^ο ΤΟΥ ΗΡ ΤΟΥ ΑΓΟΝΤΟΣ ΕΠΙ ΠΟΤ̄
4. ΜΕΜΝΟΝΕΙΟΙΣ ΤΗΣ ΛΙΒΥΗΣ ΤΟΥ ΠΕΡΙΘΗΒ$α$Σ ΤΑΦΟΙΣ
5. ΜΕΜΝΟΝΕΙΟΙΣ ΤΗΣ ΛΙβνΗΣ Τον ΠΕΡΙ͞Θ   ΤΑΦΟΙΣ

1. ΩΝ ΑΙ ΓΕΙΤΝΙΑΙ ΔΕΔ ΔΙΑ ΤΗΣ ΠΡΟΚ^ε ΣΥΝΓΡ
2. ΟΥ ΑΙ ΓΕΙΤΝΙΑΙ ΔΕΔ ΔΙΑ ΤΗΣ Π̊Ρ̄   ΣΥΝΓ͞Ρ
3. ΟΥ ΑΙ ΓΕΙΤΝΙΑΙ ΔΕΔ ΔΙΑ ΤΗΣ ΠΡΟΚΕΙΜΕ   ΣΥΝΓ͞Ρ
4. ΑΝΘ ΗΣ ΠΟΙΕΙΤΑΙ   ΛΕΙΤΟΥΡΓΙΑΣ
5. ΑΝΘ ΗΣ ΠΟΙΟΥΝΤΑΙ ΛΕΙΤΟΥΡΓΙΑΣ

1. ΟΝ ΗΓΟ͞Ρ   ΠΑΡ ΑΛΗΚΙΟΣ   ΚΑΙ
2. Ον ΗΓ̊   ΠΑΡ ΑΛΗΚΙΟΣ ΤΟΥ ΕΡΙΕΩΣ ΚΑΙ
3. ΟΝ ΗΓΟΡΑΣΕΝ   ΠΑΡ ΑΜΜΩΝΙΟΥ ΤΟΥ ΠΥΡΡΙΟΥ ΚΑΙ
4. Α ΕΩΝ^η ΠΑΡ ΟΝΝΩΦΡΙΟΣ ΤΟΥ ΩΡΟΥ
5. Α ΕΩΝΗΣΑΤΟ   ΠΑΡΑ ΟΝΝΩΦΡΙΟΣ ΤΟΥ ΩΡΟΥ
6. ΟΝ ΕΩΝΗΘΗ   ΠΑ͞Ρ ΠΑΜΩΝΘΗΣΤΟΥ   ΚΑΙ

1. ΛΟΥΒΑΙΤΟΣ ΚΑΙ ΤΒΑΙΑΙΤΟΣ ΤΩΝ ΕΡΙΕΩΣ ΚΑΙ
2. ΛΟΥΒΑΙΤΟΣ ΚΑΙ ΤΒΑΙΑΙΤΟΣ ΤΩΝ ΕΡΙΕΩΣ ΚΑΙ
3. ΨΕΝΑΜΟΥΝΙΟΣ ΤΟΥ ΠΥΡΡΙΟΥ
6. ΣΝΑΧΟΜΝΕΩΣ ΤΩΝ ΠΕΤΕΨΑΙΤΟΣ ΣΥΝ ΤΑΙΣ ΑΔΕΛΦΑΙΣ

152 VARIOUS REGISTRIES COMPARED.

1. ΣΕΝΕΡΙΕΥΤΟΣ ΤΗΣ ΠΕΤΕΝΕΦΩΤΟΥ ΚΑΙ ΕΡΙΕΩΣ ΤΟΥ
2. ΣΕΝΕΡΙΕΩΣ   ΤΗΣ ΠΕΤΕΝΕΦΩΤΟΥ ΚΑΙ ΕΡΙΕΩΣ ΤΟΥ

1. ΑΜΕΝΩΘΟΥ ΚΑΙ ΣΕΝΟΣΟΡΦΙΒΙΟΣ ΤΗΣ ΑΜΕΝΩΘΟΥ
2. ΑΜΕΝΩΘΟΥ ΚΑΙ ΣΕΝΟΣΟΡΦΙΒΙΟΣ ΤΗΣ ΑΜΕΝΩΘΟΥ

1. ΚΑΙ ΣΠΟΙΤΟΣ ΤΟΥ ΚΑΙ ΕΡΙΕΩΣ ΤΟΥ ΑΜΕΝΩΘΟΥ
2. ΚΑΙ ΣΠΟΙΤΟΣ   ΚΑΙ ΕΡΙΕΩΣ ΤΟΥ ΑΜΕΝΩΘΟΥ

1. ΕΝ ΤΩΙ ΚΗ ΠΑΧΩΝ|$\overline{\text{Κ}}$
4. ΕΝΤΩΙ Λς $\llcorner$ ΑΘΥΡ Κ$\eta\varsigma$

1. $\overline{\text{Χ}}\overline{\text{Χ}}$ τελος
2. $\overline{\chi}$ $\overline{\chi}$ a δ τελος
3.   ΧΑλ$\varkappa$ ΓιΒ $\overset{c}{\text{Τ}}$
4. ΣΥΙΝΕΤΡΑΠΗΣΘΗΙ ΧΑΛΚΟΥ ¿ΧΣ? ΤΕΛΟΣ
5.   ΧΑΛΚΟΥ ΖΓ $\overline{\text{Τ}}$
6. $\overline{\text{Χ}}$ Ζ α

1. τ$\eta\varsigma$ $\overset{.}{\delta}$ Ρ | Ρ ΔΙΟΝ $\overline{\text{ΥΡ}}$
2. ου $\overline{a\varkappa}$ Φ   ΔΙΟΝ^v ΥΡ
3. ου $\hat{\Lambda}$ R, R ΛΥΣΙΜΑΧ   Υ$\overline{\text{ΓΡ}}$
4. ΕΝΑΚιοΟΥΣ | Ι ΛΥΣΙΜΑΧΟΣ   Υ$\overset{\varepsilon}{\gamma}$$\rho$
5.   Τ | Τ ΛΥΣΙΜΑΧ   Υ$\overline{\text{ΓΡ}}$
6. $\hat{\eta}$ $=$ χ Δ $\overset{.}{a}$ Υ$\overline{\text{ΓΡ}}$

APPENDIX II.

SPECIMENS OF HIEROGLYPHICS:

From the Article EGYPT.

1. GOD; *powerful*
2. GOD; *judge*
3. GODDESS
4. GODS
5. AGATHODAEMON
6. PHTHAH
7. AMMON

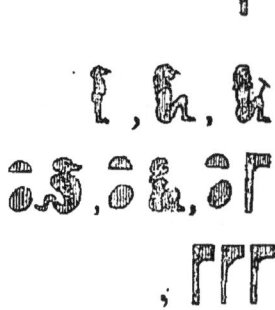

8. PHRE
9. RHEA

10. IOH

11. THOTH

12. OSIRIS

13. ARUERIS

14. Isis
15. Nephthe
16. Buto
17. Horus
20. Apis
22. Hyperion
23. Cteristes [or Cerberus]
24. Tetrarcha
25. Anubis
26. Macedo
27. Hieracion
28. Cerexochus
30. Platypterus
38. Memnon
50. Psammis

SPECIMENS OF HIEROGLYPHICS. 155

52. AMASIS

57. SOTERES

72. Ramuneus

80. EGYPT

81. MEMPHIS

83. GREEK

84. COUNTRY

85. LAND

87. TEMPLE

88. SHRINE

91. COLUMN

92. DIADEM

100. TEAR

101. IMAGE

102. STATUE

103. LETTERS

108. LIFE

109. ETERNITY

110. IMMORTAL

111. JOY

112. POWER

113. STABILITY

114. ESTABLISHED

116. MIGHTY

117. VICTORY

118. FORTUNE

119. SPLENDOUR

120. BEARING

121. ILLUSTRIOUS

122. HONOUR

SPECIMENS OF HIEROGLYPHICS.   157

123 Respectable

125. Rite

126. Worship

127. Father

129. Son

133. Child

(128.) [Wife]

[Brother; Sister]

134. Director

135. Steersman

137. King

138. Condition

139. Kingdom

140. Libation

158 SPECIMENS OF HIEROGLYPHICS.

142. PRIEST

143. PRIESTHOOD *sacerdozio*.

145. ASSEMBLY

146. SACRED

147. CONSECRATED

148. GIVE — *dare* — *donare*

149. OFFER *offerta Sforio*.

151. LAWFUL — *giusto legitimo*.

152. GOOD

153. BESTOWING

154. MUNIFICENT

155. UPPER; LOWER *sopra*
                  sotto

156. OTHERS *gl'altri*

160. ENLIGHTENING

162. LOVING *amah*

SPECIMENS OF HIEROGLYPHICS.

164. SET UP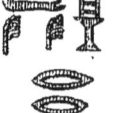

165. PREPARE

166. IN ORDER THAT

167. WHEREVER

168. AND }
169. ALSO, WITH }

170. MOREOVER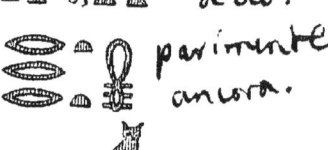

171. LIKEWISE

172. IN

173. UPON, AT

174. OVER, ON

175. FOR

176. BY THE

177. OF, TO

178. DAY

179. MONTH

SPECIMENS OF HIEROGLYPHICS.

180. YEAR

181. THOYTH *Septembre.*

182. MECHIR *Februar.*

183. MESORE *august.*

184. FIRST DAY

185. THIRTIETH *trentesimo*

186. ONE

187. FIRST

188. TWO

192. THRICE

197. TEN *dieci.*

200. FORTY TWO *quaranto*

201. A HUNDRED *cento.*

202. A THOUSAND *mille*

SUR LES

TROIS SISTÈMES D'ÉCRITURE

DES ÉGIPTIENS.

IMPRIMERIE DE H. FOURNIER,
RUE DE SEINE, N° 14.

SUR LES

TROIS SISTÈMES D'ÉCRITURE DES ÉGIPTIENS.

Par M. le Marquis de FORTIA D'URBAN,

MEMBRE DE L'INSTITUT DE FRANCE (ACADÉMIE ROYALE DES INSCRIPTIONS ET BELLES-LETTRES), DE LA SOCIÉTÉ DES ANTIQUAIRES DE FRANCE, DE CELLE DES BIBLIOPHILES FRANÇAIS, DE LA SOCIÉTÉ ASIATIQUE, DE L'ACADÉMIE D'ARCHÉOLOGIE ET DE CELLE DES LINCÉES, DE ROME, DES ACADÉMIES DE NAPLES, DE CORTONE, DE BRUXELLES, DE FRANCFORT-SUR-LE-MEIN, DE VETTÉRAVIE, D'AVIGNON, DE MARSEILLE, DE MONTPELLIER, DE NIMES, DE TOULOUSE, ETC.

PARIS,

CHEZ H. FOURNIER JEUNE, LIBRAIRE,

RUE DE SEINE, N. 14;

ET CHEZ L'AUTEUR, RUE DE LA ROCHEFOUCAULD, N° 12.

1833.

SUR LES

TROIS SISTÈMES D'ÉCRITURE

DES ÉGIPTIENS.

J'AI dit dans mon Essai sur l'origine de l'écriture que les hommes avaient commencé par peindre les signes des objets (art. xxv), et par tracer quelques signes de convention qui avaient formé une écriture de pensées : c'est l'enfance de l'écriture.

On imagina ensuite de substituer l'instrument réel ou métaphisique à la chose même ; le soleil annonça la divinité, l'œil un monarque, l'épée nue un tiran. Ainsi naquit l'écriture simbolique ou hiérogliphique des Égiptiens, c'est l'écriture des Mexicains.

Cette écriture multipliant trop les volumes, on substitua au contour de la figure une sorte de marque abrégée. De là naquit l'écriture des Chinois.

Enfin, la difficulté d'exprimer une infinité de pensées intellectuelles et métaphisiques fit inventer l'écriture des sons qui est la nôtre et qui a été celle des Phéniciens, des Hébreux et des Grecs.

Les Égiptiens ont eu toutes ces écritures à la fois et les enseignaient successivement dans leurs écoles ; mais ils commençaient par la dernière qui était la plus facile pour transmettre les idées, et qui était ainsi devenue populaire, tandis que les deux autres étaient réservées aux prêtres dont elles cachaient les mistères.

Tel est le principe de l'explication d'un passage de Clément d'Alexandrie, qui a trompé jusqu'à présent la sagacité de tous les interprètes. Cet écrivain souvent obscur l'a tellement été en cette occasion, qu'il n'a pas été bien compris. On a cru qu'après avoir nommé les trois sistèmes de l'écriture égiptienne, les trois définitions qu'il en donnait n'appartenaient qu'à la troisième, ce qui leur composait en tout cinq écritures dont les deux premières n'étaient point expliquées par l'auteur, et dont les trois dernières étaient absolument inintelligibles. La traduction que je vais donner de ce passage célèbre, nécessaire pour la pleine intelligence des principes que j'ai posés et pour la connaissance de l'écriture ancienne, sera comprise si facilement, qu'elle prouvera par sa clarté combien elle est conforme au véritable sens du texte. C'est Clément d'Alexandrie qui va parler (1) :

« Ceux qui reçoivent l'instruction parmi les Égip-
« tiens apprennent d'abord la méthode de toutes les

---

(1) *Stromata*, livre V, § 9, p. 245-680, de l'édition de Potter.

« écritures égiptiennes, appelée *epistolographique*; la
« seconde, ou l'*hiératique*, est celle dont se servent les
« écrivains sacrés; enfin, et en dernier lieu, est l'*hié-*
« *rogliphique.*

« La première méthode, » c'est-à-dire l'épistologra-
phique, « comprend les caractères *curiologiques* » (ou
qui représentent la forme propre), « par le moyen des
« premières lettres.

« La seconde, » (l'hiératique) « est simbolique : ou
« elle conserve sa forme propre par imitation, ou elle
« exprime les objets d'une manière *tropique* » (c'est-à-
dire figurée); « ou bien encore elle s'énonce par des
« sortes d'énigmes. Les Égiptiens veulent-ils peindre le
« soleil? ils font un cercle; la lune? un croissant : telle
« est la forme curiologique » (ou propre à ce genre);
« dans la méthode tropique » (ou figurée), « suivant
« l'analogie, ils détournent, changent et transportent
« le sens des objets. Ils sculptent ces caractères en di-
« versifiant leurs formes ; c'est ainsi qu'ils se servent de
« mithes sacrés pour célébrer les louanges des rois, et
« ils les retracent sur les bas-reliefs.

« Quant au troisième genre dont l'expression est
« énigmatique » (l'hiérogliphique), « en voici un exem-
« ple : pour exprimer la marche oblique des astres, ils
« les représentent par le corps d'un serpent; ils figurent
« le soleil par un scarabée, parce que cet insecte, après
« avoir construit une masse sphérique de fumier de
« bœuf, la roule par un mouvement rétrograde. Ils
« croient qu'il passe six mois sous la terre, et qu'il vit
« sur sa surface le reste de l'année. Ils ajoutent qu'il

« jette, dans le sphéroïde qu'il a formé, un germe sper-
« matique; que c'est ainsi qu'il se reproduit, et qu'il
« ne naît aucun scarabée femelle. Il est donc vrai,
« pour le dire en un mot, que tous ceux qui se sont
« occupés de matières religieuses, soit chez les Bar-
« bares, soit chez les Grecs, cachèrent le principe des
« choses : ils ne montrèrent la vérité que sous le voile
« de l'énigme et de la métaphore, ainsi qu'au moyen
« d'autres figures semblables. »

Tel est le passage très-curieux d'un auteur qui, né
en Égypte, élevé dans la religion païenne, a bien
connu le peuple dont il parlait. Il vivait vers la fin
du second siècle de notre ère et dans les premières
années du troisième. Le culte du paganisme ne se
soutenait plus guère alors que par sa longue pres-
cription et par le charme des poësies d'Homère. Clément fit ses premières études à Athènes; il les con-
tinua en Italie et dans l'Asie Mineure, et vint les
achever dans la capitale de l'Égypte, école célèbre
où, de toutes les parties de l'empire romain, on ve-
nait étudier l'éloquence et la philosophie platoni-
cienne; mais sans doute il ne négligea point de s'instruire de la sagesse des Égiptiens, dont il reconnaît
que les lettres étaient les premières. Il écrivit en grec;
son stile, dans le *Pédagogue* et dans l'*Instruction
aux Gentils*, est toujours fleuri, souvent éloquent,
quelquefois sublime : c'est la justice que lui rendent
Eusèbe et Photius; mais on trouve de l'obscurité, de
la négligence, et même de la dureté, dans celui des

Stromates, dont il est malheureux qu'il n'existe pas un seul manuscrit dans nos bibliothèques. Voici le texte du passage que j'ai traduit, d'après l'édition de Potter, regardée comme la meilleure. Je ferai seulement un léger changement dans la ponctuation; j'y joins la version latine de Potter (1), à laquelle je ne ferai que les changemens nécessaires pour rendre le sens littéral du texte.

(1) *Stromata*, V, § 9, p. 245-680 et suiv., dans l'édition de Potter. On trouvera le même passage dans l'édition de Paris, 1641, pag. 555 et 556. Mais la version latine y commet une faute grossière, au commencement, en écrivant : *Jam verò qui docentur ab Ægyptiis, primùm quidem docent ægyptiarum literarum viam ac rationem*, au lieu de : *Jam verò qui docentur ab Ægyptiis, primùm quidem discunt*, etc. C'est une des corrections très-justes de Potter.

Αὐτίκα οἱ παρ' Αἰγυπτίοις παιδευόμενοι, πρῶτον μὲν πάντων τῶν αἰγυπτίων γραμμάτων μέθοδον ἐκμανθάνουσι, τὴν ἐπιστολογραφικὴν καλουμένην· δευτέραν δὲ, τὴν ἱερατικὴν, ᾗ χρῶνται οἱ ἱερογραμματεῖς· ὑστάτην δὲ καὶ τελευταίαν, τὴν ἱερογλυφικὴν·

Ἧς ἡ μὲν ἐστὶ διὰ τῶν πρώτων στοιχείων, κυριολογική.

Ἡ δὲ συμβολική· τῆς δὲ συμβολικῆς ἡ μὲν, κυριολογεῖται κατὰ μίμησιν. Ἡ δ' ὥσπερ τροπικῶς γράφεται· Ἡ δὲ, ἄντικρυς ἀλληγορεῖται κατὰ τίνας αἰνιγμούς. Ἥλιον γοῦν γράψαι βουλόμενοι, κύκλον ποιοῦσι· σελήνην δὲ, σχῆμα μηνοειδὲς, κατὰ τὸ κυριολογούμενον εἶδος· τροπικῶς δὲ, κατ' οἰκειότητα μετάγοντες καὶ μετατιθέντες· τὰ δ' ἐξαλλάττοντες· τὰ δὲ πολλαχῶς μετασχηματίζοντες, χαράττουσιν. Τοὺς γοῦν τῶν βασιλέων ἐπαίνους θεολογουμένοις μύθοις παραδίδοντες, ἀναγράφουσι διὰ τῶν ἀναγλύφων.

Τοῦ δὲ κατὰ τοὺς αἰνιγμοὺς, τρίτου εἴδους, δεῖγμα ἔστω τόδε· τὰ μὲν γὰρ τῶν ἄλλων ἄστρων διὰ τὴν πορείαν τὴν λοξὴν, ὄφεων σώμασιν ἀπείκαζον. Τὸν δὲ Ἥλιον τῷ τοῦ κανθάρου· ἐπειδὴ κυκλοτερὲς ἐκ τοῦ βοείας ὄνθου σχῆμα πλασάμενος, ἀντιπρόσωπος κυλίνδει. Φασὶ δὲ καὶ ἑξάμηνον μὲν ὑπὸ γῆς· θάτερον δὲ τοῦ ἔτους τμῆμα, τὸ ζῶων τοῦτο ὑπὲρ γῆς διαττᾶσθαι· σπερμαίνειν τε εἰς τὴν σφαῖραν, καὶ γεννᾶν· καὶ θῆλυν κάνθαρον μὴ γίνεσθαι.

Πάντες οὖν, ὡς ἔπος εἰπεῖν, οἱ θεολογήσαντες, βάρβαροί τε καὶ Ἕλληνες, τὰς μὲν ἀρχὰς τῶν πραγμάτων ἀπεκρύ-

Jàm verò qui docentur apud Ægyptios, primùm quidem discunt ægyptiarum literarum methodum, quæ vocatur epistolographica : secundam autem hieraticam quâ utuntur hierogrammates, extremam autem et ultimam hieroglyphicam.

Cujus (methodi) prior quidem species est cyriologica per prima elementa :

Altera verò symbolica. Symbolicæ autem una quidem est juxtà imitationem cyriologumena; alia verò scribitur veluti tropicè : alia verò ferè significatur per quædam enigmata. Quùm solem itaquè volunt scribere, faciunt circulum : lunam autem, figuram lunæ cornuum formam præ se ferentem, convenienter ei formæ quæ cyriologumena dicitur. Tropicè autem per convenientiam traducentes, et transferentes, et alia quidem immutantes, alia verò multis modis transfigurantes, insculpunt. Regum itaquè laudes sacris fabulis immiscentes, anaglyphis describunt.

Tertii autem generis, quod fit per ænigmata, hoc sit indicium : alia quidem astra, propter obliquam conversionem, assimilabant corporibus serpentum : solem verò scarabei; quoniàm cum rotundam ex bubulo stercore effinxit figuram, eam vultu adverso convolvit. Aiunt autem hoc quoque animal, sex quidem mensibus sub terrâ, alteram verò partem anni vitam degere super terram, et semen in globum emittere et gignere, et non nasci fœminam scarabeum.

Omnes ergò, ut semel dicam, qui de rebus divinis tractârunt, tàm barbari quàm Græci, rerum qui-

ψαντο· τὴν δὲ ἀλήθειαν αἰνίγμασι καὶ συμβόλοις, ἀλληγορίαις τε αὖ καὶ μεταφοραῖς καὶ τοιουτοισί τισι τρόποις παραδεδώκασιν. κ. τ. λ.

dem principia occultaverunt; veritatem autem ænigmatibus, signisque ac symbolis et allegoriis rursùs et metaphoris, et quibusdam talibus tropis modisque tradiderunt, etc.

Le Marquis DE FORTIA D'URBAN.

Paris, 4 juillet 1833.

Post-scriptum. La raison de l'erreur commise par les interprètes est que le traducteur latin, n'osant employer le mot *methodus*, plus grec que latin, a traduit μέθοδον par *viam ac rationem*. Mais, ne comprenant pas que le pronom ἧς, en grec, peut se rapporter à μέθοδον qui est un peu éloigné, il a traduit *cujus* au lieu de *quarum* qu'exigeait la traduction du pronom ἧς en l'appliquant à *viam ac rationem*.

Il résulte de ce passage d'une très-haute importance que les Égiptiens sont le seul peuple de l'antiquité qui ait possédé à la fois les trois écritures, savoir : celle des Mexicains, celle des Chinois et la nôtre. La première est une écriture des sons, ou alfabétique, qui avait vingt-quatre lettres, comme le dit Plutarque (1). Les deux autres écritures indiquées dans ce passage sont des écritures de pensées, dont la première est celle des Chinois, et la seconde celle des Mexicains.

Il est naturel de conclure de ce fait que les Égiptiens ont inventé les trois écritures. Il y a donc eu un tems où l'Afrique a communiqué avec l'Amérique ; et les monumens récemment découverts dans l'ancienne ville de Palimbram, à quelque distance de Mexico, prouvent en effet que cette ville avait des monumens analogues à ceux de l'Égipte. Il y a peut-être eu aussi un tems où l'Égipte a donné son écriture hiératique à la Chine ; c'est ce dont la connaissance des livres d'histoire si nombreux, que nous avons sur cet ancien empire, pourra nous instruire. Enfin je crois avoir déjà

(1) Symposiaques, livre IX, quæst. 3, à la fin.

prouvé, dans mon Essai sur l'origine de l'écriture, que les Phéniciens ont puisé en Égypte leur écriture alfabétique qu'ils nous ont transmise. C'est donc à l'Égipte que nous devons notre civilisation ; et nous n'avons rien de mieux à faire que de dire avec Solon (1) qu'auprès de cette ancienne nation, les Grecs et nous ne sommes que des enfans.

Paris, 5 juillet 1833.

(1) Voyez le Timée de Platon.

Ce Mémoire a été lu à l'Académie des Inscriptions, le 5 juillet 1833, par M. le marquis de Fortia d'Urban, membre de cette Académie.

ON TROUVERA CHEZ LE MÊME LIBRAIRE :

Les deux Mémoires suivans du même auteur.

Homère et ses écrits. Paris, 1833, in-8°; prix : 5 fr.

Essai sur l'origine de l'écriture, sur son introduction dans la Grèce et son usage jusqu'au tems d'Homère, c'est-à-dire jusqu'à l'an 1000 avant notre ère, avec quatre planches dont l'une est coloriée. 6 fr.

OEuvres choisies de M. le vicomte de Châteaubriand, édition publiée par M. le marquis de Fortia, avec trois cartes pour l'Itinéraire de Jérusalem, 18 vol. in-12. 27 fr.

SAGGIO

SOPRA IL SISTEMA DE' NUMERI

PRESSO

GLI ANTICHI EGIZIANI,

LETTERA

DEL

CAV. GIULIO DI S. QUINTINO

Conservatore del Museo Egiziano di S. M. il Re di Sardegna.

Al Prestantissimo Signore

IL SIGNOR ABATE

GIO. BATTISTA ZANNONI

*Segretario della Reale Accademia della Crusca,
R. Antiquario nell'I. e R. Galleria di Firenze ec.*

GIULIO DI S. QUINTINO

L'approvazione, colla quale V. S. volle pur onorare que' pochi fogli che ultimamente mi sono fatto un dovere di presentarle, e di sottoporre al suo esame, vale per me assai più di una corona d'alloro, perchè so in qual conto s'abbiano a tenere i suoi giudizi, non solo in fatto di amena letteratura, ma negli studi ancora più gravi, ed in quelli soprattutto spettanti all'Archeologia. Confortato da sì gentile accoglienza mi prendo oggi la libertà di pregarla a voler gradire alcune nuove osservazioni, e scoperte risguardanti, come le precedenti, le cose dell'antico Egitto; vale a dire un saggio sul sistema, e sulle cifre de' numeri altrevolte adoperati in quella classica contrada; il quale fu già argomento d'una mia lezione in questa R. Accademia delle Scienze, nel dì 13 del corr. mese di gennaio.

Finora, com' Ella ben sa, nulla è stato detto o pubblicato ad illustrazione di questa parte rilevantissima delle antiche scritture degli Egiziani, ed appena tre o quattro segni del loro sistema numerale erano stati fin qui ben accertati, col mezzo de' confronti fatti sui pochi testi bilingui già conosciuti. Io ho avuto la sorte, nello scorso mese, di trovarne tutti gli elementi ne' papiri di questo R. gabinetto; ed è loro mercè che finalmente la dottrina de' geroglifici, per la quale abbiamo già contratte tante obbligazioni cogli Oltramontani, verrà oggi ad avere qualche incremento anche fra noi, che, per buona sorte, siamo di tutti i più ricchi di antiche scritture atte a promuovere l'avanzamento.

I papiri di cui mi sono maggiormente giovato nelle mie ricerche sono i contratti demotici, e certi preziosi registri ieratici, che sono qui in buon numero, pieni in ogni loro parte di date, e di quantità numerali: ma più ancora mi sono stati opportuni i miseri avanzi di un antico codice cronologico egiziano, che presso di noi pure si conserva, ridotto però dal tempo in centinaia di frammenti.

Primo a visitare questo ammasso confuso di vetuste memorie fu l'illustre sig. Champollion il minore; e non sì tosto egli ebbe preso ad esaminarle che, nei mesi ora scorsi, i migliori giornali d'oltremonte sì politici che letterari già annunziavano quel rarissimo papiro: come un vero canone reale fatto a somiglianza di quello di Manetone; come un tesoro per la Storia, di cui non si potrà mai deplorare abbastanza la perdita, per ciò che ne manca; come un'appendice inestimabile alla celebre tavola genealogica d'Abydos, e contenente una serie di oltre cento Monarchi egiziani. Le quali cose quando sieno vere è forza il dire che quel gran numero di Faraoni, ignorati finora, abbiano regnato sull'Egitto in tempi anteriori ai trentaquattro Re ascendenti del gran Sesostri, nominati nella citata tavola d'Abydos, vale a dire sette in otto secoli prima dell'età di quel conquistatore; giudicando della durata di tutti i divisati trentaquattro regni da quella della metà di essi, cioè de'Monarchi della celebre dinastia detta la diciottesima presso Manetone, i quali ci sono ben noti d'altronde pei loro stessi monumenti; giudicandone pure dalla durata delle altre dinastie meno antiche ed oscure dello stesso Scrittore, e finalmente dalle tavole cronologiche degli imperi moderni, colle quali que' regni medesimi si potranno facilmente confrontare. (1)

---

(1) I quattordici Faraoni della così detta diciottesima dinastia, che sono i meno antichi fra quelli registrati sulla tavola d'Abydos, hanno regnato fra tutti, secondo Manetone, anni trecento quarant'otto. — I novantadue Re che, giusta lo stesso autore, tennero lo scettro d'Egitto dalla duodecima fino alla vigesima sua dinastia, regnarono per lo spazio di anni duemila cento vent'uno. — I successori di Carlo Magno, i quali tengono la corona dell'impero d'Occidente già da mille e più anni, sono cinquantanove. — I Principi della R. casa di Savoja che, in numero di trentasette, governarono fin qui le nostre contrade, da Umberto I all'Augusto Regnante CARLO FELICE, occupano già più di ottocento anni di gloria ne' fasti delle umane vicende ec.

Ora egli è evidente che aggiungendo quei settecento od ottocento anni, all'anno mille quattrocento settantatre avanti l'era volgare, nel quale, con molta ragione, si crede dagli Eruditi che il Re Sesostri abbia cominciato a regnare, noi saremo trasportati dalla sola tavola d'Abydos oltre i tempi d'Abramo, in un'epoca già assai vicina al diluvio, secondo la cronologia de' libri santi. (1) Eppure Ella dee sapere, sig. Abate pregiatissimo, che i nomi dei Faraoni che si trovano sparsi in que' frammenti sono veramente assai più di cento; io stesso ne ho riscontrato poco meno di dugento; ed è cosa probabilissima che nell'intiero papiro il loro numero fosse anche maggiore, se si pon mente allo stato infelicissimo nel quale esso si vede ora ridotto.
 Questo nostro canone cronologico tanto celebrato non sarebbe egli mai per avventura quello stesso codice nel quale erano registrati i trecento quaranta Re, i quali, secondo ciò che i sacerdoti di Tebe voleano far credere ad Erodoto (*Her.* II. c. 142.), tennero lo scettro di Egitto per lo spazio di undici mila trecento e quarant'anni, da Menes loro primo Monarca fino a Sethos Re e sacerdote di Vulcano?

Ma i mentovati giornali contenti di aver dato notizia di questo nostro tesoro come di un monumento pregevolissimo pel numero, e per l'età dei Regnanti,

---

(2) Il Patriarca Abramo, giusta la più comune opinione, nacque poco prima dell'anno duemila avanti Gesù Cristo, e secondo la autorità della Vulgata, e del testo ebraico della Genesi, anni mille novecento quarant'otto dopo la creazione del primo uomo, cioè dugento novantadue anni dopo il diluvio, il quale, secondo la stessa venerabile autorità, ebbe luogo nell'anno 1656. del mondo.

quivi, col mezzo dei loro prenomi accennati, non credettero opportuno di aggiungere che in quel papiro, dopo il nome di ciascun Principe, vedesi pure segnato in cifre numerali il periodo del suo regno, diviso, non solamente in anni e mesi come presso il sacerdote di Sebennito, ma ancor in giorni con somma precisione. La quale circostanza è appena credibile nella serie di dugento regni, i quali, giusta i confronti dianzi proposti, non possono abbracciare uno spazio di tempo minore di trenta in quaranta secoli; seppure que' regni non si volessero supporre contemporanei gli uni agli altri, e quindi non conformi a quelli registrati ne' libri di Manetone, co' quali, come ho notato, furono trovati somiglianti.

Io mi avvidi con gratissima sorpresa di questo nuovo pregio de' nostri frammenti, mentre, per obbligo del mio uffizio, li stava esaminando ne' giorni passati, per vedere se fossevi ancor modo di riordinarli. Conobbi allora di qual sussidio quella faragine di date cronologiche, e di nomi poteva ancora riuscire, insieme cogli accennati registri, onde manifestarci il valore dei geroglifici propri dei numeri nelle diverse scritture egiziane; ed in breve n'ebbi raccolto un numero sì grande, e sì vario da non lasciarmi più in forse sull'esito felice delle mie investigazioni.

Abbandonai quindi al suo destino tutta quella turba disordinata di Faraoni, nascosti sotto il velo di oscuri prenomi per lo più mutilati; perchè, com'Ella può credere, non mi vanno punto a genio sì fatti antichi monumenti cronologici, che non so trovar modo di conciliar facilmente coi testi delle Scritture sante, ed in particolare colle otto generazioni che precedettero, dopo il diluvio, la nascita d'Abramo. (*Gen.* c. XI.) Mettendole perciò in un fascio colle dinastie del primo libro del citato Manetone, coi troppo vantati zodiaci, e colle tradizioni dei sacerdoti egizi riferite dai greci scrittori, ne farò di buon grado un olocausto all'autorità irrefragabile dei libri di Mosè, che la religione egualmente che la ragione c'impongono di preferire ad ogni altra. E ciò tanto più volontieri che quella nuda serie di nomi, e di date non presentando, per quanto pare, alcun mezzo di connessione nè co' suoi propri elementi, nè colla tavola d'Abydos, nè con altro monumento, od epoca qualunque conosciuta, non so vedere in qual modo possa giovare ai progressi della Storia, ed essere un motivo di molte speranze. Nè vorrei che venisse a volgersi in argomento di scandalo il dono prezioso di tanti rarissimi monumenti che la Reale munificenza ha ora voluto fare alle lettere, ed al decoro di queste nostre contrade. Duolmi perciò non poco che, mentre io sto scrivendo queste osservazioni, una gazzetta italiana, in un certo suo articolo posto sotto la rubrica di Parigi del giorno sei del corrente gennajo, nel voler privar me del picciol merito della priorità in queste mie ricerche numerali, nel che non vi è gran male, abbia inavvedutamente fatto eco anch'essa ai giornali stranieri accennando quel codice pericoloso come uno di quei documenti, i quali *debbono giovar tanto per rischiarare la serie delle antiche dinastie, ed i tempi primitivi degli antichi Faraoni ..... di un' epoca remota intorno alla quale rimangono tanto poche nozioni*; senza accorgersi, che vantava tempi, e dinastie non solamente più antiche di tutti i più vetusti monumenti di questa R. collezione, messi ora in sì chiara luce dal predetto sig. Champollion, e dagli Accademici torinesi, ma anteriori al diluvio, ed allo stesso Adamo; giustificando così le accuse, che i detrattori di questi buoni studi vanno movendo contro chi li coltiva, di tendere, cioè, segretamente *a distruggere l'infallibilità della sacra storia scritta da Mosè*.

Attenendomi pertanto alla sola parte veramente pregevole di questi nostri frammenti, voglio dire alle date cronologiche, ho preso ad esaminare le diverse quantità dei numeri che in essi si presentano ad ogni tratto, e confrontandole fra loro, e deducendone le necessarie conseguenze, ne ho tratti i corollari che sono ora per esporre, e che V. S. troverà riuniti, come in un quadro, nella tavola qui annessa.

Gli Egiziani delineavano sul papiro i loro numeri, come le altre loro scritture, in tre diverse maniere di segni, cioè in caratteri sacri ora geroglifici, ora ieratici, ed in caratteri di forma demotica, ossia volgare. Si servivano dei segni numerali geroglifici per registrare sui loro principali monumenti, e talvolta ancora sui maggiori rotoli sepolcrali, le date de' tempi, e le altre quantità che loro occorreva di accennare. Ma convien dire che il facessero assai di rado, perchè sono pochissimi ancora gli esempi che ne sono stati publicati finora; così che non più di tre o quattro ne ho veduto fra le otto mila e più cose antiche d'Egitto che sono in questo R. Museo. Trattandosi di cose già note abbastanza, io sarò contento di produrne uno solo nella tavola quì unita, il quale sarà sufficiente a far vedere come nello scrivere le quantità numerali nella scrittura geroglifica gli Egiziani non adoperavano, per solito, che due soli segni, vale a dire la linea verticale per esprimere l'unità, ed il così detto ferro da cavallo pel numero dieci. In questo R. gabinetto abbiamo però ancora alcuni esempi del numero cinque rappresentato dalla metà del detto ferro da cavallo. Ma avevano pure un altro geroglifico per esprimere il cento, ed un altro ancora pel mille, dei quali non mancano esempi nelle opere dei signori Champollion, e Young.

I caratteri numerali della scrittura ieratica, come V. S. potrà verificare nella tavola, fino al numero sei non differiscono quasi in altro dagli esposti elementi delle quantità geroglifiche, se non per la forma loro più corsiva, e meno regolare. Il loro numero per salire al cento, e quindi anche fino al mille, è almeno di quindici. All'incontro tutte le cifre demotiche, che ho potuto trovare nei mentovati frammenti, e negli altri papiri della nostra collezione, sono appena cinque o sei; nè credo che ve ne sieno di più. È però cosa degna di considerazione la somiglianza che passa fra i segni numerali demotici, ed i moderni numeri arabici, che, ne' bassi tempi, ci sono stati probabilmente portati dall'Oriente, e fors'anche dall'Egitto, dove gli Arabi aveano allora dominio.

Vero è però che tanto le cifre ieratiche come le volgari vedonsi del continuo adoperate promiscuamente come se appartenessero in egual modo ad amendue quelle scritture; in maniera per altro che, nelle date cronologiche soprattutto, i numeri ieratici vedonsi di preferenza impiegati nello accennare gli anni, ed i mesi, e le cifre demotiche per lo più nello indicare i giorni, e le quantità dei registri. Questa regola non è tuttavia costante, come il dimostrano gli esempi che presento nella tavola. La vedo però seguita generalmente anche in altri papiri ieratici che un amico ebbe la compiacenza di comunicarmi, ne' quali pare sieno scritti affari di publica o privata economia, siccome nei sopraddetti registri di questo gabinetto.

Tutte le tre divisate foggie di note numerali si scrivevano dagli Egizi nell'ordine stesso delle altre loro scritture, cioè dalla parte destra alla sinistra; e per lo più nei manuscritti ieratici si vedono delineate in color rosso, per farle meglio distinguere dal rimanente dello scritto.

I numeri iniziali delle decine rappresentavansi con particolari caratteri o gruppi, gli uni diversi dagli altri; e dopo di essi segnavansi le unità nell' ordine solito. Ma nel far ciò gli Egiziani non tenevano sempre la via più breve; ed il loro metodo di numerare sia per la quantità delle cifre, come per la maniera di collocarle era molto lontano ancora dall'eccellenza di quello che adoperiamo noi di presente; ed è facile il convincersene gettando gli occhi sugli esempi proposti nella tavola.

In tutti i manoscritti egiziani che ho veduto le quantità destinate ad indicare la durata del tempo nelle sue varie divisioni, ossia le date cronologiche, sempre sono precedute dai segni propri di ciascun periodo: vale a dire o dall'asta ricurva, indice dell'anno: o dalla luna crescente rovesciata, simbolo del mese: ovvero dal disco solare, emblema dei giorni.

I segni determinativi dell'asta annuale sono pure sempre gli stessi in tutte tre le scritture, cioè il disco, ed il segmento del circolo: ma negli avanzi dell'accennato nostro canone cronologico i geroglifici che servono a dare il proprio valore al simbolo dei mesi variano quasi sempre, e sono di due sorta, come si può osservare nella tavola. Gli uni, veri caratteri geroglifici, sembrano dover rappresentare il nome proprio di ciascun mese egiziano; gli altri, cioè quelle unità che si vedono replicate fino a quattro volte sotto la luna crescente rovesciata, potrebbero essere abbreviature ieratiche del simbolo geroglifico proprio di alcuni mesi, il quale, nell'iscrizione del cippo di Rosetta, vediamo le tre e le quattro volte replicato nello stesso gruppo per significare un solo mese. Ma per essere certi dell'una e dell'altra mia supposizione converrebbe trovare qualche monumento nel quale que' segni si vedessero accompagnati dal nome dei mesi medesimi, scritto in caratteri fonetici, od altrimenti dichiarato; od almeno dove gli stessi segni si vedessero collocati nell'ordine loro naturale, dopo uno di que' pochi mesi il cui simbolo geroglifico è già stato prima d'ora riconosciuto. Ed allora sembra che le quantità, o date cronologiche del nostro codice si dovrebbero leggere nel modo seguente, per dir vero, alquanto straordinario: *Il Re NN. regnò, per esempio, anni* xx *e mesi* viii, *avendo cessato di vivere nel giorno* xxv *del mese di Choiac.* Il tempo rischiarerà un giorno tutte queste incertezze.

Ma dopo aver messi insieme, e distinti gli elementi tutti dell'abbaco egizio, com'Ella ben vede, o Signore, rimaneva ancora ad assegnarsi a ciascuno di essi il proprio valore. La qual cosa non sarebbe stato affare da condursi a fine sì agevolmente senza l'opportunità di multiplicare i confronti, che mi fu somministrata dalla gran quantità delle cifre contenute nei nostri papiri, le quali si trovano anzi talvolta scritte nell'ordine loro progressivo, e naturale. Ma oltre a ciò mi furono ancora di molto ajuto le seguenti preliminari notizie, ed osservazioni.

Primieramente essendo già conosciuti i caratteri della scrittura geroglifica propri dei numeri uno, cinque, e dieci, come si è avvertito di sopra, non restava più dubbio sul valore dei segni numerali ieratici che loro somigliano, e corrispondono, benchè di forma alquanto più corsiva, cioè l'uno, il due, il tre, il quattro, il cinque ed il dieci.

In secondo luogo nel porre a confronto l'epitafio greco, e la leggenda egiziana, che stanno sulla cassa della mummia torinese di Petemenofi (Vedi queste mie *Lezioni Archeologiche* facc. 127.), io aveva già fatto osservare, e messo in chiaro le seguenti cose. 1.° I segni ieratici, o demotici, che si voglian dire, corrispondenti ai numeri quattro, ed otto. 2.° L'uso in cui erano gli Egizi, nelle loro due scritture abbreviate, di giovarsi delle prime quattro unità o replicandole ciascuna due volte, ovvero combinandole diversamente fra loro, a fine di esprimere le unità susseguenti. Così, per modo di esempio, scrivevano due volte la cifra del quattro per rappresentare il numero otto, come l'ho fatto vedere nella leggenda della mummia anzidetta; scrivevano parimente due volte la cifra del tre per esprimere il sei; accoppiavano il segno del due, e quello del tre per dare il numero cinque; e quello del tre coll'altro del quattro per segnare il sette. 3.° Nello interpretare quelle iscrizioni funerali io avea pur fatto conoscere un nuovo esempio dei vari simboli adoperati nelle scritture egiziane per indicare gli anni, i mesi ed i giorni nelle date cronologiche.

In terzo luogo ho osservato che, nei mentovati numeri rappresentati da più d'una cifra, era pratica costante degli Egizi di far precedere il segno del numero maggiore a quello del numero minore. Quindi, nella moltitudine delle quantità numerali sia ieratiche come demotiche, essendomi già noto il numero quattro, io non dovea più incontrare difficoltà nel verificare il valore delle cifre proprie delle tre unità minori di quello, e delle loro diverse combinazioni con altre cifre nella progressione dell'abbaco.

Ma ciò che favorì più d'ogni altra cosa le mie indagini fu l'osservare che nel numero grandissimo delle note numerali registrate negli accennati frammenti, a fine di manifestare la durata del regno di ciascun Faraone, divisa, come si disse, in anni, mesi e giorni, mai il numero dei mesi poteva presentarmi una cifra superiore all'undici, nè quello dei giorni un numero maggiore del trenta, nè finalmente il numero degli anni poteva eccedere la durata probabile della vita dei Monarchi colà nominati. Talchè, col sussidio delle nozioni preliminari testè esposte, sicura e facile ne derivò la scienza di quelle cifre, essendo esse, nel caso nostro, ristrette in sì angusti confini.

Per questa favorevole circostanza io non indugiai a trovare, nell'esempio quinto della tavola, una nuova dimostrazione che il segno ivi rappresentante il numero dei mesi, già d'altronde abbastanza indicato e dalla sua forma corsiva del ferro da cavallo, e dalle unità dalle quali si vede quasi sempre seguito, era veramente il segno ieratico del dieci. Conobbi che la prima cifra del gruppo, che serve ad accennare il numero dei giorni nell'esempio terzo, e nel sesto, non poteva essere che il dieci demotico; ed, accertato questo, vidi per conseguenza che, negli esempi primo e quinto, i primi segni delle due quantità che vi esprimono i giorni dovevano figurare il numero demotico iniziale della terza decina, cioè il numero del venti per l'una, come per l'altra delle due scritture corsive. Nè potendo essere più di trenta i giorni nei mesi egiziani, ed essendo già noti, per gli esempi precedenti, i segni con cui si scrivevano nelle tre prime decine tutti i giorni del mese, dovetti conchiudere che il nuovo carattere che, nell'esempio quarto, occupa il luogo dei giorni, dopo il noto simbolo del disco, non poteva essere che il numero che rimaneva a trovarsi per compiere il mese, cioè il trenta, iniziale della quarta decina.

Ebbi ancora opportunità di verificare il valore della cifra ieratica del num. sette in certi contratti o quitanze demotiche scritte sopra papiro di questo R. museo, appartenenti al regno del primo Psammetico della dinastia detta la ventesima sesta presso Manetone, i quali, siccome fu già avvertito dal sig. Champollion, presentano il numero progressivo degli anni del suo regno dal xxxi. fino al xxxviii. Quindi, per conseguenza, ottenni il valore dei segni ieratici corrispondenti ai numeri sei, e nove nella tavola medesima, essendo già note tutte le altre unità della prima decina.

Più difficilmente, per la minor frequenza degli esempi, delle somme, e quindi dei confronti, ho potuto fondare le mie idee sopra i segni propri dei numeri iniziali delle decine superiori al numero quaranta fino al novanta, e sopra quello delle varie frazioni che tratto tratto si vedono scritte dopo le quantità intiere. Egli è per questa ragione che non le ho registrate nella tavola se non accompagnate coll'indice dell'incertezza, e del dubbio, benchè io sia già per me stesso persuaso che il posto che tengono nella tavola sia veramente quello stesso che debbono avere. Col sussidio di nuovi documenti, per altro, che si troveranno forse ancora in questa grandiosa collezione, io mi affido che non sarà a me, o ad altri difficile di dare al valore di queste poche cifre, non meno che alle altre, tutta quella certezza che è di dovere.

Ma troppi esempi, e troppi numeri io le dovrei presentare, preg.^{mo} mio Signore, s'io volessi renderla pienamente informata dei raziocini che ho dovuto fare su di essi, e delle varie conseguenze che ebbi a dedurne; eccederei i limiti di un semplice saggio epistolare, nè credo che vi sia mestieri di più parole con V. S. avvezza a vedere sì addentro, e sì bene nell'oscurità delle cose antiche, e ad illustrarle sempre con pari ingegno ed evidenza. Gradisca però la mia buona volontà di provarle, anche con queste inezie letterarie, come nessuno più di me le sia sinceramente devoto ed affezionato.

Torino, questo dì 15 gennaio 1825.

Con permissione.

SULL' USO

CUI ERANO DESTINATI

I MONUMENTI EGIZIANI

DETTI COMUNEMENTE SCARABEI

LETTERA

DEL

CAV. GIULIO DI S. QUINTINO

Conservatore del Museo Egiziano di S. M. il Re di Sardegna.

All'egregio e Nobile Uomo

IL SIGNOR

GIO. BATTISTA VERMIGLIOLI

Professore di Archeologia nella Università di Perugia.

GIULIO DI S. QUINTINO

Ho letto con pari mia istruzione e piacere l'erudita vostra lettera intorno alla moneta unciale, unica ed inedita, di cui fu largo a cotesto vostro museo perugino il sig. Dott. Speroni, e che voi attribuiste, con molta ragione, all'antico *Heretum* dei Sabini; città ignota finora nella serie delle vetuste zecche italiane. Così, mercè i vostri studi profondi, e le indefesse vostre ricerche, noi veggiamo ogni giorno farsi più chiara non solo la storia patria, e la lingua ed i monumenti degli Etruschi, ma la numismatica ancora de'più antichi tempi di questa nostra beatissima Italia. Perciò io vi debbo essere gratissimo per sì bel dono, e ve ne rendo mille e mille ringraziamenti: ma acciò che questi non si rimangano nel suono di poche parole io ve li offro accompagnati da qualche nota, che sono andato segnando in questi giorni scorsi, mentre attendeva a mettere in ordine la numerosa serie dei così detti *Scarabei*, che fanno parte di questa celebre collezione di cose egiziane, che il Re mio Signore ha voluto affidare alla mia custodia. Forse, leggendo queste note, avverrà che non ne troverete il tema così lontano dall'argomento della vostra lettera, qual si presenta in sulle prime; e se in ciò il vostro giudizio autorevole sarà conforme al mio parere, io mi terrò sicuro di non aver vaneggiato in questi miei divisamenti, e d'aver pur recata qualche luce a questa parte dell'archeologia egiziana.

Sotto nome di scarabei intendo parlare di quei piccoli monumenti dell'antico Egitto, figurati o scritti nella loro parte liscia, fatti di terra cotta ovvero di pietra, ed aventi, per lo più, la forma di quello scarafaggio che si vede tutto dì fare per terra la pallotta, o d'altro animale, o cosa non molto diversa dalla figura ovale e tondeggiante di quell'insetto.

Questi monumenti, che formano la serie più numerosa di quasi tutte le collezioni di cose antiche egiziane, si debbono dividere in due principali categorie, vale a dire in iscarabei sepolcrali, ed in iscarabei destinati per gli usi civili della società.

I primi sono pochi in paragone de' secondi: ma generalmente sono alquanto più grossi, e privi, il più sovente, d'iscrizioni e di figure; quando però ne hanno, queste si riferiscono sempre ai defunti, sul petto de' quali si trovano nelle tombe. Per questa classe di scarabei è cosa essenziale la forma simbolica dello scarafaggio. Il loro numero in questo R. gabinetto supera di poco gli ottanta; fra questi alcuni mostrano tuttavia di essere stati anticamente indorati, e quindi involti nell'asfalto, affinchè meglio si conservasse la doratura; in altri le iscrizioni, invece di essere intagliate sullo scarabeo, sono semplicemente scritte con inchiostro di vari colori: dal che si fa sempre più manifesto l'unico fine per cui erano fatti, cioè di rimanersi perpetuamente colle mummie. Quì il più voluminoso di tutti è lungo circa sette centimetri nel suo asse maggiore, e tre soli centimetri il più piccolo. Non pochi sono fatti di lapislazzolo, di basalte, d'agata, di serpentino, e di altre pietre assai pregevoli.

Ne' secondi all'incontro nulla si ravvisa che abbia relazione coi sepolcri; pare anzi che in essi la forma precisa dello scarafaggio non fosse necessaria per l'uso cui erano destinati. Tutti sono traforati nella direzione, per lo più, del loro diametro maggiore; e così praticavasi sicuramente dagli Egiziani per poterli mettere in filze, in quel modo che gli Orientali portano anch'oggi per vezzo le ambre, e le loro paste profumate. Questo carattere, tutto ad essi particolare, serve a farli subito distinguere dagli scarabei che facevano parte degli arredi sepolcrali, per lo scopo de' quali il foro non era punto necessario.

Degli scarabei di questa seconda classe nessun museo al mondo ne possiede tanti quanti ora ne ha il Re nostro Sovrano in questa sua collezione di antichità egiziane, dove ve ne sono pochi meno di mille e settecento. È bensì vero che tra questi ne abbiamo circa dugensettanta ch'io credo dover essere annoverati fra loro, quantunque non abbiano precisamente la stessa forma degli altri. I più grandi, tranne un solo, nella loro maggior lunghezza non superano i quattro centimetri, ed i più minuti toccano appena i sette millimetri: la maggior parte però tiene una proporzione di mezzo fra questi due estremi.

Gli scarabei appartenenti ai sepolcri si facevano piuttosto di pietra che di altra sostanza, perchè in tal guisa erano più atti a ricevere l'intaglio delle lunghe e minute leggende di cui li vediamo spesse volte ricoperti. I nove decimi de' secondi, all'incontro, non sono composti che di una tenacissima terra cotta, anzi, per lo più, d'una vera porcellana, poco men dura e consistente degli stessi macigni, quasi sempre coperta di smalti di vari colori, verdi, gialli, celesti, turchini, screziati ec. d'ogni tinta e gradazione, ad esempio delle pietre, dalle quali talvolta quelle porcellane appena si possono distinguere. Il costo di quegli scarabei veniva così ad essere assai tenue, e minore di molto il loro peso; condizioni assai rilevanti, come vedremo, per l'uffizio cui erano destinati.

Ma a che cosa dunque servivano in Egitto questi curiosi, numerosissimi lavori? Degli scarabei sepolcrali non è d'uopo dire molte cose: erano senza dubbio monumenti religiosi, i quali accompagnavano i defunti nella tomba, come simboli, probabilmente, dell'universo, e del suo facitore. Ma, intorno agli altri, vario tuttora ed incerto è il parere degli Eruditi; e niuna delle cose che ne furon dette fin qui parmi consentanea alla ragione, od alle cose rappresentate dagli stessi monumenti. Non erano certamente cose spettanti nè alla decorazione de' mobili, o degli edifizi, nè all'ornamento della persona, nè all'uso de'santuari, perchè in tanto numero di bassirilievi, e pitture, ed utensili egiziani che già si conoscono, neppur uno di questi piccoli monumenti si è mai veduto adoperato in simili uffizi. La loro forma, ed anche il soverchio loro numero sono sufficienti per farli distinguere dai sigilli, e dagli anelli; la vera conformazione de' quali ne è fatta abbastanza palese per forse cinquanta esemplari che ne abbiamo in questo gabinetto, e per tanti altri che si vedono per tutto altrove. Io sono ora per dirne il mio parere, e per esporre ad un tempo le ragioni che me ne fanno persuaso.

Non ebbi fin qui, a dir vero, opportunità di vedere la collezione dei trecento e più scarabei dell'Imp. gabinetto di Vienna, testè publicati per ordine sovrano, nè ciò che ne fu scritto dal valente loro illustratore il sig. Steinbüchel; e nè pure conosco l'altra, senza paragone più copiosa, stampata, or sono pochi anni, in Costantinopoli. La raccolta del nostro museo torinese è però abbastanza numerosa per se stessa perchè io possa trarne, senza ricorrere ad altri sussidi, se non un sicuro sistema, un'opinione almeno più d'ogni altra probabile, e simile al vero.

Fa veramente meraviglia come fra l'infinito numero delle cose antiche d'ogni forma e sostanza che, già da più secoli, si vanno scavando nella valle del Nilo, non siasi scoperta mai una sola moneta di vero conio egiziano; quando, all'incontro, se ne trovano ogni giorno in gran copia di quelle battute colà non solo dai Romani, e dai Greci, ma talvolta ancora dagli stessi Monarchi Persiani, che furono a contatto cogli ultimi Faraoni. Io tengo quindi per certo che l'uso delle monete metalliche, quali le ebbero quegli stranieri conquistatori, e quali le abbiamo noi, era sconosciuto in Egitto ne' più antichi e migliori tempi di quell'impero. È per altro impossibile che un popolo ricco, ingegnoso e potente, che traeva oro ed argento da' suoi monti, come abbiamo da Diodoro di Sicilia, che seppe innalzare le piramidi e gli obelischi, che sì di buon'ora toccò l'apice della civiltà e delle arti, abbia potuto rimaner sì gran tempo privo di uno de' primi cardini della società, voglio dire della moneta, o di altra cosa che la rappresentasse.

Nelle maggiori contrattazioni è facile lo imaginare che il valore delle cose fosse contraccambiato con metalli preziosi dati e ricevuti in massa, e, tutto al più, cautelati nella loro bontà per qualche publico marchio; così praticavasi appunto in Italia ne' più barbari periodi de' secoli di mezzo. Ma pei traffici di minor conto gli Egizi dovevano necessariamente avere ricorso ad altra cosa che tenesse luogo del nostro rame monetato, il quale, comechè non abbia comunemente in se medesimo il valore de'metalli nobili di cui fa le veci, è però ricevuto da ognuno pel bisogno che se ne ha, giunto al vantaggio d'un peso moderato, e d'un piccolo volume.

Quel succedaneo della moneta in Egitto dovea avere in sè tutte, od in parte almeno, le proprietà de'metalli men rari; dovea essere di una materia dura, poco voluminosa, non greve, capace di lunga durata, ed atta a ricevere, e conservare gl'impronti; di una figura sempre uniforme; di una forma tondeggiante anzi che angolosa, affinchè pel continuo attrito non venisse troppo presto a logorarsi. Dovea essere in oltre di una sostanza triviale, e di facile lavoro, acciocchè il prezzo della materia, e dell'opera non superasse il valore delle cose più dozzinali per le quali si dava. Dovea essere, per ultimo, infinitamente moltiplicato, affinchè potesse bastare ai bisogni d'una nazione ricca e numerosissima.

§ Ora qual altra cosa conosciamo noi fra gli avanzi dell'antico Egitto che offra in sè riuniti tutti i divisati caratteri, comuni alla vera moneta, se non sono i piccoli scarabei, fatti, com'io dissi, per gli usi civili della società? Infatti nelle raccolte de'monumenti egiziani questi non si presentano diversamente che le antiche monete o medaglie negli altri musei, tanto pel loro numero sempre superiore ad ogni altra cosa, come per la mole, per la robustezza della materia, per la varietà infinita dei tipi, e pel nome frequente de'Principi che ne furono autori.

Si potrà quindi conchiudere essere cosa, se non sicura, almeno probabilissima, che gli Egizi, nei primi tempi, e fino a tanto che non furono costretti dalla forza delle armi a ricevere leggi e costumanze straniere, non essendo ancora fra loro conosciuto l'uso d'improntare i metalli a foggia di moneta, supplissero, nel vicendevole commercio, a tal difetto con quelle tessere che ora noi chiamiamo scarabei. E se veramente colla figura dello scarafaggio solevano essi simboleggiare l'universo (*Horap.* I. c. 10), altissima fin d'allora sarebbe stata la loro sapienza nel dare la forma di quell'insetto a ciò che fra gli uomini rappresenta, ed equivale all'universalità delle cose, la moneta.

Verisimilmente le prime vere monete coniate in Egitto furono que' Darici di purissimo argento che Ariande, governatore di quel regno per Cambise e per Dario, s'attentò di battere colà a somiglianza delle monete persiane (*Herod.* I. c. 166.).

Il corso degli scarabei dovette allora probabilmente cessare affatto nelle provincie di quella contrada sottomesse ad un popolo conquistatore, che avea propria moneta, e che forse ne provava i vantaggi già da gran tempo. Pare anzi che l'uso di quelli avesse già cominciato a scemare dopo il regno del gran Sesostri, essendo molto più rari gli scarabei improntati del nome dei Re delle dinastie susseguenti, che quelli de' più antichi tempi; ed è assai verosimile che quel Monarca, vincitore dell'Asia, ne abbia seco portato non le sole ricchezze, ma ancora le migliori instituzioni.

So che Diodoro, trattando delle cose d'Egitto (*Diod. Sic.* Bibl. I. c. 78), fa menzione di un'antica legge di quel paese per cui erano sancite pene contro i falsari della moneta, dei pesi, delle misure e de'sigilli; ma non credo che in questa parte l'autorità di quello scrittore, contemporaneo di Augusto, possa contraddire a ciò che dai fatti, e dai monumenti si deduce; perchè primieramente presso di lui non è ben determinata l'epoca in cui fosse emanata quella legge; e poi è facile il vedere come nel nome generico di pecunia, adattandosi all'intelligenza comune, potè egli benissimo comprendere tuttociò che per publica autorità avea potuto farne le veci. L'esempio de'nostri giorni, in questo particolare, dee servirci di norma per dar giudizio sul valore delle cose, e delle parole dei tempi andati.

Ora a maggior conferma delle cose fin quì ragionate, gioverà ancora por mente alle seguenti osservazioni che mi vennero fatte esaminando la collezione degli scarabei in questo R. gabinetto.

1.ª Nella serie di questi scarabei, che è poco minore di mille settecento, come si è già detto, io ne ho contato un centinaio circa, i quali invece di essere segnati colle solite note geroglifiche, ovvero con figure, presentano dei punti fatti a modo di piccoli cerchietti, regolarmente disposti, e di vario numero dall'unità fino al venti. Non è cosa improbabile che in tal guisa, come appunto sulle frazioni dell'Asse romano, venisse indicato il maggiore o minor valsente nominale di ciascuno scarabeo.

2.ª Nella maggior parte degli scarabei fatti di porcellana, i quali, come ho già notato, sono di tutti i più numerosi, i loro smalti durissimi veggonsi quasi intieramente consumati nelle parti prominenti; ed, all'incontro, in ottimo essere tuttora, dove i fianchi dello scarabeo si fanno concavi, e gli angoli rientranti. La qual cosa, come ognun vede, non può essere che l'effetto di un lungo sfregamento prodotto dall'uso quotidiano di quelle porcellane, non diversamente da ciò che noi vediamo accadere alle monete correnti nel giro di pochi anni.

3.ª Il foro, che traversa sempre questa classe degli scarabei egiziani, vedesi spesse volte solcato nella sua circonferenza, od aggrandito del doppio da quel che era. Dunque gli scarabei si portavano in filze, e non in tasca, o nelle borse come adoperiamo noi colla moneta.

4.ª Gli scarabei intagliati in pietre fine, o dure non sono anch'essi, in questa nostra collezione, che un centinaio circa; e nè pur tutti, per quanto mi pare, debbono aver servito all'uso medesimo che gli altri. Questa qualità di scarabei è, per lo più, affatto priva d'intagli, e la figura dello scarafaggio vi è stata appena accennata col mezzo della ruota. Nè ciò mi fa meraviglia, giacchè troppo in su sarebbe salito il loro valore se fossero stati lavorati di vantaggio. Ma ciò che in essi vuol essere particolarmente avvertito si è che quasi tutti sono logori in ogni loro facciata, e scantonati negli angoli; nel quale stato difficilmente si troverebbero ridotti se avessero servito per tutt'altro bisogno che per succedaneo della moneta, stante l'estrema durezza di loro sostanze. Fra questi ve ne sono oltre il numero di trenta lavorati in basalti sì neri che verdeggianti; tre di lapislazzolo; dieci in amatista; quattordici in corniola; otto in agate di più qualità, ed altri finalmente in vari diaspri, ed in altre pietre dure di somigliante natura.

5.ª Uno de' maggiori argomenti ch'io possa addurre in appoggio della mia opinione intorno all'ufzio cui dovettero servire i nostri scarabei nella società, sono finalmente i nomi dei Principi egiziani che tratto tratto si trovano scolpiti sopra i medesimi; oltre un numero grandissimo di emblemi, divinità, e figure varie, sotto il velo delle quali gli stessi Principi sono quivi chiaramente simboleggiati. I Monarchi egiziani, al regno de' quali si riferiscono gli scarabei, sono sui medesimi nominati non diversamente che sugli altri monumenti, cioè col mezzo de' soliti cartellini, ora col nome loro proprio, ora col solo prenome, ed altre volte con ambedue. In questa sola nostra raccolta ho trovato più di dugencinquanta di tali cartelli; ed eccoli, senza più, enumerati col nome del Faraone cui appartengono. Uno ve n'ha di Osimandia; quattro di Amenofis I, capo della XVIII dinastia, quattro di Amenofis II; cento settantadue di Thutmosis II, Meride: uno de' quali porta l'anno undecimo del suo regno; due di Amenofis III; due parimente di Thutmosis III; tredici di Amenofis IV, Memnone, più un altro accompagnato con quello di Taia sua moglie; tre altri della stessa Principessa; uno di Ramesses I; tre di Mandui, oppure di Osirei suo fratello; uno di Ramesses IV, Meiamonè; uno pure di Ramesses v; quattordici di Ramesses vi, Sesostri; uno di Ramesses vii; uno di Sesonchis primo Re della xxii dinastia; quattro di Osortos, tre di Psammo: ambedue della xxiii dinastia; due del primo Psammetico, ed uno del secondo Re dello stesso nome: ambedue della xxvi dinastia; uno probabilmente di Neferite, ed un altro di Acoris, l'uno e l'altro della dinastia xxix, ultima de' Monarchi egiziani. Ignoro a quai Principi, ed a quali schiatte s'abbia a riferire il rimanente di que' cerchietti Reali; non pochi di essi però sono senza dubbio anteriori alla così detta diciottesima dinastia di Manetone, di cui fu capo il precitato Amenofis 1.° Si veda ciò che ho notato nelle mie *Lezioni Archeologiche* a facc. 149, 172, 174. intorno alle dette dinastie.

Dopo tutto ciò se alcuno, paragonando il numero degli scarabei appartenenti a ciascuno dei mentovati Monarchi, mi chiedesse perchè gli scarabei distinti col nome di Meride sono tanto più numerosi in paragone di quelli di tutti gli altri Monarchi egiziani, io dimanderò a lui parimente per qual ragione, fra le medaglie imperiali di Roma, le monete dell'Imperatore Gallieno si trovino in copia sì prodigiosa, quando nella stessa serie sono in tanto minor numero quelle degli altri Imperatori, molti de' quali hanno pur avuto un regno assai più lungo del suo.

I predetti nomi de' Monarchi egiziani nei tipi degli scarabei sono non di rado accompagnati dalla figura de' medesimi Principi, rappresentati ora sotto forme umane con differenti emblemi allusivi alle loro gesta, ora colle sembianze d'una sfinge, o di altro animale fregiato delle reali divise. Ovvero, quando la forma dello scarafaggio non essendo che accennata, i tipi veggonsi replicati sulle due opposte facciate, allora avviene talvolta che da una banda si vegga scritto il loro nome, e dall'altra vi sia l'effigie del Re, ovvero della sua divinità favorita; ed in ciò, se non erro, abbiamo un primo esemplare del modo con cui un medesimo soggetto si vide poi diviso, ed espresso separatamente in parte sulla facciata diritta, ed in parte sulla rovescia della moneta medesima.

Per contrario in tutta la serie degli scarabei torinesi non v'ha esempio d'un tipo figurato di rilievo come quello delle medaglie; tutti vi furono incavati o colla ruota, o colla punta nella foggia delle nostre pietre incise; così si provedeva maggiormente alla loro conservazione in sostanze meno dure dei metalli.

6.ª Frequentissimo è pure sugli scarabei il tipo delle divinità egiziane, le quali ora vi sono ritratte nella loro propria figura, ora accennate soltanto col mezzo dei loro simboli, ovvero col nome loro in geroglifici. Questa R. collezione ne presenta poco meno di trecento esempi: ma non sarebbe facile con tutto ciò di formarne una nuova categoria, separandoli dagli scarabei con impronti Reali, o storici, perchè sovente gli uni e gli altri si trovano far parte di un medesimo tipo; come, per esempio, là dove i Monarchi si veggono in atto di adorare or queste or quelle loro divinità tutelari; ovvero dove sotto la forma di queste è simboleggiato il Monarca medesimo.

Chiuderò finalmente queste note con una settima ed ultima osservazione intorno al vantaggio che gli Egiziani doveano ritrarre dall'uso degli scarabei, quando sieno stati veramente il supplimento della loro moneta. Forse nel primo sorgere di quel popolo alla vita civile, essendo ancora ignota presso di lui e la maniera di scavare i metalli, e l'arte dello affinarli, il bisogno avrà suggerito ad esso, come suggerì di poi egualmente ad altri popoli dell'Affrica, il modo di supplire alla loro mancanza con altre cose meno difficili a procacciarsi; ma ne' tempi susseguenti, quando l'arte fusoria, e l'oriliceria in particolare erano già salite a tanta eccellenza da stare a fronte delle opere migliori de' moderni artefici, come il potrei dimostrare con cento esempi di questo museo: quando l'antico e magnifico Osimandia offeriva agli dei l'immensa copia dell'oro e dell'argento, che ritraevasi ogni anno dalle miniere d'Egitto, e ne formava quel suo celebrato circolo astronomico d'incredibile ampiezza, onde coronarne il proprio sepolcro (*Diod. Sic.* I. c. 49); quando finalmente la moneta era già divenuta comune nelle contrade circostanti: allora l'uso degli scarabei, presso un popolo che bastava a se medesimo, nè avea mestieri del traffico esterno, non fu più l'effetto della necessità, ma un compenso voluto dalla ragione, e dal più sagace accorgimento. Perciocchè, là dove noi impieghiamo tutto dì grandissime somme nel coniare e rinovare la moneta, e non poca parte del suo peso vediamo del continuo insensibilmente consumarsi nel passare di mano a mano, gli Egizi sapevano far risparmio di tutto ciò mediante que' piccoli lavori di niun costo, resi però con somma arte sufficienti all'uopo. Talchè se ora si volessero mettere insieme tutte le somme de' risparmi fatti in tal modo, nel corso di mila ottocento e più anni, chè tanti ne passarono fra Osimandia ed Acoris, de' quali abbiamo gli scarabei, io non dubito punto che si verrebbe a formare tal tesoro da rinnovare in parte le opere più stupende dell'antico Egitto.

Torino, questo dì 25 gennaio del 1825.

Con permissione.

www.ingramcontent.com/pod-product-compliance
Lightning Source LLC
Chambersburg PA
CBHW050653170426
43200CB00008B/1266